DAWN OF...

Dutch Resistance to the German Occupation of Holland 1940-1945

Richard S. Fuegner

MORI
STUDIO, INC.

Minneapolis, Minnesota

DAWN OF COURAGE © copyright 2008 by Richard S. Fuegner. All rights reserved. No part of this book may be reproduced in any form whatsoever, by photography or xerography or by any other means, by broadcast or transmission, by translation into any kind of language, nor by recording electronically or otherwise, without permission in writing from the author, except by a reviewer, who may quote brief passages in critical articles or reviews.

Edited by Leif Fedje, Soulo Communications
Cover Design by Chris Stoeckel, Soulo Communications
Interior Design, layout and typesetting by Thomas D. Heller, Soulo Communications

ISBN 13: 978-0-9778209-7-9
Library of Congress Catalog Number: 2008938838

Printed in the United States of America

First Printing: October 2008

12 11 10 09 08   5 4 3 2 1

Mori Studio, Inc. *A Division of Soulo Communications*
2112 Broadway St. N.E., Ste. 200
Minneapolis, MN 55413
1-877-788-4341
www.moristudio.com

To Mary with love

Deo Omnis Gloria

CONTENTS

Acknowledgments vii
1 The Innocent Years 1
2 The Winter of Deception 7
3 The Five Day War 14
4 The Darkening of Occupation 28
5 The Plight of the Dutch Jews 36
6 The Dutch Samaritans 44
7 The Christian Church Reaction 53
8 The Conscience of the Nation 63
9 Resistance Initiatives 78
10 A Dutch Calamity 93
11 A Spirit of Defiance 117
12 Brotherhood of Strangers 128
13 The Dutch-Paris Underground Line 139
14 The Carpet to the Rhine 152
15 The Dutch Famine of 1944-1945 178
16 Holland Rejoices 190
   Epilogue 201
   End Notes 205
   Bibliography 231
   Index 237

ACKNOWLEDGMENTS

My sincere thanks to Gerda Leland who provided me with first-hand knowledge of life under the Occupation in Holland along with original source material which I included in the final preparation of the manuscript.

I would also like to thank Pat Rohan and the reference department staff members at the Kirkwood, Missouri, public library for their timely efforts in obtaining bibliographical materials throughout the course of my research.

I am also grateful to Professor William Brennan of Saint Louis University for valuable information that he provided concerning the refusal of Dutch physicians to participate in Nazi medical practices that were incompatible with the precepts of Christian ethics.

My thanks also to Jo Hedwig Teeuwisse and the *Historisch Adviesbureau* in Amsterdam for the translation and reproduction of several Dutch Underground periodicals.

My sincere thanks also to Dr. David Murphy, Professor of Modern and Classical Languages Department at Saint Louis University for additional help in translation and to the Brunetti International Language Center.

Last, thanks to the team at Mori Studio for all their help in turning a manuscript into a book.

1

The Innocent Years

The innocence that feels no risk and is taught no caution, is more vulnerable than guilt, and oftener assailed.
—*Nathaniel P. Willis (1806-1867), American poet and journalist*

On a cloudless spring day in the Netherlands, before the light of dawn on Friday, May 10, 1940, the citizens of that small but densely populated country were roused by the droning of aircraft passing overhead. It was a familiar sound to the people of Holland, who were growing accustomed to the sounds of German heavy bombers on their way to England. But there was something different about the sounds this time: Instead of diminishing, the noise grew louder. Deceptively, the planes had turned around over the North Sea. At 4:15 AM, the return of the unsightly aircraft accompanied by the pandemonium of sirens, and the windows of houses vibrating from the explosion of bombs and anti-aircraft fire drew the populace outside onto their lawns, their balconies and patios. Standing bewildered in their pajamas and night clothes, they lifted their heads to an early rising sun that was nearly eclipsed by hundreds of German paratroopers that blanketed the pale blue sky.

Like Denmark and Norway, invaded just one month earlier without warning or declaration of war, swarms of locust-like Nazi legions had descended upon Holland, Belgium and Luxembourg, conveniently situated on Germany's northwestern border. Just one year earlier, in April 1939, Hitler gave a "binding declaration" to the three Low Countries that under no circumstances would Germany violate their policy of neutrality and strict independence.[1]

DAWN OF COURAGE

Although as a people the Germans had never been particularly popular in the Netherlands, the two countries had never been enemies. Many Dutchmen viewed the Germans as arrogant and arbitrary, and lacking in equanimity. As one German scholar put it, "the Germans are like a torrent of water without a river bed to contain it and give it form and direction."[2] Nevertheless, many of the Dutch had relatives and friends in Germany. In fact, intermarriage between Dutch and German royalty was not an unusual occurrence. The ruling Dutch dynasty, the House of Orange itself, can be traced to a German-born prince, William of Orange, who led the fight against Spain for Dutch independence in the latter half of the sixteenth century.[3] The late husband of Queen Wilhelmina was German, as was her mother; and in 1937, Crown Princess Juliana married the German Prince Bernhard. The marriage enhanced the popularity of the House of Orange, and with the subsequent birth of children to the royal couple, an earlier desire of turning the Netherlands into a republic was abandoned in favor of retaining the ruling dynasty and the constitutional monarchy.[4]

The Netherlands achieved its astounding prosperity and strength in the seventeenth century when it dominated the shipping and commerce of Europe. It was then that the Dutch began their conquests of colonies in the West Indies, to wit, Guyana, the Antilles, Curacao and Aruba; and Surinam in South America. Prosperity was further nourished by acquisitions in the rich East Indies, which became a source of raw materials for Dutch industry and provided a market for Dutch goods. The country's strength came from the wealth created by its productive activities: shipping and fishing, trading and manufacturing, and by having the most advanced agriculture in Europe. Goods could be shipped farther into Europe by means of Holland's three great rivers, the Rhine from Germany, and the Maas and the Scheldt from Belgium.

A spirit of industrialization and cooperation grew among the people as a system of canals and bridges was established to unite the provinces and various sections of the country. Since about 25% of the Netherlands is below sea level, dams, called dikes, were built to hold back water and prevent flooding. Windmills were also used to drain water off the land until mechanical pumps and more sophisticated means were developed. This small country on the North Sea depended on the maintenance of good relations with neighboring powers, especially Germany and England.

The country did not emerge as an independent monarchy until 1815, when Dutch troops, combined with the Duke of Wellington's army, defeated Napoleon at the Battle of Waterloo. For the next 125 years, from 1815 until 1940, the Netherlands experienced an almost uninterrupted period of peace.

The only significant exception occurred in 1830, when a revolt took place in the southern provinces in which Belgium broke away from Holland and ultimately gained its independence.[5]

Unlike Belgium, whose neutrality was severely violated during the First World War, Holland was not materially affected on land. However, sea commerce diminished because German minefields and U-boats made the North Sea especially hazardous. During 1914–1918, neutral Holland lost 1,200 seamen, 121 merchant ships, and 96 fishing vessels,[6] which clearly indicated that neutrality does not necessarily immunize a nation from the vicissitudes of war. Nevertheless, toward the end of the war, when most of the German merchant fleet had been destroyed, the Dutch offered to provide their ships as help. In return, the Germans sent steel to build new ships with the understanding that they not then be used against Germany.[7]

During the interwar years, Holland regained its prewar mercantile position, and common commercial interests on the Rhine hinterland made collaboration between the Netherlands and Germany necessary. There was always a market for Dutch goods in Germany, and this was facilitated by a large number of German firms that conducted business in Amsterdam, Rotterdam and other cities in Holland.

Like the Norwegians, there was a strong pacifist movement in the Netherlands that discouraged the outlay of large armament expenditures. Reliance was mainly placed upon the reputation and strength of British sea power as an effective deterrent. Furthermore, the vast majority of the Dutch populace believed that their country's neutrality, which had served them so well during and in the years following the First World War, would provide the same sense of security when war again loomed on the horizon. Moreover, it was believed that an invading army could be met successfully by Dutch inundations: the flooding of threatened locations and impassable water obstacles.

Nevertheless, both geographically and logistically, Holland was ill-suited to military deterrence. In a total area of less than 13,000 square miles, this small, densely populated country of nearly nine million people made the problem of defense extremely difficult. Most of the country was essentially flat and well cultivated. There were scarcely any forests of appreciable size, which made hiding far more difficult. In the southwestern-most part of Holland, the fingerlike province of Zeeland often seems to be more a part of the North Sea than of the Netherlands, and its landscape is a stitched pattern of little islands mostly below sea level, loosely protected from the sea by dikes and sand dunes.

In the far south are scores of rolling hills averaging heights of no more than twenty or thirty feet. Unlike the mountainous regions of Poland, Czechoslovakia, Greece, Yugoslavia, Italy and France, there are no natural features in the Netherlands suitable for rural guerilla warfare or conducive to the establishment of organized armed resistance groups like the French *Maquis*. Most inhabitants lived in highly urbanized areas. They still do. The coastal region is a land of flat fields and interconnecting canals, consisting of a long range of beaches and sand dunes. The land was intersected by bus transportation and a large railway network and by excellent and numerous roads. A rural telephone and telegraph system existed, which extended into the smallest villages.

Additionally, Holland was isolated from its western European allies by Germany, which lay alongside the long Dutch eastern frontier; by Belgium to the south (which was also soon to be occupied); to the west, England, its only unoccupied ally, separated by more than a hundred miles of the North Sea, one of the fiercest bodies of water in the world; and by neutral Sweden, more than six hundred miles to the north. Squeezed between Germany and the sea, Holland lay farthest from the neutral sanctuaries of Switzerland and Spain.

Hitler's rise to power in 1933 did not unduly disturb the Dutch people, even though the Nazi seizure of power was somewhat unsettling to a people who generally shunned extremism of the Right or the Left. The people were very well informed about what was going on in Germany. Great concern was expressed in the Netherlands about the Nazi brutalities and their anti-Semitic policies in the early years of the Third Reich, but ironically, as conditions in Germany grew worse in the succeeding years, the less the average Dutch citizen wanted to know about it. As one Dutch writer expressed it, "the entire country lived in an atmosphere of cheerful disbelief and deliberate self-deception."[8] Problems of trade, an influx of refugees and food shortages would exist, but otherwise there would be nothing of major importance in Holland to worry about.

In the years after the First World War there were a few Fascist and National Socialist groups in Holland, but none managed to win seats in Parliament. In 1931, an engineer, Anton Mussert, founded the Dutch National Socialist Bond (N.S.B.), whose supporters were small shopkeepers, unemployed white-collar workers and laborers and hard-pressed farmers, principally victims of the severe Depression of the thirties.[9] The N.S.B. program was, in part, an exact translation of Hitler's Nazi platform, as outlined in *Mein Kampf*, in addition to vague slogans and glittering generalities.[10] In 1935 the party received 7.91 percent of the vote, but late in the following year, with the introduction of anti-Semitic racial theories, its strength diminished, and in the last election before the occupation (1939) the party polled only 3.7 percent of the vote.[11]

The Innocent Years

Throughout the tumultuous thirties, the collapse of collective security after the League of Nations failed to act decisively against Italian aggression in Ethiopia in 1935, and especially after German remilitarization and reoccupation of the Rhineland in 1936, brought about a change in Dutch defense policy. A build-up of the armed forces became a definite necessity, even to those in the Labor Party who opposed it so bitterly in the years immediately after the First World War.

Nevertheless, despite the ever darkening war clouds, the refusal to recognize danger on the horizon, even by the seemingly better-informed, prevailed in Holland. In fact, in 1937, during a visit with Winston Churchill, the earlier Dutch Prime Minister Hendrik Colijn made the overly ambitious claim that the mere push of a button would be enough to deter an invader with impassable water obstacles.[12]

When it was becoming increasingly obvious that Germany was emerging from its state of isolation and embarking upon its pursuit of territorial expansion—the years during which Hitler and Mussolini formed the Rome-Berlin Axis; when the German annexation of Austria took place; and when the shameful Munich appeasement regarding Czechoslovakia and that country's final absorption by the Reich occurred—the Dutch defense budget rose from 93 million guilders to 261 million.[13]

On August 28, 1939, the Dutch ordered the mobilization of 250,000 men in anticipation of the outbreak of hostilities. Mobilization of the armed forces was maintained until Germany invaded Holland. Everything directly related to the defense of Dutch territory was under strong political control. The government, a national coalition, was composed of all major political parties, but neither the cabinet, now headed by D.J. de Geer, a pacifist at heart, nor most other high-ranking political and military authorities, had the foresight to recognize the importance of proper military preparedness.

Within the army there was a lack of motivation, limited fighting spirit, insufficient training in the field—a problem compounded by senior officers who had little or no experience in leading larger detachments of troops—and the shortage of modern military equipment and materiel. Strategic positions were defended by obsolete field artillery. There were no tanks, and only eighteen armored vehicles. The reliance on field telephones with ground cables was of little use when troops were engaged in a campaign of ongoing mobility.[14]

The growing importance of air power was equally neglected. The small air force possessed 120 aircraft, of which only 23 were combat competitive.[15] Certain bombers had to be modified for use as fighters because there were no bombs available, and others had no proper bomb racks, or sights to aim their bombs properly. Air defense was ineffective due to the absence of radar. Searchlights lacked the equipment to point them in the right direction. Air observation posts throughout the country did not have modern communication equipment; public telephones had to be used. Anti-aircraft guns were short of ammunition. Conversely, the Germans had a powerful, well-balanced air force of 260 bombers and 240 modern fighters, as well as transport planes ready for use against Holland.[16]

The navy, whose chief concern was protection of the Dutch East Indies and defense of the homeland, was somewhat better off than the other services. Some modern ships had been built, and scientific advancements were being made in the fields of radar, gun stabilization and fire control, and snorkels for submarines, to enable them to recharge batteries while remaining submerged. The navy was the only branch equipped for coding and decoding. Nevertheless, much of the new equipment was being introduced for the first time, and most of the ships were not combat-ready.[17]

On September 1, 1939, immediately after the German invasion of Poland, the Dutch war announcement, in the words of one former member of the Dutch Underground, "produced no more than a ripple in our peaceful lives. ... No clash of arms occurred anywhere near us. So we relaxed."[18] The Dutch Government, concerned at the specter of a fully mobilized German army deployed on its eastern frontier, maintained its army of trained conscripts, but was careful so as not to provoke Germany in any way.

Like Poland, which sought its strength from horse-drawn cavalry, and France, which placed a misguided reliance on an obsolete complex of fortifications known as the Maginot Line,[19] Holland staked its faith on its numerous canals and inundations as adequate defense in the event of an attack. Clearly, the Dutch, who had no notion of air supremacy or modernized land warfare, still thought in terms of World War I tactics, while clinging to the tenuous belief that the long-standing posture of neutrality that served them so well a generation earlier would meet their needs on the eve of World War II. For the people of Holland, the years of innocence were coming to an end.

2

The Winter of Deception

*It is as easy to deceive one's self without perceiving it,
as it is difficult to deceive others without their finding it out.*
—*Francois Duc de La Rochefoucauld (1630-1680),
French moralist*

In the fall of 1939, the interlude that followed the German conquest of Poland until hostilities broke out on a large scale in the spring of 1940 is commonly known in the West as the "Phony War" (*Sitzkrieg*). Yet how any considerable segment of public opinion familiar with the aggressive nature, the accumulating military strength and the all-too-recent record of territorial expansion of Nazi Germany could regard the war as "phony" remains inexplicable; especially when one considers the massive destruction Poland had suffered. Nevertheless, in the eyes of the world, as the eminent British military analyst B.H. Liddell Hart eloquently stated, "people everywhere could only see that the battlefronts remained quiet, and concluded that Mars had fallen into a slumber."[1] Realistically, however, behind the scenes the situation in Europe was growing ever more ominous.

As the Polish campaign was drawing to a close in mid-September, Hitler began to give serious consideration to an offensive in the West. His ultimate concern was what he called the "life and death struggle with Britain," but he was not yet ready to challenge her world power. His armed forces had only been developed and equipped for a continental war. He knew that he could not wage a prolonged world-wide struggle against England and her Empire until he had increased the size of his army and navy, and obtained the necessary reserve stocks of oil to support such a conflict. A long war with Britain would exhaust Germany's resources, and expose her to a deadly attack from Russia. The Nazi-Soviet Non-Aggression Pact, which enabled Hitler to attack Poland without fear of Soviet intervention, would not guarantee the latter's neutrality any longer than it suited her purpose.

The Fuehrer's failed attempt to obtain a peace agreement with Britain that would recognize his hegemony over continental Western Europe prompted him to set the stage for an early offensive against France. He believed that after an early victory in France, the conditions for a successful war against England would be secured. England could then be blockaded from the French coast by the *Luftwaffe*, while the navy with its U-boats could extend the range of the blockade. Daily attacks by the air force and navy would cut Britain's lifelines, and once her supply routes were severed, she would be forced to capitulate.[2]

However, in a War Directive on the conduct of the war addressed to his military commanders, Hitler reiterated his anxiety about a long war with France and Britain. He expressed particular concern about the possibility of a surprise occupation of Belgium and Holland by Anglo-French forces based in close proximity to the German frontier, and the resultant danger that Allied air attacks posed to the heart of the German munitions industry: the Ruhr, which lay along the Rhine just behind the southern Dutch border. If this were to occur, he said, it would "lead to the collapse of the German war economy and thus of the capacity to resist."[3]

Consequently, Hitler believed that if his forces successfully occupied neutral Holland and Belgium, both of which constituted a "protective zone in front of the Ruhr,"[4] and if France was also defeated, he would have a base from which he could then launch a promising sea and air war against England.

The final top-secret directive for the invasion of the Low Countries, code named *Fall Gelb* (Case Yellow), was issued by Hitler in an order to the Armed Forces High Command (OKW) on October 9:

> *Preparations should be made for offensive action on the northern flank of the Western Front crossing the area of Luxembourg, Belgium and the Netherlands. This attack must be carried out as soon and as forcefully as possible. The object of this attack is ... to acquire as great an area of Holland and Belgium and Northern France as possible.*[5]

When the Fuehrer summoned his military commanders to a conference to disclose his plan to attack in the West, the news was met with objections from both his Commander-in-Chief of the Army, Field Marshal Walther von Brauchitsch,

The Winter of Deception

and General Franz Halder, the Chief of the General Staff. Both tried to dissuade the Fuehrer from invading France. Along with most of the senior German generals, they did not share Hitler's belief that he could overcome the opponents' superiority in military trained manpower. They believed that the German Army was not nearly strong enough to defeat the Anglo-French forces. Of even greater concern was their belief that the war in the West would spread into another world war, and this would mean a disastrous ending for Germany.[6] Determined to carry out his plan to attack, Hitler rebuked his military leaders, rebuffed their arguments, and set a tentative date for the offensive: November 12.

Meanwhile, unaware that Holland's fate had already been sealed the previous May when Hitler secretly declared his intention to break his pledge to the Low Countries,[7] Queen Wilhelmina, like her Scandinavian neighbors, formally announced official neutrality. This neutrality, however, did not prevent the sinking of eleven Dutch ships on the high seas, including the passenger liner *Simon Bolivar*, which involved considerable loss of life.[8]

Nor did strict official neutrality prevent individuals from freely entering the Netherlands, which in turn, enabled both Germany and England to engage in certain types of unofficial activity. For example, espionage and subversive activities from within the country; by Germany, to continue its preparation for the invasion of Holland, and by England as a base to secure information from Germany. It was a period of covert activity, fortuitous events, and ultimately, calamitous consequences for the people of Holland.

Early in November, British Secret Intelligence Service (SIS) agents operating in The Hague learned that a military conspiracy against Hitler existed in Germany, and certain of the plotters wished to make contact with England. Through a Dutch wireless interception, the Chief of Dutch Intelligence, Major-General J.W. van Oorschot, caught the British agents communicating with a German officer in the Rhineland who wanted assurances that London would deal fairly with the new anti-Nazi regime.[9]

The conspiracy had already been disclosed to the British by one of the plotters on September 3, the day Britain and France declared war on Germany, but the London government wanted further assurances from the conspirators. The two British intelligence officers, Major R.H. Stevens and Captain S. Payne Best, were provided a Dutch security officer, Lieutenant Dirk Klop, to accompany them at all times. Secret meetings were held with the anti-Nazi officer, "Major Schaemmel," who in reality was Major Walter Schellenberg, a Nazi SS counter-espionage agent. He convinced the British agents that the German generals were determined to overthrow Hitler and initiate peace negotiations with Britain and France. After renewed conferences with a higher authority in London, and after numerous wireless communications and further meetings in various Dutch towns between the two parties, the British agents met with "Schaemmel" on November 7 in Venlo, a Dutch town on the edge of the German border. The agents gave "Schaemmel" a rather vague message from London to the anti-Nazi plotters, stating in general terms the basis for a just peace with a new German regime. It was agreed that the ostensibly dissident "Schaemmel" would bring one of the leaders of the anti-Nazi resistance to Venlo to begin negotiations. The objectives of both sides were clear. The British wanted to establish contact with the German conspirators to encourage and support them. The Germans were trying to discover through the British who the German plotters were and what their connection was with the British.[10]

On November 9, at a frontier café near Venlo, the Nazi SS Major Schellenberg awaited the arrival of the Anglo-Dutch agents. After they pulled up behind the café, they were suddenly fired upon by waiting Nazi agents in an SS car. During the encounter, Klop was critically wounded, and along with both British agents, was forcibly taken a short distance across the border into Germany. The Dutchman died a few days later in a German hospital, and the two kidnapped British officers remained prisoners in Germany for the duration of the war. According to an official Dutch account, the Dutch government sent nine written complaints to the Germans demanding an investigation because the incident was a clear violation of Dutch neutrality, but no replies were ever given.[11]

At a conference on November 23, Hitler simply told his military leaders that "a breach of the neutrality of Holland is meaningless, and no one will question it when we have won. If we do not break the neutrality, then England and France will. Without attack the war is not to be ended victoriously."[12]

The Dutch government, and especially Prime Minister de Geer, who had always believed that Germany's superior strength could not be resisted, clung tenaciously to the notion that anything that was contrary to the spirit of neutrality should be scrupulously avoided. Dutch Intelligence involvement in the "Venlo Incident" was seen as a violation of that spirit. Consequently, Intelligence Chief van Oorschot was dismissed, and the Dutch government felt itself fortunate that it had escaped being charged with non-neutral conduct and invaded by Germany immediately.[13] Later, however, on the day of the invasion, Hitler used the incident as partial justification for his attack on the Netherlands, claiming the Dutch acted in collusion with the British SIS.

In many European countries threatened by Germany just before the war, alleged subversive elements known as a "fifth column" were encouraged by the

The Winter of Deception

Nazis to demoralize a population dreading an imminent attack. For the most part these forces were nonexistent, but the notion was encouraged, nevertheless, by the Nazis to incite nervous rumors and divisive suspicion among the populace. Holland was no exception. The same euphemistic term was used to describe activities useful to the enemy. Just one month prior to the German invasion, twenty-one Dutch Nazis were arrested for espionage activity for providing Germany with information regarding Dutch defense installations.[14] And some five weeks before the invasion, a German commanding general who led one of the first divisions into the Netherlands, while dressed in civilian clothes, was able to get a bird's-eye impression of a defense layout from a high tower in a zoo overlooking an area that he found very useful. Prime Minister de Geer had recently refused to demolish the tower on the grounds that a neutral country had nothing to fear.[15]

"Fifth Column" also applied to espionage conducted by German Counter-Intelligence (*Abwehr*).[16] One such activity involved smuggling Dutch uniforms into Germany, which were used in the early stages of the invasion. The *Abwehr* was ordered to prepare a plan for the seizure of certain key bridges on the Dutch-German frontier by means of a deception that involved German troops dressed in Dutch uniform disguise. The agent who had been told to procure the uniform patterns was captured by the Belgians with the uniforms in his possession. But astoundingly, the ruse aroused no suspicion either in Holland or Belgium.[17] The tactical surprise that resulted from the failure to issue precautionary instructions to Dutch border guards after the intended treachery was discovered will be dealt with in the following chapter.

Although the Dutch and the Belgian general staffs had no knowledge of Hitler's secret war directive, they knew from their own intelligence sources near the border there were some fifty divisions of German troops situated along their frontiers.[18]

They also received warnings of an attack from an unexpected source. Certain of those high-ranking members of the German General Staff who favored the removal of Hitler believed that the hour of liberation from the Fuehrer's yoke would come when the German offensive against France got bogged down after short-lived initial success. A German military setback would then provide the opportunity to launch a coup to save Germany from ultimate disaster; and the failure of the campaign against France would provide the right psychological moment for such a coup.[19]

With this in mind, one of the anti-Nazi conspirators, Colonel Hans Oster, Chief of Staff of the *Abwehr*, warned the Dutch military attaché in Berlin, and close personal friend, Colonel G.J. Sas, to expect a German attack on November 12, the target date for the autumn offensive.[20] But because of inclement weather the invasion was delayed.

With the start of the New Year, Hitler rescheduled the date of the offensive for January 17. However, on January 10, a *Luftwaffe* liaison staff officer flying from Munster to Bonn with certain operational details of the plan to attack in the West lost his way in bad weather, and was forced to land his plane in Belgium. He tried to burn the incriminating plans, but vital parts of the document were salvaged by the Belgians and submitted to the British and French authorities. Although the Germans did not know at the time what had happened to the secret papers, they took no chances and changed their operational plan.[21]

Now that the plan had been compromised, the Germans had an additional four months to organize a new plan of attack that proved especially unfortunate for the Allies. The original arrangement was hastily formulated in the fall of 1939 to meet Hitler's expectation of an early offensive in mid-November. It called for a principal German drive on the right flank through Belgium and northern France, with the object of occupying the Channel ports. This plan to sweep through Belgium, and possibly Holland by flanking a complex of fortifications known as the Maginot Line, failed to anticipate a head-on clash with the entire British Expeditionary Force (B.E.F.), the major part of the French Army and a combined force of Dutch and Belgian troops—a force numerically comparable to that of the Germans.[22]

The revised proposal was conceived by General Erich von Manstein, the Chief of Staff of Field Marshal von Rundstedt. He believed that the main German assault should be launched by a massive armored thrust through the Ardennes forest, then into France by flanking around the left wing of the Little Maginot Line extension near Sedan, and across the River Meuse, where it would be least expected by the Allies. The main force would then swing northwest and break out into open country and drive for the Channel coast, trapping the French Army and the B.E.F. with their backs to the sea. On February 24, 1940, the Manstein proposal was formally adopted in a new OKW directive, a grand design to encircle and destroy the Anglo-French armies in northern France.[23]

On May 1–2, news of the evacuation of British forces from central Norway signaled the beginning of a victorious end to the campaign in Scandinavia for the Germans, and prompted Hitler to turn his attention to the West. After several last-minute postponements, the Fuehrer finalized the date of the German offensive in the West as May 10.

Nevertheless, because of the numerous delays of the German attack, the forewarnings, both from The Hague and Brussels, were not taken seriously by either Britain or France. On May 3, the *Abwehr* conspirator, Colonel Oster, informed the Dutch attaché, Sas, the date the attack was to occur. The following day, The Hague received confirmation from its envoy in the Vatican. The information was immediately transmitted to the Belgians. On May 9, Oster and Sas met for dinner when the German intelligence officer told his Dutch friend that the final order for the offensive was given. But again, the general staffs of both Britain and France discounted the warnings.[24] In London itself, a critical turning point of another kind was being resolved. At 6:00 on the evening of May 10, a new British government was being formed by Winston Churchill, who was appointed the new Prime Minister.

Earlier that same day, just before the break of dawn, a far graver crisis was taking place across the English Channel: A massive Nazi war machine was being unleashed, creating havoc from the skies above Holland and on the fields of the Low Countries. The battlefronts, quiet for the past eight months, now resounded with the screech of dive bombers overhead and a mounting land assault as the clamorous grinding of armored columns swept across the borders of Holland, Belgium and Luxembourg. Mars had awakened from slumber, as did the Dutch people, whose sanguine expectation that they would be bypassed, as in the First World War, proved to be a most disastrous illusion.

3

The Five Day War

If we were in possession of Holland, Belgium, or even The Straits of Dover as jumping-off bases for German aircraft, then, without a doubt, Great Britain could be struck a mortal blow.
—*OKW Directive 6 for the Conduct of the War (Signed) Adolf Hitler, October 9, 1939*

Strategically, the German Western Offensive was a single assault operation launched simultaneously against the Low Countries. But from a tactical standpoint, the German invasion of Holland was a separate engagement from the major attack through Belgium and Luxembourg. In fact, the Battle of France, the purpose of which was the defeat of the Allied armies and acquisition of the French Channel Coast, could have succeeded without encroachment on Dutch soil. Nevertheless, occupation of the Netherlands, like German operations in Denmark and Norway, was believed to be of immense significance in the later prosecution of the air war against Great Britain.

The first German operation was an airborne assault involving 4,000 parachute troops, carried by 475 heavy Junker (Ju-52) troop-carrying transports and 45 gliders.[1] The Seventh German Airborne Division under the command of General Kurt Student, reinforced by three regiments of the 22nd Infantry Division and one from the 46th, under the command of Major General Hans Graf von Sponeck, were especially trained for air landing operations. These

The Five Day War

comprised the major part of the troops landed near The Hague and the neighboring cities of Rotterdam, Leyden and Delft.[2] This was preceded by bombing attacks against the barracks, hangars and defensive emplacements at the Dutch airfields by Stuka dive-bombers to soften up ground resistance.

Among those awakened by the roar of the German planes overhead on the pre-dawn morning of the attack was the Dutch Foreign Minister Eelco Van Kleffens at his home in The Hague, Holland's seat of government. He was immediately informed that airfields were being bombed, after which he sent urgent appeals for aid to London and Paris before rushing to an emergency Cabinet meeting at the prime minister's residence. Two hours later, at about 6:00, the German ambassador, Count Julius von Zech-Burkersroda, requested a meeting with Van Kleffens. The German Minister had resided in Holland for the past seventeen years and was completely astounded and deeply ashamed over what was happening.[3]

At the German Foreign Ministry, Van Kleffens was handed an ultimatum calling for an end to all resistance to the German forces. At the instruction of Berlin, the German Minister read the message accusing Holland, Belgium and Luxembourg of collaborating with Great Britain and France in an imminent invasion of the Ruhr and that the German action was taken to prevent this alleged aggression. The note also included the promise of a guarantee for the Royal Dynasty if the Dutch would halt all resistance. Van Kleffens's reply was simply a refusal to negotiate with the Germans and a pronouncement that because of the unprovoked invasion of Holland, "We must consider ourselves at war with Germany."[4]

Indeed they were. The first German objective was to land a strong force of airborne troops on the three airfields surrounding The Hague—Valkenburg, Ockenburg and Ypenburg. At Valkenburg, the airstrip was initially taken by the Germans, but later in the day, Dutch infantry reservists supported by artillery regained their equilibrium after the initial shock and confusion of the unannounced attack, and reclaimed control of the airstrip. At the small Ockenburg airfield, where twenty transports landed, the defenders were able to restrain the invaders. And at Ypenburg, several groups of transports were severely damaged by the defending forces; one was unable to land because of widespread aircraft wreckage on the field. By evening all three airfields had either been held or retaken by the Dutch.[5] The Germans retreated into nearby villages and established defensive positions from which the Dutch were unable to dislodge them. This enabled General Sponeck's force to tie down the Dutch reserves in considerable numbers at a time when they were sorely needed elsewhere.

In North Holland at Bergen, a number of Dutch fighter planes were destroyed before they could get off the ground. By the end of the day a superbly equipped *Luftwaffe* had virtually written a new chapter in the story of air power. Half of the minuscule Dutch air force—62 out of 125 aircraft—were destroyed, most on the first day of the attack.[6]

The airborne assault was delayed somewhat when the airfields were unable to cope with the heavy transports, many of which, after landing, were hampered by getting stuck in the soft Dutch soil. Additionally, hundreds of the paratroopers were dropped too widely, and spread outside of their designated landing sites in the sand dunes and meadows. Most were found and taken prisoner.[7] By the evening of the first day, a total of 1,100 German prisoners were captured and taken to the port of Ijmuiden and sent to England.[8] An attempt by advanced German detachments to capture Queen Wilhelmina, the Royal Family and government ministers, and thereby disrupt the functioning of government, failed because of the strong Dutch resistance and the rapid recovery of the airfields near The Hague.

Additional forces were dropped near the neighboring cities of Waalhaven, Dordrecht, Moerdijk and Rotterdam where the German assault was far more formidable. General Student's main objective was to quickly seize control of the bridges and canal locks just south of Rotterdam over the Maas River.

Approximately 240 landings were made on the first day of the assault. A large body of troops landed at the Waalhaven airport in Junker transports several miles southeast of the city. Despite desperate resistance efforts by the Dutch, the Germans were able to establish an operational base from which to attack Rotterdam, which was already being assaulted from a second airborne infantry force that had landed in twelve hydroplanes on the Nieuwe Maas River.[9]

In the skies above the captured Waalhaven airfield, five of the six British Fighter Command Blenheim bombers of the British Expeditionary Force that took part in the clash were shot down by German Messerschmitt (Me-110) fighters. Fortunately for the British, attacks by Bomber Command on similar targets were, if not notably effective, at least much less expensive.[10] The only ray of light in the air war on this first of many dark days for the Allies was the performance of the British Hawker Hurricanes, which claimed thirty-six German bombers shot down.[11] On May 11, Dutch artillery fire and air bombing by British aircraft rendered Waalhaven unusable, but at this interval the Germans were landing their transports southeast of Rotterdam.

Now that Waalhaven was firmly in German hands, both infantry and paratroopers headed to the several Maas bridges to relieve the troops that landed on water. Despite a counterattack by Dutch forces and bitter fighting, the Germans were able to maintain control of the bridges.

In southern Holland, initial ground fighting was launched by a task force of German infantry, combat engineers and rifle regiments of the Fourth Panzer Division, who were hastening across the narrow southerly projection of Dutch territory known as the "Maastricht Appendix," wedged between Germany and northern Belgium in the province of Limburg. Straddling the Maas River, it was at this juncture that the Germans made their way into northern Belgium.

When the bridges spanning the Maas River, along with the more southerly branches of the Rhine-Maas estuary, were firmly in the hand of the Germans, General Georg von Kuechler's Eighteenth Army would be able to break into "Fortress Holland," the central section of the country, which included the cities of Rotterdam, Amsterdam, The Hague, Utrecht and Leyden. The Dutch relied heavily on their numerous canals and flooding devices and fortified defense positions to seal off their western stronghold from the Germans. There was some hope that Kuechler's forces might be stopped before reaching the Moerdijk bridges by French General Henri Giraud's Seventh Army, which had reached the southern province of North Brabant on the afternoon of May 11. The Dutch Commander-in-Chief, General H.G. Winkelman, called Giraud, and asked for immediate aid. But the French, like the Dutch, lacked crucially needed air support, armor or antitank and anti-aircraft guns, and were easily pushed back by heavy Stuka dive bomber attacks.

The bridges at Dordrecht and Moerdijk that had to be crossed by the German forces were wired for destruction, but the Dutch were reluctant to blow them up because it was the fastest route for sending reserves from Holland to the Peel Marshes in North Brabant (the southern end of the eighty-mile-long Grebbe-Peel defense line)[12], and the only route by which Allied ground troops from Belgium could reach Holland.[13] Exploiting this hesitation, German paratroops overtook the Dutch sentries by surprise before they could destroy the bridges. The bridges were attacked from both sides and quickly occupied.

The loss of the Moerdijk bridges was a severe setback to the Dutch defenders. The severity was compounded by their inability to send reinforcements from Holland because the Germans also controlled the bridges south of Rotterdam. On May 12, the way was now open for the German Ninth Panzer Division, and part of an SS motorized division, to cross the bridges and, by the next day, arrive at the south bank of the Nieuwe Maas across from Rotterdam, where the German airborne troops still held the bridges. The Germans then drove through light Dutch frontier positions, skirted or penetrated the Peel Marshes despite obstacles and some flooded terrain, connected up with the airborne troops that were dropped south of Rotterdam and thus penetrated Fortress Holland from the south.[14]

A major German concern was whether it would be possible to seize the bridges over the Maas intact. In the early planning stage of the invasion, the German High Command (OKW) ordered the *Abwehr* to prepare a plan for the seizure, by means of a *ruse de guerre*—by troops dressed in Dutch and Belgian uniforms—of the most important bridges over the Maas, the two road bridges and one railway bridge at Maastricht and the one road and one railway bridge at Gennep. In November 1939, Admiral Wilhelm Canaris, the head of the *Abwehr*, established a combat battalion with Dutch linguistic skills. Only if that could be done would the army be able to reach the Peel Line and thereafter relieve the paratroops dropped in the vicinity of Rotterdam.[15]

In the early hours of May 10, 1940, this advance German guard under the command of a bogus Dutchman, Lieutenant Hocke, dressed in Dutch military police uniforms and fittingly cover-named "Trojan Horse," drove to Maastricht, where they were stopped by Dutch forces that had blown the Maas bridges. Whole columns of tanks and lorries blocked the roads leading to Maastricht, but the Germans, albeit delayed, crossed the river in rubber boats and in the afternoon the first rifle units joined up with airborne troops pushing their way through northern Belgium.[16]

Farther north at Gennep on the Dutch-German frontier, a more carefully planned and executed subterfuge took place. A unit of the Brandenburg Special Duty Battalion 800, under the command of Lieutenant Wilhelm Walther, more or less, compensated for the failure at Maastricht. A reconnaissance unit—members of the Brandenburg Regiment—were disguised as German prisoners under Dutch "escort," and concealed hand grenades and automatic pistols under their greatcoats. The "escorts" were agents of the Mussert Dutch Nazi movement disguised as Dutch frontier guards. At about 4:00 in the morning, the Dutch Nazis and the Germans in Dutch uniforms captured the guards at the bridge, and, before the Dutch could recover from the shock of being deceived and taken by surprise, German tanks were rolling across the bridge.[17]

On May 11, the Cabinet recommended to Queen Wilhelmina that for her safety and that of the Royal Family, they leave the country. The following morning, Crown Princess Juliana, her husband, Prince Bernhard, and their children sailed for England on a British destroyer. On May 13, the Queen was taken to England, and members of the government followed later that day. London was proclaimed the Netherlands Government-in-Exile throughout the duration.

The Five Day War

General Winkelman, Commander-in-Chief of the Dutch armed forces, was instructed by the Queen to continue the fight for as long as he felt there was reason for further resistance.

The Dutch put up very little resistance in the northern border provinces. The territories east of the Yssel River, a northern tributary of the Rhine that includes the provinces of Overyssel, Drente, Groningen and Friesland, were held by a few frontier battalions, but only for a short time. They did succeed in blowing all the bridges on the Yssel, but this only delayed the German advance for a few hours. Supported by Dutch gunboats, Dutch troops were able to retreat across the Zuider Zee barrier dam, a magnificent piece of land reclamation that turned a part of the North Sea into cultivable drained land. In less than forty-eight hours, the fertile fields of northern Holland were overrun by several regiments and a few tanks of the German First Cavalry Division. And by the evening of May 11, a vanguard of troops reached the town of Den Helder at the northwestern end of the Zuider Zee (now reduced to the Ijsselmeer), which links North Holland and Friesland. At the northeastern end of the dam, the Germans met determined Dutch resistance, and neither air attacks nor artillery could dislodge them. Heavy fighting continued from May 12 to 14. A German infantry attack over the dam was pushed back on May 13 involving heavy casualties, and the German artillery was hushed by the Dutch gunboat *Johann Maurits van Nassau*.[18]

Meanwhile, at the Grebbe Line, the central Dutch defense position where the main body of troops was deployed, German forces were steadily advancing. The Dutch air force had practically been eliminated, and since the Royal Air Force was now engaged in air battles over France and Belgium, there was no sign of help from the Allies. Consequently, they were constantly exposed to air attack from German planes, which were able to direct artillery fire from forces on the ground as they circled over the Dutch fortifications. Nevertheless, the Dutch were able to hold their position until the afternoon of May 13, when the situation became so critical that they had to evacuate the area. They fell back behind the defenses of Fortress Holland toward Utrecht, which they continued to occupy when the final surrender took place.

The Germans were now faced with the task of completing the defeat of Fortress Holland north of the Rhine-Maas estuary by taking Rotterdam, the principal port city of Holland, and The Hague. Dutch forces were still maintaining an unbroken line along the East Front of Fortress Holland, which proved to be an unexpectedly formidable barrier to the *Wehrmacht*. It was here that the Germans met their fiercest opposition. The Dutch had time to close off the bridgehead into the city and were in strong defensive positions.[19] Incited by anger, courage, and in desperation, Dutch forces fought valiantly against superior German forces. On May 13, the Germans were still deadlocked at the bridges over the River Maas where they were confronted by determined Dutch resistance, and there was no opportunity to deploy their tanks. The Germans were becoming impatient, as they were anxious to move their armored division and motorized troops out of Holland and into France as soon as possible.

Since the occupation of Rotterdam was a principal German objective, and the city was taking too long to conquer, more drastic measures were being considered. Lieutenant Colonel Dietrich von Choltitz, commanding the battalion at the Rotterdam bridges, sent a Dutch priest and a Dutch merchant into Rotterdam to the Dutch Commander, Colonel Pieter Scharroo, urging him to surrender the city. His only response was that civilians had no responsibility meddling in military affairs and there were no further contacts until the next day.[20]

The Rotterdam Controversy

On the morning of May 14, Hitler issued a war directive stating that "the power of resistance of the Dutch army has proved to be stronger than was anticipated… and that this resistance be broken *speedily*."[21] Hitler and his *Luftwaffe* Commander-in-Chief, Hermann Goering, decided to send a bomber group, against which the Dutch people were practically defenseless, to attack in the heart of Rotterdam. The German Corps Commander in Rotterdam, General Rudolf Schmidt, was issued orders demanding a Dutch surrender under threat of an all-out destruction of the city.

Shortly thereafter, in a telephone discussion with Goering, Field Marshal Albert Kesselring, commander of the Second German Air Force, told the Reichsmarshall that under threat of air bombardment, the city might surrender. He also expressed concern over the possibility of German casualties on the ground in the event of an all-out air attack against the city. Undisturbed by this very real possibility, Goering ordered the air strike at 1:20 that afternoon. Nevertheless, Kesselring remained in contact with the ground forces at the Maas bridges, and was informed that the city had been told to surrender. It was then decided that German ground forces would send up red flares if the Dutch agreed to surrender, and as a sign to cancel the air strike. That information was to be transmitted to the bomber squadron, which, at about the same time, was taking to the air from Bremen. Radio contact was to be maintained between the air forces and the German ground troops.[22]

Later in the morning, a German officer under a white flag crossed over the Maas River Bridge and handed Dutch commander Colonel Scharroo an ultimatum for surrender. The document was not signed by a German commander, and Scharroo treated it as a possible deception and refused to accept it. At 11:45 AM., after receiving further instructions from Commander-in-Chief Winkelman, a Dutch officer, Captain Bakker, was sent across under a white flag where he met with General Schmidt on the left bank of the Maas and demanded an officially signed and authorized ultimatum. The general agreed and a new duly authorized document was issued at 1:20 PM that was timed to expire three hours later. Schmidt then correctly informed the *Luftwaffe* to cancel the air strike. But as the Dutch officer was returning over the bridge to General Winkelman's headquarters with the new surrender demands, the sound of approaching Heinkel 111 bombers could be heard overhead. Schmidt immediately fired the red flares into the air, but at the same time, the bombers released their munitions in the heart of the city with devastating results. Terrified and confused, thousands of inhabitants, mostly civilians, ran through the streets for shelter, many not knowing where to go. Civilian casualties who were not killed by the shelling or concussion of the bombs either burned alive or were choked to death by the fumes and density of the smoke. Fires erupted throughout the city, but the Rotterdam fire brigade was powerless: Immediately after the start of the attack, the water mains had burst. In the aftermath of the attack, the people were in no position to offer any resistance. The wounded were tended to and the dead removed from the wreckage and debris. Thousands of buildings were demolished, including twenty-one churches, seventy schools, and four hospitals. The fires smoldered for weeks.

On the afternoon of May 14, several thousand leaflets were dropped over the city of Utrecht that stated:

> *The Dutch lines at the Grebbe have surrendered! The outnumbering German troops are ready in the east, southwest and south to attack the city of Utrecht by the simultaneous use of strong tank and air forces. Therefore I order the Utrecht commander to stop the useless fight and surrender the city in order to spare the city and its inhabitants the fate of Warsaw. If not, I regret to say, I will be forced to view the city as a fortress and attack with all military means.*
>
> *The consequences will only be yours.*

It was now all too clear to General Winkelman that any unwillingness to capitulate would have resulted in further cowardly air attacks and the wanton destruction of one or more of the heavily populated cities of Amsterdam, The Hague and Utrecht. That same afternoon all Dutch naval vessels were ordered to sail for Britain. And at dusk, to avoid further bloodshed and the useless sacrifice of thousands of innocent citizens, the Dutch Commander ordered his armed forces to lay down their arms. On the following day, he signed the formal surrender proclamation.

The devastation of Rotterdam created a controversy as to who was responsible for this act of callous ruthlessness; a dispute that continued after the war. It has never been completely resolved and lacks consensus even today.

There seems to be general agreement that when General Schmidt fired the flares they were only seen by one side of the *Luftwaffe* squadron of planes. This was either because the flares were obscured by the smoke over the city, or the air squadron was under orders by higher command to ignore them. Dutch Colonel Scharroo maintained that because the bombing occurred before the second surrender ultimatum expired, the Germans were guilty of a "breach of faith."[23] He further believed that the Nazi leaders wanted to "terrorize the Western nations into submission by their determination to destroy entire cities in the West… in pursuit of German victory."[24]

Both Goering and Kesselring defended the bombing on the grounds that Rotterdam was not an open city, but staunchly defended by Dutch forces. They also denied that they knew surrender negotiations were being discussed when they authorized the release of the bombers from Bremen. However, there is strong evidence from information obtained from the German army archives that they did know negotiations were under way.[25] But did Goering decide not to cancel the attack, which he thought might hasten the Dutch surrender, by withholding a message from the field commanders to the air squadron, as one Dutch scholar has suggested?[26] According to Kesselring's later testimony, he spoke of "hours of heated conversation" with Goering "as to how the attacks were to be carried out, if at all."[27] Professor Werner Warmbrunn cites the testimony of the *Luftwaffe* Squadron Commander Hoehne who claimed that "one-half of the German aircraft understood and obeyed the red warning signals fired from the ground," from which the eminent professor assumes "the bombing was a failure in communication. This position," he hastens to add, "in no way denies that Goering and his generals were more willing to take the risk of bombing Rotterdam 'unnecessarily' than to pursue a more cautious policy which might have delayed the Dutch capitulation."[28]

Whatever the truth of this outrageous act may be, none of the facts presented at the post-war Nuremberg war crime trials concerning the bombing of Rotterdam were sufficient to warrant criminal convictions of any of the defendants involved.

Nevertheless, several unequivocal facts clearly stand out. The bombing of this major port city, the second-largest city in the Netherlands—like that of Warsaw, London and Coventry—was a Nazi symbol of unprovoked ruthlessness against a helpless civilian population. Hitler well knew that the Dutch could not hold out and were in the process of being demolished. Yet the overriding concern of Hitler and the German High Command was to defeat the Dutch forces as quickly as possible so that the Nazi mechanized ground forces could be moved to France. By this tactical advantage, and unhindered by any adversary in the air or anti-aircraft guns on the ground, the *Luftwaffe* transformed Rotterdam into a blazing inferno of orange and thick black suffocating smoke that killed 814 people and left some 78,000 homeless.[29]

While the Dutch forces, in accordance with the surrender terms, were returning to their barracks to dispose of their arms, a motorized regiment of SS troops was heading north through Rotterdam toward The Hague to join still-isolated airborne troops. Possibly unaware of the surrender terms, the SS men noticed the Dutch soldiers on the road carrying their weapons and suddenly opened fire with machine guns. General Student, the senior German officer at the nearby command headquarters, was accidentally struck by a stray bullet. Fortunately, Lieutenant Colonel Choltitz, who was also on the scene, ordered the Dutch soldiers into a nearby church. Gradually the incident ended.[30] The only remaining hostile activity involved those Dutch troops under French command in the southwestern most province of Zeeland, and not covered by the capitulation order. They continued to hold out for another two days before being overcome by German infantry and motorized troops. This concluded the war in the Netherlands.

Militarily, the German conflict in the Netherlands was strikingly similar to the Norwegian campaign. Air power was the decisive factor, which not only immobilized the Dutch Air Force (such as it was); it also provided the airborne troops that paved the way for the panzers over the numerous bridges and fields into the heart of Holland. The canals, flooding devices, trenches and fortified, albeit outdated, defense positions, really did accomplish what they were intended to do, namely, delay the German advance. This was done at the Peel Marshes in the south; a line along the east front of Fortress Holland that remained intact; the Maas bridges that slowed the German access to Rotterdam and The Hague; and later at the Zuider Zee dam near Den Helder. These delaying positions did slow or at least hold back the Germans until aid from the Allies arrived. But without air support, the French were no more able than the Dutch to deter the German assault.

In the Five Day War, approximately 2,100 Dutch soldiers were killed and 2,700 wounded. The number of German casualties was never published, but since the number of destroyed German aircraft exceeded 500, one can assume that the heaviest casualties were suffered by the *Luftwaffe*. The Dutch air force was practically destroyed.[31] Some 700 Dutch ships managed to escape capture, which, with the 500 already on the high seas, made a total of 1,200 available to the Allied cause.[32]

The defeat of the Dutch forces was but the first phase of a more protracted *Blitzkrieg* in the West against the Allied forces of France and the English Expeditionary Force that ended three weeks later with the surrender of Belgium and the capitulation of the French at Dunkirk. But for the people of Holland, the Five Day War was the first phase of a five-year occupational nightmare of Nazi barbarism, only to be matched by a far greater degree of heroism by the most extraordinary of ordinary people.

A Dutch Critique of the German Invasion

The following analysis of the Five Day War appeared in an Underground newsletter by Pieter 't Hoen two months after the occupation. As early as 1933, the Amsterdam journalist recognized the threat Germany posed to Western European democracy and to Dutch independence.

> *Exactly as we could have expected has happened. Without an ultimatum, without a declaration of war, the German army invaded our country. In the depth of night German air squadrons threw themselves on our airports, and German tanks and flame-throwers burned our border defenses. A few hours later the German Roller rolled over Groningen, Gelderland and Brabant, bringing death and despair to a peaceful population, brutally awoken from their innocent slumber of neutrality, in which the de Geer Cabinet had cradled and lulled it since September 1939.*
>
> *In this night of the 9th-10th of May it became suddenly clear that the politics of neutrality was an insufficient means to keep the country out of the war and to save it from a German invasion. These politics were based on the illusion that the country, by careful movement, by painfully accurate impartial behavior and by avoiding any kind of offence, could remain neutral. This illusion was a serious ignorance of the target and stake of this war. The fight is in the first place about the hegemony in Europe and in a further stadium, world domination.*

Why would Germany that strives for this world domination, leave our country out of the matter? There was even less reason for such an assumption because our country and Belgium, the obvious and natural headway area would be for a German army that would want to invade France by by-passing the Maginot Line. That is why it was obvious beforehand that Germany would never respect our neutrality, regardless of all the sacred assurances regularly made in the Wilhelmstrasse on this matter. The November 11, 1939 panic and the January 14 crisis of this year were already a consequence of the existing plan in Berlin to invade the Netherlands and Belgium. Only the unfavorable weather circumstances saved us then. But this was only delay, not cancellation.

This became obvious on the 10th of May. The consequences of the unfortunate politics of neutrality became clear then. It was purposely neglected to organize the necessary coordination between the Belgian and Dutch defense system, so that our Peel Division for instance, was left on its own and the Dutch troops, retreating from Limburg, and who were looking for cover behind the River Maas on Belgian territory, were shot upon at some locations. Instead of a thoroughly prepared attack on the German army, an improvised Belgian-Dutch cooperation had to be put in motion, but the beloved fiction of neutrality, cherished in The Hague, were an insuperable obstruction to this.

Cooperation with our natural allies against the German threat, namely France and England, was also not pursued. On the contrary, it was intentionally omitted, what could have ensured a speedy assistance; all this just because of the neutrality misunderstanding. But when push came to shove, the Allied help had to be improvised as well. Was it a miracle that these improvisations failed against the perfect German army organization, of which it was known that it has been preparing for this battle since 1933? Admittedly on the 10th of May British planes appeared above our country, but this help (that admittedly was very effective in certain places) could by lack of preparation not be of the desired scope. The safety of the country had to be sacrificed to the illusion of neutrality.

In five days the battle had been fought. Besides the bitter results of the foreign policies we also had to suffer the consequences of the neglect of our armament. A people of eight million souls can certainly bring forth an army of 800,000 men. We only had 400,000. Heavy border fortresses we did not have at all. They never wanted to spend the money for that. When five years ago Professor Goudriaan proposed to build a Maginot

Line on our German border, he was laughed at. The regents, the bankers and the aristocracy, who have been in charge here for ages, refused to pay the necessary millions for this purpose.

There were no airplanes either. It's estimated that we had nearly 400 planes, but barely 15 per cent of these were of sufficient quality to fight the Heinkels and Messerschmitts. The rest consisted of old wooden crates that could barely fly 200 kilometers an hour, and brave men who were sent into the skies faced certain death. Fokker and Koolhoven were two modern airplane builders. If one had combined their factories and invested the necessary money for mass production, we could have had at least 2,000 first class planes to use against the German invader. But all of this was overlooked. The puny rich classes are to blame for this.

The remaining air defense was also miserable. There was a terrible shortage of anti-aircraft guns. Deserving patriots, who had seen the danger coming for some time, organized collections in several towns to buy anti-aircraft guns. But the money came slowly and insufficiently. The cheapskates kept their money boxes shut and in the country's capital for instance, where about a hundred millionaires live, they had to beg for more than a year to collect one million; they even had to hire an advertising agency to entice the people to open their wallets, and when finally, after much trouble succeeded in collecting 900,000 guilders, the city council paid the last few thousands. If I am not mistaken, the flak batteries hadn't all arrived by the time Herman Goering's first squadrons flew over the city.

We haven't any tanks at all. It was said that those would be completely useless here with the type of land we have. The German invasion proved that point wrong. There were nowhere near enough anti-tank guns. In Limburg for instance, there were only two anti-tanks on a border stretch of four kilometers. Against the German tank techniques that one could have learned from the war in Poland, they could only have the effect of a children's toy pistol.

All we had was our Waterline and our courage. But unfortunately this Waterline was a strategic defense work built in the 17th century, but in our time was clearly deficient in stopping General Keitel's armies. This Waterline was a rattrap that we had locked ourselves in and presented ourselves to the German airmen on a presenting tray. And our courage? Yes that was magnificent. The airmen, marines, sailors and many troops have fought as men. But teeth grinding and cursing with powerless anger, they had to realize that they stood opposite the German enemy just as Abyssinians stood opposite the Italians. Because of the thriftiness and the lack of European insight by the countless ministries Colijn and de Geer cabinet, they were withheld the weapons needed to resist the aggressor. The good village politicians in The Hague, who didn't understand what was going on in the world and who didn't want to listen to the urgent advice by the responsible military, who kept their hands on their wallets; after all that's why we already had to capitulate after five days.

Pieter 't Hoen 33
25 July 1940

4

The Darkening of Occupation

We felt like the bees of a bee colony deprived not only of their queen bee, but also of their hive. Every individual had to decide for himself. Not a few found such decisions distressing; most decided to wait and see. The government had gone, the military were in captivity, parliament suspended, newspapers restricted. Consequently leadership was completely absent.

—Herman Friedhoff, *member of the Dutch Resistance*

After the German conquests in Scandinavia and in the Low Countries, the defeat of a large part of the British army, and with France on the verge of collapse, the Nazi leaders were ever more confident that they could triumph over those unoccupied territories of Europe not yet under their domination. The successful German victories also produced a severe psychological reaction on the part of the Dutch population. Blighted hopes and disillusionment led many to accept the German presence as a *fait accompli* of a *Pax Germania* on the European continent. Like the beleaguered citizenry of Denmark and Norway, the Dutch accepted their downfall with relative acquiescence. Once in control, and assured that the Dutch had laid down their arms and were demobilized, the Germans allowed the Dutch prisoners of war to return to civilian life. All of Holland now lay under the heel of the hated Hun.

The Five Day War left town and country in a state of utter chaos. Families were separated, small towns and villages were abandoned, and larger cities were

The Darkening of Occupation

overcrowded with thousands of evacuees. For the 9 million citizens of Holland who realized that they were suddenly being ruled by a tyrannical foreign power, ambiguous reactions of fear, indignation, anguish, shattered hopes and resignation combined to create varied emotions. For some, the feeling that the occupation was a temporary, albeit unpleasant, phase that would end as quickly as it had begun; but for others it was a dark impenetrable abyss of unknown duration. As one seventeen-year-old Dutch girl remembers, the Nazi legions paraded through the cities of Holland:

> *The Dutch citizens, their faces stern, black, immobile with inner rage and disfigured with shed and unshed tears, watched the grand entrance of the German war machine. Along the streets we stood huddled together, shivering in the bright May sunshine watching, watching… endlessly. We saw armored cars, powerful guns, panzerwagons, trucks, and then rows upon rows of marching soldiers, like automatons, their boots lifting and falling on the pavement in minutest cadenza and precision, their arms swaying up and down like a machine. This relentless pounding of the boots on the pavement became for me the symbol of impending danger, of fear and of hatred. What was in store for us now? What kind of life awaited us?* [1]

The Dutch authorities were immediately ordered to release some 6,000 Dutch Nazi collaborators—the N.S.B.'ers as they were called—imprisoned during the conflict. Their leader, Anton Mussert, unwilling to expose himself too soon to a large majority of patriotic countrymen, remained in hiding somewhere east of Amsterdam. Once he reappeared in public, wherever he went he met with distrust and animosity.[2]

In Amsterdam conditions were particularly grim for the thousands of German refugees who sought a safe haven from endless suffering under Nazi tyranny. Throughout the cities and smaller towns, countless persons—both Netherlanders and German refugees—took their own lives to avoid the anguish of Nazi persecution and atrocities of the type in Poland they had read about in their newspapers. On the first day of the occupation, the number of suicides was so large that the Health Department was unable to handle the bodies of the unfortunates with its ambulances; large trucks were hired to assist in the removal of the bodies.[3]

Nevertheless, the first several months of the occupation were not as bad as many people expected. The German troops were instructed to conduct themselves courteously toward the Dutch civilians. They were well-behaved, and abused no one. They were seen enjoying themselves in the cafes, restaurants and night clubs, often in the company of Dutch female sympathizers. Within a few weeks, stores, theaters, bars and movie houses reopened, and people resumed their daily activities.

But at the same time, numerous prohibitions were announced. It was forbidden to show the national flag or the flag of the House of Orange; any distribution of pamphlets that called for resistance to the German authorities was a punishable offense. All means of private transportation required the granting of special permits, and stocks of gasoline were requisitioned by the German High Command to be used for the transfer of troops and arms to Belgium and Northern France.[4] Yet despite these measures, life went on pretty much as usual.

On May 25, less than two weeks after the capitulation, a German civilian administration for the Netherlands was established under the rule of Hitler-appointed *Reichskommisar*, Dr. Arthur Seyss-Inquart, the Austrian pro-Nazi Chancellor who was mainly responsible for the German annexation of Austria two years earlier. Prior to his assignment to Holland, he was the Deputy Governor General of Occupied Poland.

Of the several German officials who accompanied Seyss-Inquart to Holland, clearly the most influential was Hanns Albin Rauter, also an Austrian, the "Higher SS and Police Chief," who dominated the intricate German security mechanism in the Netherlands. As head of all police services in Holland, Rauter controlled the dreaded SS including the *Waffen-SS* military troops, the *Staatspolizei*, commonly called the *Gestapo*, and the Order Police, more familiarly referred to as the "Green Police" because of their green uniforms, who engaged in mass raids, street arrests, deportations, actions against strikes and executions; internal subversion was handled by the *Sicherheitsdienst* (SD), the intelligence service that made use of hundreds of Dutch undercover agents called V-men, who infiltrated Underground organizations. Rauter received his orders directly from Heinrich Himmler, the head of the *Schutzstaffel* (SS), Hitler's elite black-uniformed praetorian guard.

In his inaugural speech at The Hague four days after his arrival, Seyss-Inquart, in hypocritical Nazi fashion, bitterly accused the Dutch Government of cowardly taking flight, making common cause with the enemy (England), thus "forcing" the Germans to occupy Holland. "Rather would we have come here with our hand lifted in salute than with weapons in our fist," he said. "We are to build a new Europe based upon the foundations of honor and common labor. We all know that the ultimate purpose of our Fuehrer is peace and order for all who are of good will."[5]

Then, in a more flattering tone, the new German High Commissioner told the Dutch people that their laws and basic rights would remain in force until further notice. Assurances were given that the occupation was exclusively military, and that Germany had no imperialistic designs or claims on Dutch territory in Europe or overseas, and there was no obligation to accept Nazi political convictions.[6] Many Netherlanders were naively taken in by this ambiguous proclamation, and wanted to believe that the Germans would not import their hated Nazi creed. Initially the German leaders wanted to keep the Netherlands ostensibly independent so as to create a minimum of trouble during the early period of adjustment. They realized that only an insignificant number of the Dutch people favored annexation to Germany.[7]

Of greater significance and of more far-reaching concern for Hitler was the role he expected the Netherlands would play in the long-range vision of a postwar Europe. He believed that a common hereditary bond existed with the Dutch both racially and nationally. Like the Norwegians, the Netherlanders were viewed as "racially pure" and as the best representatives of the Germanic race, subject to incorporation in the Greater German Reich. It was always the Fuehrer's belief that his vision of a "Germanic Empire" would need all of the soil and territory to which he considered it entitled, and that the establishment of civilian administrations in the Netherlands and Norway would produce the superior stock necessary to improve the racial composition of the German Nation.[8]

With clever manipulation, the Nazi leaders expected cooperation from the Dutch populace, but the Germans lacked subtlety. Less than a month after the occupation, the true intentions of the Nazi administration gradually began to surface. One discriminatory measure after another was introduced that resulted in a growing anti-Nazi sentiment. Resentment was frequently augmented by the *Wehrmacht* troops parading through the streets singing *"Dan wir fahren gegen Engeland"*—Next we go to England.

On June 24, Seyss-Inquart terminated the Parliament and dismissed the existing Council of State, the body charged by the Constitution with the appointment of a regent in the event of a vacancy.[9] In his quest for power, N.S.B. leader Mussert submitted a plan to the *Reichskommisar* prepared by the former's legal adviser to reappoint a new Council of State composed of Dutch Nazis and others sympathetic to Mussert that would appoint him regent, because the position of Head of State was vacant since the departure of the Queen. However, the plan was rejected by Seyss-Inquart as too far-reaching.[10] The next few months were marked by the introduction of new German ordinances and decrees. On July 4, a prohibition against listening to the B.B.C.; on July 14, food regulation and rationing were introduced; on July 16, a Dutch Nazi commissar was appointed to run the unions; on July 20, the Communist party was dissolved. Then on July 31, Seyss-Inquart announced the first, albeit innocuous, anti-Jewish measure: the prohibition of ritual animal slaughter.[11]

Some pacifist-minded Christians claimed that there should be no interference with the Germans "because the occupation itself was God's will." Other resistance-minded people, many of whom were filled with passionate contempt for the hated invaders, cited passages from the Bible in support of a more realistic position that clearly expressed the direction they believed should be taken. Still others felt betrayed by the flight of their queen, and that she no longer had the right to lead the people.[12]

However, on July 28, 1940, the official Free Dutch broadcasting station in London under the name "Radio Oranje" made its first appearance, and when Queen Wilhelmina delivered her inaugural speech expressing her firm resolve to stand firm against Adolf Hitler and all others who believed as he did, those feelings were reversed, feelings of hostility against Germany increased, and people began to realize the value of a legal Government-in-Exile.[13]

Fortified by a fervid patriotic spirit, the people began to express their true feelings in what might be called acts of "symbolic Resistance," personal gestures or actions that expressed one's instinctive aversion to the presence of the *moffen*—a pejorative term used by the Dutch to describe the German occupiers—and allegiance to his or her country, its individuality and right to exist. For example, stamps were now placed on the top-left corner of envelopes because the right side was reserved only for stamps bearing the image of the Queen. And since there was no greeting more commonplace than "hallo," the letters of this word were regarded as an acronym for the sentence: *Hang alle landverraders op*, which means "Hang all traitors."[14] As a sign of "keeping together," safety pins were worn on coat lapels and other outer garments. Probably the most symbolic gesture that helped energize a resistance mentality was the V-for-Victory campaign that originated in London and the B.B.C. The four notes or simply four beats of the drum from Beethoven's Fifth symphony harmonized with the Morse code for the letter V: three dots and a dash. Often the letter V was plastered on walls or over German propaganda placards or next to the initials R.A.F., not only in Holland, but throughout all of Occupied Europe during the war years.

One of the largest displays of symbolic Resistance occurred less than two months after the occupation on June 29, 1940, the birthday of Prince Bernhard. The Germans banned the flying of patriotic flags and the singing of the national anthem. Nevertheless, many Dutch citizens celebrated the day by joining together and singing the national anthem, and either carrying red, white or pink carnations—the Prince's favorite flower—or wearing one in their buttonholes. In the town of Wageningen, policemen showed their support for the Royal Family by wearing ribbons in the Dutch royal colors.[15] All of these symbolic gestures of passive Resistance helped keep the spirit of resistance alive in the hearts and minds of the Dutch people.

But even within the government there were those who still advocated a policy of cooperation with the Nazi occupiers. Chief among them was the exiled Cabinet Minister de Geer, who even tried to convince his fellow ministers that an all-out war against Hitler was impossible. After having lost all willingness to fight, he advocated a separate negotiated peace with Germany. In August, the Queen informed de Geer that she had lost all confidence in him; he offered his resignation the following month and she promptly accepted. He was succeeded by the Minister of Justice, Professor Pieter S. Gerbrandy, a staunch patriot who helped restore high regard for the government that was sadly lacking under the previous cabinet leadership.[16]

Within Holland it was becoming increasingly obvious that the six remaining political parties could no longer operate effectively so long as the country was occupied by the Germans. It was simply a matter of time before they would be disbanded; thus leaving the Dutch Nazi Party (N.S.B.) the only political party. Consequently, a new political movement, the Netherlands Union (*Nederlandse Unie*), was formed on July 24, 1940, to counteract the influence of the N.S.B. It was headed by J. Linthorst Homan, the Queen's Commissioner for the northern province of Groningen; Professor J. E. de Quay of the Roman Catholic Party; and L. Einthoven, Police Commissioner of Rotterdam and member of one of the Liberal parties.[17] It declared itself as standing for national independence, the principles of Christianity, freedom of religion, education and speech. It repudiated class distinctions and the accompanying materialism, and it envisaged a corporate economic structure that guaranteed the right and the obligation to work. Politically, it stood for a strong nation in close relationship with its overseas territories, the Netherlands East and West Indies.

Since the founders of the Union believed that Parliamentary democracy had come to an end in Holland, and wanted to keep the country united, they harbored the hope that some sort of cooperation with the German administration might be possible by granting certain concessions in the interest of collaboration. Consequently, Union members were warned against joining Underground groups. But when the Labor Service was introducing National Socialist practices, and when Jews were being excluded from full membership in the Union, the leaders began to realize that collaboration with the Germans was possible only at the price of complete surrender. In its weekly publication *De Unie*, the Union refuted the Dutch Nazi allegation that the N.S.B. was the sole representative of the people of Holland.

During the summer of 1940, membership in the Union increased tremendously, and street fights between patriots and members of the N.S.B. were frequent occurrences. By February 1941, the Union had 800,000 members as compared to a peak membership of 100,000 claimed by the N.S.B., an obvious sign of growing patriotic activity.[18]

The earliest widespread public-spirited demonstration occurred on June 29, when people all over the country expressed their allegiance for the House of Orange. Thousands flocked to the Royal Palace in The Hague; flags were displayed from homes; flowers were laid before royal statues; and many people wore carnations or orange-colored flowers in honor of the Prince. Seyss-Inquart viewed this nationwide celebration as expressed opposition against Germany.

In its ongoing battle against the Royal Dynasty, the Germans enacted a number of measures that were aimed specifically at the Queen. Her picture was removed from all government offices, postage stamps bearing her image were replaced, references to the Royal House were eliminated from newly published textbooks and street names of living members of the House of Orange were no longer permitted.[19]

In the summer of 1941, when the Germans invaded Russia, the Queen declared the Netherlands to be an ally of Soviet Russia, after which she was declared an enemy alien by Seyss-Inquart, and her property was confiscated.[20] And when the Nazi administration called upon the Netherlands Union to promote a crusade against Bolshevism ,the Union leaders, like the Queen, refused to comply on the grounds that Russia was an ally of the Netherlands. In retaliation, the Germans suspended publication of *De Unie* for six weeks and later subjected it to censorship, whereupon the weekly halted publication, and the organization was terminated.[21] By the fall, the only remaining party in Holland was the Dutch Nazi Party.

Throughout the late autumn and winter of 1940–41, three major factors led to an ever-growing patriotic fervor among the Dutch population, augmented by an ever-growing hostility toward the goose-stepping conquerors. In the first place, there was heightened admiration for the British, an aftereffect of the resolve of that island nation to "go it alone," and notably by the success of a resilient R.A.F. in repelling Nazi air attacks from an equally determined *Luftwaffe*. This provided some encouragement and hope for the future. Second, a provoked antagonism by the black-shirted *Weer Afdeling* (W.A.), an unarmed paramilitary branch of the N.S.B., led to street fights, which were becoming persistent occurrences in an atmosphere where permissible lawlessness was becoming the order of the day.

The third and clearly the most compelling phenomenon that elevated the social consciousness of the Dutch populace was a hatred of the Nazi occupiers caused by a growing number of anti-Jewish measures forced upon a people doomed by the biological accident of race. By early 1941, that hatred was beginning to swell to fever-pitch, creating a deep-seated revulsion marked by a nationwide contamination of the brown leprosy that was soon to spread like the medieval plague.

5

The Plight of the Dutch Jews

We Nazis do not consider the Jews a part of the Netherlands people. They are our enemies, with whom we neither wish to conclude a truce nor a peace.
—Reich's Commissioner Arthur Seyss-Inquart
March 12, 1941

Unlike Germany and Eastern Europe, very little anti-Semitism existed in Holland before the Nazi occupation. Clearly, social divisions were observed by both Jews and Gentiles, just as between Catholics and Protestants, but the atmosphere in the Netherlands was distinguished by religious tolerance. In 1930, approximately 113,000 Jews were living in Holland.[1] With the rise of Nazism in Germany, energized by a racial superiority and intensified by the rapture of a militant nationalism, an influx of Jewish refugees flooded into the Netherlands. After the German annexation of Austria and the dismemberment of Czechoslovakia in 1938, some 15,000 German Jews and about 10,000 other foreign Jews entered Holland in a desperate attempt to avoid the encroaching Nazi tentacles. By the end of the year, immigration was dramatically reduced because most of the new arrivals had no visible means of support, but also out of Holland's fear of alienating Germany. By 1939, an additional 10,000 indigent foreign Jews entered the country, many of whom were interned at the newly constructed refugee camp, Westerbork, in the northeastern province of Drenthe. By the time the country was under Nazi rule, there were approximately 140,000 Jews in the Netherlands.[2]

The Plight of the Dutch Jews

During the first eight months of the occupation, the German authorities proceeded reluctantly toward the Jews. The purpose was to segregate the Jewish inhabitants from the rest of the Dutch population. In early August 1940, the first anti-Semitic decree prohibited the Jewish ritual slaughter of animals. No longer able to kill their cattle by the severing of arteries and bleeding, Jewish butchers were now required to follow the more commonly accepted method of stunning and shooting. The Dutch Nazi daily, the *Nationale Dagblad*, hastened to applaud the decree as a "measure which will cleanse our Dutch national honor of this Palestinian smudge of cruelty to animals."

About the middle of September, the next ruling involved hundreds of small Jewish merchants, most of whom were poor traders, who were no longer allowed to eke out a living peddling their wares, mostly odds and ends, in carts on public streets.[3]

In the early autumn, Civil Service and municipal government jobs were no longer open to Jews, or to Gentiles married to Jews. Those already employed were barred from promotion. In October, some 30,000 Jewish businesses were required to register with the German authorities; the beginning of a slow process of pauperization for tens of thousands of Jewish citizens.[4]

Additional measures of discrimination involved the forcible dismissal of all Jewish professors from Dutch universities. In late November, after the dismissal of Jewish professors and students at Leiden University, the Dean of the Law School, Professor R.P. Cleveringa, responded by delivering a stinging denunciation of the German authorities, followed by a staccato outburst of the *Wilhelmus*, Holland's national anthem, by the student gathering. That same day Professor Cleveringa was arrested and locked in an SS prison situated in the dunes in Scheveningen, a beach resort on the North Sea near The Hague, and generally referred to by the Dutch as the "Oranje Hotel."[5] The students responded by going on strike at both Leiden and at the Institute for Technology at Delft. The Germans reacted immediately by closing both universities. Leyden remained closed for the duration of the war; Delft was closed until April 1941.

The following January, Seyss-Inquart required a complete registration of the entire Jewish population, and in July a large "J" had to be stamped on new identity cards issued to every Jew. Inspections could be conducted at any time on streets, trains and public places. Anyone caught without his identity card was subject to arrest. There followed a measure requiring Jewish owners to sell their firms far below their real value.[6]

With Teutonic thoroughness the Nazis were determined to make life unbearable for the Jews. All public places posted a sign that read: *Verboden voor Joden*—Forbidden for Jews. Theaters, cafes and restaurants were closed to them.[7]

Among the numerous amenities now being denied the Jewish population was the possession of radios. Anyone caught listening to the news could be deported. The reason given by the German authorities was that Jews were propagating detrimental rumors obtained from listening to London broadcasts of Radio Orange. Ironically, the forbidden radio was covertly listened to more enthusiastically than before. Those who took the risk and retained their radios would remove them from concealment while designated family members would stand guard within their own homes to keep a lookout for N.S.B. traitors looking for Jews with hidden radios. A teenage son might stand sentinel in the hall listening at the front door for footsteps in the street while his mother would be posted in the kitchen ready to receive a signal for forwarding to the back room. Another member would serve as translator from English into Dutch. Christians invited Jews into their homes on a regular basis to listen to the broadcasts. Additionally, Gentiles expressed their disdain of the sadistic anti-Semitic decrees by special acts of kindness and thoughtfulness toward their Jewish neighbors. In the shops and other public buildings where the Jews were still allowed to visit, they met with great friendliness and sympathy.[8]

The hospitality and kindliness did produce some unfortunate repercussions. On one occasion at The Hague a Jew was elected President of a High School Parents' Association. Later that same day when the matter was discovered by the Germans, the man was arrested and sent to a concentration camp, accused of "presumptuous behavior." Henceforth, the Nazi authorities warned all Gentiles that if any such "scandalous elections" were ever to occur again they would be met with severe reprisals.[9]

In February 1941, rioting erupted in Amsterdam, The Hague and Rotterdam. The first physical attacks took place between small Jewish action groups called *Knokploegen* (K.P.), and the Dutch Nazi street fighting *Weer Afdeling (W.A.)*. The large Jewish district in the north of Amsterdam was the scene of violent assaults precipitated by the *W.A.* who staged a provocative march that soon degenerated into attacks on passers-by and on houses occupied by Jews who were dragged into the streets and from the streetcars. Assisted by Gentiles, the Jews clashed with thugs, killing one Nazi and injuring several others. At the height of the riots and demonstrations, the Nazis sealed off the Jewish quarter. On February 17 and 18, the Communists succeeded in forcing a strike of Amsterdam metal and shipyard workers, and obstructed German plans to forcibly deport workers to Germany.[10]

On February 19, the German police raided an ice-cream parlor that was a known action group front. During the struggle, acid was sprayed on the police

The Plight of the Dutch Jews

by one of the defenders. On February 22, in retaliation, in what became known as the Black Sabbath, 425 men below the age of 35 were rounded up and severely beaten in full public view. The prisoners were then transported to the sulphur mines of Mauthausen concentration camp in Austria, where all but one died.[11]

When news of the round-ups and brutalities was received by the people of Amsterdam, the citizens, including the Gentile populace, seethed with deep-seated revulsion. Within two days of the arrests, the Communists were the first to react to the ill-treatment of the Jews. Their political party had been dissolved earlier, but was reorganized illegally in November 1940 despite the German non-aggression pact with the Soviet Union. Thousands of leaflets were circulated urging a work stoppage.

The Communists assembled in a large public square in a working-class district and called for a protest strike. On February 25, all tram conductors were persuaded to strike, and by noon all streetcar traffic ceased. Within hours, businesses and shops, offices and stores also closed their doors. Later in the day, hundreds of people who were not working circulated in the center of the city and encouraged others to join the strike. By the end of the day, almost half of the municipal workers were on strike. The work stoppage persisted and extended to the nearby towns of Haarlem and Zaandam.[12]

The strike had taken the German authorities completely by surprise. Seyss-Inquart was in Vienna, leaving his Security Police Chief, Hanns Rauter, in charge. Once the authorities realized how serious conditions had become, a stage of siege was immediately declared. Executive power was transferred to General Friedrich Christiansen, the military head of the Nazi occupation troops. Large numbers of Nazi SS death's-head units and Dutch military police were moved into the city to patrol the streets. A curfew was announced both by broadcasts and loudspeaker vans, which forbade anyone on the streets in the evening after 7:30. To avoid any further reaction by the Germans, the Mayor of Amsterdam ordered all municipal officials to return to work immediately or face punishment or dismissal. However, the strike did not finally end until February 27, when normal activities were resumed and men returned to their jobs.

The number of those who took part in the strike varied from between 200,000 and 300,000 out of a total population of 800,000.[13] In retaliation for the strike, 1,000 workers, both Communist and others, were arrested, followed by deportation. Heavy fines in the amount of fifteen million guilders were imposed on Amsterdam and corresponding collective fines went to the other municipalities where the strikes had occurred.[14]

Even though the short-but-widespread strike produced no material benefits to the strikers, the work stoppage made unequivocally clear to the Germans the Dutch opposition to the anti-Jewish measures; that the Nazi hold on the country was based solely on their military presence; that Nazi propaganda was a failure; and that the strike was an active repudiation of both the German regime and Mussert's Nazi Party, which had proved itself to be totally dependent upon German military superiority.

In connection with the Amsterdam riots, the Germans established a Jewish Council to oversee and control the Jewish community. It also assisted Jews in legal and financial matters, provided educational programs, and later supervised the distribution of food. But since it was the intention of the Nazis to destroy the Jews, the Council was soon constrained to follow the directives of its German masters, which made it a more pliable instrument in the hands of the Nazi authorities.[15]

On March 12, 1941, in a move to discourage any further protests, Seyss-Inquart took particular care in a public speech to point out that "we Nazis do not consider the Jews a part of the Netherlands people. They are our enemies, with whom we neither wish to conclude a truce nor a peace."[16] In May, all Jews were banned from entrance into the Stock Exchanges of Amsterdam, Rotterdam and The Hague. Further decrees ordered Jewish doctors, dentists and pharmacists to treat Jewish patients only. Furthermore, Jewish musicians were forbidden to play in subsidized orchestras, and in The Hague, a stipulation was issued that excluded Jewish citizens from hotels, boarding houses, furnished rooms and public parks; boulevards adjacent to seaside resorts were also off-limits.[17]

By the summer of 1941, scarcely any freedom of movement was left to Holland's Jewry. No amusements were available to them. Throughout the country, however, Gentiles were forced to attend theaters where the scurrilous anti-Jewish film, "The Eternal Jew," was being shown. It was so unbelievably crude that no one in his right mind could take it seriously. For most of the Gentiles who viewed the film, it merely strengthened their resolve to oppose the Nazi regime. Toward the end of June, the Jews were forced to keep their shops closed on Sundays. In the northern part of the country where many were engaged in the cattle trade, they were forbidden entry into the cattle markets.[18]

One of the most vicious measures during the summer months was the confiscation of all arable land belonging to the Jews, and the concentration of all Jewish capital in a single bank, which had previously been placed under German control. No Jew was allowed to possess more than one thousand guilders, or about $540, and he was completely dispossessed of the power to dispose of his own possessions for money. In August, they were required to register all their real estate, whereupon they lost all authority over immovable property.[19]

With the reopening of the schools in early autumn, the Jewish Council was instructed to organize a separate system of education for Jewish children in which Jewish teachers would perform the instruction, since Jewish pupils were forbidden to attend schools with Gentiles. And while in The Hague and Amsterdam a few primary schools were opened, nothing was done in the provinces for Jewish children.[20]

In the early spring of 1942, Jews from all over the Netherlands were now being transported to large urban centers, particularly Amsterdam, where they were resettled into crowded ghettos, leaving behind all their possessions, which were requisitioned by the Germans. Hundreds of Jewish families were often forced to share one foul-smelling room with two or three families. The narrow streets were overfilled with the continuous influx of dispossessed souls from all over Holland.[21]

For most of the Jews, this "resettlement" was a temporary condition; it was soon replaced by the so-called "final solution." On January 20, 1942, at the quiet Berlin suburb of Wannsee, orders verbally given earlier by Hitler to Reich Marshal Hermann Goering, were carried out by the diabolical SS Security Service (*Sicherheitsdienst*) head, Reinhard Heydrich. The order was rather simple. All the European Jews were to be transported to camps in the conquered Eastern territories to be used as slave laborers. They would then either be worked to death or, for those who survived, exterminated.[22]

In May, German Security Police Chief Hanns Rauter issued an order requiring all Dutch Jews to wear a clearly visible "Star of David," on a yellow background, the size of the palm of one's hand bearing the inscription *Jood* (Jew) in black Hebrew letters. A similar star was to be conspicuously displayed at the entrance of each Jewish home or apartment.

Gentiles expressed their denunciation of this new Nazi measure by going out of their way to show their support for their Jewish fellow citizens. Non-Jewish girls made it a point to walk arm in arm with star-marked Jewish boys; the reverse was an equally common occurrence. As a further sign of support, Gentiles would offer their seats on trolley cars to star-marked Jewish neighbors. And many of the non-Jews displayed an emblem resembling the Jewish Star, but with the word "Duchman" written across it in black letters.[23]

In the summer of 1942, for the vast majority of the Jews in Holland, the worst was yet to come. The Jewish Council was informed by the German authorities that all Jews between the ages of 18 and 40 were now ordered to go to work in armament plants and other industries in Germany. On July 14, the date of the departure of the first group, relatively few Jews reported voluntarily to the deportation office. As a result, the German police arrested 750 Jews as hostages in a mass raid to force compliance of the first group's scheduled for departure. The scheme worked well. Within the last two weeks of July, more than 6,000 Jews were shipped to the former refugee camp at Westerbork, which was now a transit camp where families were transported to their ultimate destination: extermination camps in the East. Between July 1942 and September 1943, 93 freight trains left Westerbork in the north and two other trains from the overflow camp at Vught in the south; 60,000 Jews were deported to Auschwitz, and 34,000 to Sobibor; another 9,000 went to Theresienstadt and Bergen-Belsen.[24]

During the early fall of 1942, immunity from deportation was granted to certain classes. Jews married to Gentile women with children could apply for exemption; Jewesses married to Christian men were eligible for this favor, even if childless. But later in the autumn, the stipulation was rescinded.[25] Exemptions were allowed for certain other categories. For example, a *sperrstempel* (exemption stamp) was provided on the identity card of a Jew who somehow had helped a high-ranking German officer. Similarly, a young Jewish nurse who worked at a Jewish hospital was given a *sperr* on her identity card.[26] An exemption stamp was the Jews' most priceless possession during 1942–43. But even those Jews who possessed an exemption stamp but were caught on the street during a raid couldn't be certain as to their fate. Some capricious German officials were erratic and unreliable and paid no attention to the exemptions.

Nevertheless, for the vast majority of Jews in the days and weeks that followed, the situation was unbearable. Jews were rounded up in day and night raids and marched off in large groups into the unknown. Suicides were not uncommon and many Jews lost their reason. One anguished victim whose letter somehow managed to reach Allied territory gave this account:

> *We are on the point of death. You cannot imagine the suffering that goes on here. Throughout the long nights we listen for the sound of footsteps, and wonder whether they will halt before our door. Age no longer makes a difference. Several of our friends and neighbors, including a woman of 80, have disappeared. Presumably they have been sent to the slaughterhouses of Poland.*[27]

Gradually divested of their rights, their social standing, their worldly possessions and now their very lives, the Jews were finally reduced to frightened, hungry and humiliated creatures with only one instinct—to survive at whatever cost. And while denunciation and oppression were looked upon as a national virtue by the Nazi occupiers and their Dutch collaborators, the vast majority of the Dutch population viewed it as a stigma on the national soul.

6

The Dutch Samaritans

Courage is never alone for it has fear as its ever-present companion. An act deserves to be called courageous if, and only if, it is performed in spite of fear. The greater the fear, the more courageous the action that defies it. Thus, it is only when fear and anxiety rule supreme that courage can truly assert itself.
—*Schlomo Breznitz, Israeli Professor of Psychology, Haifa University*

The terrible anguish of the martyred Jews of Holland evolved into something more than an historical example of demonic cruelty and indifference to man; the personal eyewitness testimony to the inhumanity to which the Jews were subjected became an index of the spiritual wretchedness of the vast majority of the Dutch Christian population. The Jewish community had long been regarded as an integral part of Dutch society. As early as the seventeenth century, Jews were permitted to settle and worship in many cities of Holland without distinguishing identification or without being required to live in ghettos or pay special taxes, as was the practice in other parts of Europe; unfortunately, that was not the case in all of the countries of Occupied Europe.

The extent to which the Jews were victimized throughout Occupied Europe varied from country to country depending on several factors. The severity and amount of control that the SS exercised over the civilian population of the country was a principal factor. It was the SS who were charged with the responsibility of eradicating the Jewish people. Then there was the extent of discretionary power that was left in the hands of indigenous national leaders and the degree of restraint or resistance to Nazi demands for the persecution or deportation of Jews to death camps. The SS frequently relied upon local governmental agencies to register Jews, deny them their rights and property and arrest and deliver them to transit camps supposedly for "resettlement" in Eastern European labor camps. For example, both Bulgaria and Slovakia were autonomous German allies. In Slovakia the ruling power concurred with most of the German requests for the deportation of its Jews, whereas the Bulgarian regime did not. By the end of the war, 80 percent of Slovakian Jewry perished, whereas 80 percent of the Bulgarian Jews survived.[1]

An additional factor in determining the extent of Jewish decimation was the level of pre-war anti-Semitism and the degree to which Jews were assimilated into the society at large. This greatly impacted the amount of sympathy and support Jews received during the occupation. For example in Poland, where anti-Semitism was widespread, Jews formed an ostracized subculture. Aid was scarcely extended to Jews even by many Poles who joined anti-Nazi resistance movements. Conversely, in Denmark, where Jews were regarded as an integral part of Danish society, a daring rescue operation saved almost an entire Jewish community.[2]

In pre-war Holland, Jews constituted less than two percent of the population and benefited from a long tradition of religious tolerance and civic equality.[3] After the occupation, it was the Germans, by their own barbaric behavior, who created an ever firmer solidarity between Jews and Gentiles than had existed before. That feeling of kinship was strengthened when the N.S.B. and its 80,000 members aided the German occupiers by filling vacated political offices, intimidating Jews and assisting in raids and round-ups of Jews for deportation.[4] No Gentile could remain indifferent to the fate of the Jews without being indifferent to his or her own fate.

Lastly, there was the topographical condition of the region that contributed to the success or failure of the concealment of the Jews, and whether the location facilitated smuggling Jews into adjacent neutral countries such as Sweden, Switzerland or Spain. In Holland, borders on the North Sea and parts of Nazi-occupied territory made concealment and escape difficult and dangerous. The flat terrain, lack of heavy forestation and high population density afforded little opportunity or safe refuge for those attempting to hide in remote areas; there were no easy escape routes for those on the run.

Despite the numerous obstacles to evasion and escape, it is nothing short of incredible that so many evaders were able to elude capture by going into hiding.

These were what the Dutch called *onderduikers*, a colloquial term that literally means "underdivers" because they had to "dive" Underground to evade capture by the Germans. Anyone who has studied the European resistance movements during the war knows that this was not an exceptionally Dutch phenomenon. This form of Underground activity occurred all over Occupied Europe.

What was typical of Holland was the scale on which persecuted people were helped into hiding. The problem became particularly urgent in the summer of 1942, when the Germans started deporting Dutch Jews to the death camps in Poland and Germany. Several studies have suggested that 24,000–25,000 Dutch Jews went into hiding and 16,000–17,000, including about 4,000 children, lived through the war.[5] Generally, in those places where Jews lived in sizable numbers, there were far fewer opportunities for going into hiding. Thus, Jews from the rural provinces had a far better chance of surviving the war in hiding than those from the major cities in North and South Holland.[6]

The decision to go into hiding was not always an easy one to make; and for the majority of Jews the attempt was not made for any number of reasons. Many were so firmly attached to their personal belongings that they simply refused to leave their family home. Age, illness and aging parents whose adult children did not want to abandon them were additional factors. Other considerations involved small children who were bound to make noise while in hiding places where silence was absolutely necessary for at least part of the day; providing for the education and entertainment of older children kept in confinement for weeks and even months. Orthodox Jews found it particularly difficult to conceive of performing their religious observances underground. Finally there were those who believed that deportation offered a better chance of survival than evading the German authorities. These and numerous other issues were enough to discourage many families from going into hiding.[7]

For those who did go into hiding, the arrangements varied considerably and frequently involved moving to several locations. They were frequently hidden in basements, back rooms and attics, even in dwellings used or lived in by the Germans that contained places to hide. Sometimes entire families lived in upstairs rooms in homes, cafes and other office buildings. Anne Frank and her family found refuge in a secret annex above a ground floor warehouse where Anne's father had a spice-importing business. A moveable bookcase that served as a revolving door concealed a narrow staircase on the second floor that led to their living quarters. False walls and ceilings would conceal cupboards, rooms and even suites of rooms; certain portions of attics were partitioned off or accessed by hidden staircases. In older homes such as were found in Amsterdam, there might be another house connected to the house that faced the street (as was the case where the Frank family took refuge), such that it was difficult to tell where the one building ended and the other began. If the one dwelling was connected to the other by a small corridor, some hosts might allow their guests to spend time in other parts of the house at meal times or at other times during the day. But even then the guests needed a place to hide in the event of an unexpected knock at the door. In that event concealed trapdoors, coal cellars, and even spaces between floorboards were used for temporary concealment.[8]

As conditions worsened in the cities, especially in Amsterdam where German raids increased, *onderduikers* sought temporary refuge in the dunes along the seashore and in small towns and villages, particularly in the rural northeast part of Holland. Places of concealment where farmers hid their guests ranged from barns, haystacks, storage huts and dugouts, uncultivated areas of heath land, turf shelters, chicken houses, outhouses and inside farmhouses.

Without a job, money or income, each day was filled with the uncertainty of how one would survive the Occupation. *Onderduikers* were totally dependent upon others to provide them with food, shelter, valid ration and identity cards and many other essentials of everyday life. For those who were permanently consigned to a room or an attic with no end in sight, life could become unbearable. There were cases of Jews who were prone to fits of depression and even suicide as the result of prolonged incarceration. In one case, a boy of ten who was left in a room for six months lost the power of speech.[9]

Some were better equipped psychologically to deal with loneliness, and particularly the terrible anxiety and pressures created by the fear of being discovered. For example, one woman went into hiding with her husband in the draughty attic of a farmhouse in September 1942. With the approach of winter, she wrote in her diary, "This is the thirty-eighth day of our hiding; I so hope there won't be thirty-eight more." In fact, she and her husband spent a further 933 days in the attic, until the liberation in 1945.[10]

Anne Frank, who spent 25 months hiding before being discovered by the Nazis, wrote in her diary that *"we passed the time in all sorts of crazy ways: asking riddles, physical training in the dark, talking English and French, criticizing books, but it begins to pall in the end" (28 November, 1942)*. And when she was tempted to complain because of boredom she wrote, *"If I just think of how we live here, I usually come to the conclusion that it is a paradise compared with how other Jews who are not in hiding must be living."*[11] There were some who could leave their hideaway and perform odd jobs for their hosts, or find things to do to pass the time. But for the most part, the *onderduikers* were severely constrained by their circumstances. And there was always the constant fear of being discovered, and thus of endangering the lives of their courageous hosts in addition to their own.

A principal question that concerned the Dutch fugitives seeking help was a safe "address," where a trustworthy and amenable host could provide refuge. And financial rewards were offered to anyone who disclosed the whereabouts of the *onderduikers*. Doubtless, it was far more difficult for Jews to find places to hide than for non-Jews. People were either afraid of the severe punishments decreed by the Germans for hiding a Jew, or they viewed the Jews as aliens unworthy of outside help.

In spite of these fears and predilections, there was a minority in Holland willing to help. These were persons who, like that certain Samaritan in the Gospel parable refused to "pass by on the other side," as their neighbors and fellow citizens were being shipped like so many cattle to death camps. Not only did they not turn away, they refused to excuse themselves from responsibility when there was something to be done to save the life of a brother or sister in great need. Throughout the course of the occupation, clearly the most remarkable and doubtless the most admirable achievement of the Dutch Resistance was the assistance provided to the *onderduikers* who were helped into hiding. Truly, they were the heroes of Nazi-occupied Europe. They were ordinary men and women, young and old, who came from the cities, rural villages and farms; they included Catholics, Protestants, Jews, agnostics and atheists. And whatever help they provided was done at the risk of their lives. The consequences for the rescuers in a Gestapo raid most certainly would be torture, imprisonment, deportation or death.

For the most part they acted as individuals, sometimes for purely emotional or humanitarian reasons, or from profound religious convictions. In a comprehensive study, Malka Drucker and Gay Block spent three years interviewing more than a hundred rescuers from ten Nazi-occupied countries and arrived at the following conclusions:

> *Rescuers do not easily yield the answer to why they had the strength to act righteously in a time of savagery. It remains a mystery, perhaps a miracle. Many helped strangers, some saved friends and lovers. Some had humane upbringings, others did not. Some were educated, others were barely literate. They weren't all religious, they weren't all brave. What they did share, however, was compassion, empathy, an intolerance of injustice, and an ability to endure risk beyond what one wants to imagine.*[12]

The Dutch Samaritans

One for whom the decision to help the *onderduikers* was not easy to make was Bill Bouwma, a farmer who lived with his wife, Margaret, just outside the small village of Ternaard, in the northern province of Friesland, adjacent to a dike. He never stopped to consider his motivation for helping to hide Jews until a "diver" queried him. After giving it some thought, he then asked himself the same question. Maybe what he was doing was all wrong. What was right, protecting his family or saving strangers? To ponder the issue more deeply he strolled back and forth on the dike, lost in thought amidst the rhythmic pounding of the waves, seeking the right answer. After several hours of reflection, he considered how his parents raised him to help the disadvantaged, that his faith taught him to welcome the homeless, and also that he was conditioned to cope with this kind of risky adventure as a result of his military training. But the real explanation was simply that "a voice inside me told me that I had to do it. Regardless of everything else, that's all there is to it. If I disobeyed that voice in me, I would no longer be me."[13]

Others, when asked why they helped, would answer humbly that *they believed it was the right thing to do and what God would want*. They witnessed the Jews being beaten, robbed of their human dignity, dispossessed of their personal belongings, arrested on the street for no apparent reason, only to be transported to a railway station and herded into waiting freight trains and deported east to unknown destinations.

One such witness was Marion van Binsbergen Pritchard, a social worker who, at age 22, witnessed for the first time the Nazi brutalities that she had previously only heard about. On her way to school one morning in 1942, she was passing a Jewish orphanage when she saw Nazi SS soldiers picking up small crying children by an arm or a leg, and even by their hair when they didn't move fast enough, and tossing them into trucks. When two women on the street tried to interfere, they too were thrown into trucks. Outraged at what she was seeing, she was determined to assist the Jews in any way that she could. She and a number of friends organized an informal network that involved locating hiding places, providing food, clothing and ration cards for host families.

On one occasion during a raid in a large home in the country, she was hiding a Jewish family friend and three small children in a hole beneath some floorboards concealed under a rug. When a Dutch Nazi policeman returned to investigate after an initial search failed to disclose their whereabouts, Marion shot and killed the collaborator to save the family from arrest and deportation. With the help of the Underground, the corpse was disposed of in a coffin with a legitimate body. Marion, who estimates having saved about 150 Jews during the occupation, attributes her motivation and concern for others to her Anglican upbringing and the respect and consideration that she received from her own parents as a child, which helped nourish the conviction that we are our brothers' keepers.[14]

Similarly, and with that same sense of moral outrage, Arie van Mansum, a young Dutch lad who lived in the southeastern town of Maastricht, said that for him "the Holocaust did not start when Jews were being sent to concentration camps, but rather it started in the hearts of the people. As soon as you put one race higher than another, that's where it starts." As a distributor of the underground newspaper, *Vrij Nederland*, he was soon accompanying Jewish families into hiding. Soon he was providing families with several hundred ration cards that he was able to forge with the help of a contact who worked in a food-stamp office. Van Mansum was arrested first in October 1943 and incarcerated in Haaren Prison, where he spent six months in solitary confinement. Later he was sent to a concentration camp in Amersfoort in the province of Utrecht, where he was held until that area was liberated by the Allies. He was arrested again in February 1945 for delivering copies of *Vrij Nederland*, and was held there until the end of the war.[15]

Others, like Theresa Vander Burg, considered rescue work a call from God to fulfill a divinely destined mission of mercy. After persuading her husband of the righteousness of aiding Dutch dissidents, their home became a temporary refuge for anyone being hunted by the Germans. The family informed the Underground that only those persons who would be difficult to place with other families, such as expectant mothers and persons with physical disabilities, could remain for extended periods. Whenever Theresa was faced with a moral decision, she would ask herself what Jesus would do in this situation. Throughout the course of the war, on an average night, the Vander Burgs housed twelve strangers in addition to their own six children sleeping in their modest six-room house. By the end of the occupation, the family had harbored about 450 people, mostly Jews; others included striking railroad workers, forced labor evaders, members of the Resistance on the run and downed Allied pilots.[16]

In the case of Aart and Johtje Vos, "Holland was like a family and part of that family was in danger." The aid and protection that they provided for the Jews was a spontaneous reaction that they attribute to their upbringings, their happy marriage, their love for people and most of all, their love for God. In their home in Laren, a small artists' colony near Amsterdam, they concealed 36 people at one time, including 32 Jews and four others being sought by the Gestapo. An underground tunnel extended from a shed on the back of the house, under a false bottom below the coal bin, under their garden and out into the open woods. Whenever they received a warning that the village was surrounded and that a raid was immanent, the *onderduikers* would move into the tunnel where they would remain until it was safe to return to the house. In this way many lives were saved and none were ever lost.[17]

A small, albeit effective, rescuer network was formed by Arnold Douwes and Seine Otten, two men living in Nieuwlande, a farm district in the northeast. Seine, a teacher, and his wife, along with his best friend, Arnold, was part of a network of 250 people who found and provided shelter for hundreds of Jews. For Arnold, it was "the time of the Nazi boots. How I hated those boots! We heard them everywhere, together with those despised songs with which those creatures, whose legs were stuck into those boots, contaminated the cities, towns, villages, and countryside."[18] Located on a farm, they made room for the *onderduikers*, no matter how many came, even though the very small living quarters had only two rooms and a lavatory outside in the garden area. There was a small kitchen and a stairway that led up to an attic with a false hiding place. The real hiding place was under the house, which was also a workplace with a mimeograph machine where Underground leaflets were being produced. They also used carrier pigeons to send messages to England. One day the Gestapo came to the house searching for hidden Jews, and found nothing but the false hiding place in the attic. After they left the house Arnold and another member of the Resistance who was hidden in the basement managed to get a message by carrier pigeon to London that Nazi V-2 rocket parts were known to be hidden underground at a nearby airfield. The next day the airfield was bombed by the British and a returning pigeon carried a message that read *Carpe diem*.[19]

These are but a few of the dedicated men and women who provided the food, shelter and other necessities of life for the *onderduikers*, who defied the certainty of torture and death if arrested, and who survived the most savage decade of the twentieth century. Living in a persistent state of tension and fear, rescuers placed themselves in constant danger by lying, stealing and sometimes killing to successfully protect those in their care. And besides the rescuers there were others who, as Marion Pritchard stated, "risked his or her own life, such as the milkman who never asked why the family needed an extra liter of milk, or the postman who didn't ask about the dark-haired child peering around the open door, who also helped to save Jewish lives."[20]

Unlike the Allied military effort, which purpose it was to wipe out the physical presence of the enemy, this silent rebellion of ordinary citizens stood

DAWN OF COURAGE

in the very presence of the enemy for five long years, and whose courage to care for their Jewish brethren and others became the moral imperative within the Dutch Resistance by doing what they believed was the only right thing to do—preserve human dignity and the sacredness of the individual person by saving human lives.

7

The Christian Church Reaction

The present war is not only a conflict between nations. It is a war of the false gods of Teutonism against all that Christianity stands for; an onslaught upon the Christian foundations of society.
—*J.H. Boas, Religious Resistance in Holland*

Unlike the religious divisions of the 16th century, when the most important issues of the day were the threats of Protestant heresies dividing Europe and the danger posed by Muslim Turks threatening to conquer the Continent, the overriding concern of the Christian churches of Occupied Europe in the mid 1940s was the spiritual danger posed by the potential introduction of Nazism, a pre-Christian ideological view of life based on the principle of absolute authority of a single leader, a racial hatred of all non-Aryans, and German domination in a "New European Order."

Like their Norwegian neighbors to the north, the Dutch were viewed by their Nazi captors as having a common racial and national bond with the Aryan master race (except for the Jews, who were viewed as *Untermenschen*—"subhumans"), and were therefore worthy of assimilation into it.[1] This is why, as some believed, Seyss-Inquart, a civilian administrator, was put in charge as High Commissioner in Holland, as opposed to Belgium and France where military governors were installed. The Germans believed that a majority of the Dutch people would recognize the former Austrian Chancellor as an instrument for Holland's annexation into the "Greater Germanic Realm."[2] However, the Dutch citizenry, like the Norwegians, are a proud and patriotic people, and would renounce any such attempt to make Holland a part of Germany.

Nationally, Holland had become a nation-state long before Germany had acquired that status. Her struggle for independence began as far back as 1568 at the inception of the Eighty Years' War. And before William of Orange was chosen to lead the revolt, the provincial regents had formed a spiritual and social unity. By the seventeenth century, the Dutch United Provinces had grown into highly prosperous regions. Amsterdam was for a while the leading shipping and commercial capital of Europe. In 1830, after a brief civil war in the southern provinces when Belgium seceded to form a separate kingdom, the country remained united as a consolidated nation.

Conversely, Germany, some seventy years ago, was still a loose federation of kingdoms and dukedoms that fought continually until unification in 1871, without a true capital or center of its own.[3] The establishment of a German Empire and its subsequent demise after the abdication of Kaiser Wilhelm II was followed by the collapse of a parliamentary government of no less than 33 political splinter parties so riddled with bitter multi-party factionalism that the German people were unable to forge a nation able to survive any form of national catastrophe.[4] Nevertheless, as the dominant occupying power, the Germans believed that they could control the territorial and external affairs of Holland.

It was also their intention to impose their fascist ideology upon the subjugated Dutch populace. This would require the suppression of religious liberty and the Christian conception of life as practiced in the Roman Catholic and various Protestant churches in Holland.

> *There were two main reasons why Nazism did its utmost to destroy the influence of the Christian Churches:*
>
> *(1) the ethical principle of Christian charity is incompatible with the merciless policy on which the Nazis rely for the final victory of Teutonism*
>
> *(2) no community can be expected to become really devoted to the Nazi view of life while the Churches retain any influence upon its educational and social development.[5]*

In the census of 1930, the Roman Catholic population, 2.75 million strong, was the largest single religious group in Holland (36 percent) because Protestants were divided into a number of sects. The two largest denominations were the Dutch Reformed or Calvinists (34 percent), which became the state church and was similar to the Presbyterian Church in the United States, and the

Reformed Churches (8 percent).[6] Protestants and Catholics alike had their own well-organized trade union movements, their own schools, colleges and universities and probably the most highly developed daily newspaper press in the world with large circulations.

Long before the outbreak of war, Holland publicly denounced National Socialism, with its idolatry of race and of the State. In 1934, having recognized how rapidly the infection had taken hold in Germany, the Dutch Roman Catholic hierarchy threatened severe penalties against those members who joined the National Socialist Bond (N.S.B.).[7] In March 1937, Pope Pius XI issued an encyclical, *Mit Brennender Sorge* (With Burning Concern), that was read in all German churches, in which he condemned in a solemn way the injustices of National Socialism, accusing it of sowing "the tares of suspicion, discord, hatred, calumny, of secret and open hostility to Christ and His Church."[8] Protestant leaders were no less severe in their condemnation of the N.S.B. If the church leaders were to remain true to their mission, they had to speak out against the Nazi ideology and its paganistic practices. Practically without exception, priests and ministers decided that there could be no question of a compromise with any kind of totalitarian dictatorship.

Resistance to the discriminatory anti-Jewish decrees was the first public expression of church opposition to Nazification after the occupation. However, there was a difference between the Protestant and the Catholic approaches in their opposition to anti-Semitism. Within the Reformed Churches, championship of the Jews was the most rigorous form of opposition to the excesses of Nazi tyranny, whereas Catholic interference on behalf of the Jews was more or less incidental to the entire Catholic plan of defense against the enemy's abuse of power. But whether they acted in common—as they did on many occasions—or separately, the General Assemblies of the Reformed Church in their public statements and the Catholic Hierarchy in its Pastorals did not speak on behalf of sections of the population; they each spoke for the entire nation.[9] Christian solidarity was an established fact.

In the fall of 1940, the Reformed Churches signed a joint declaration in which Seyss-Inquart was reminded of his solemn promise not to impose Nazi ideology upon the Dutch people. This same reminder was embodied in a letter of Oct. 24 protesting the removal of all Jewish civil servants.[10]

The relations between Catholics and Jews had been most friendly in Holland for many centuries, but in the course of the last twenty years there was a growing interest among Dutch Catholics in the work of the so-called mission under Israel.[11] The Archconfraternity of Prayer for the conversion of Israel numbered hundreds of thousands of members in Holland—more than in any other single country—and the Dutch branch of the Catholic Guild of Israel was extremely active, perhaps not making many converts, but certainly many friends among the Jews.

Yet no religious community since Hitler's advent to power had more militantly opposed the rise of National Socialism in Holland than the Catholic Church; and because anti-Semitism was an essential element in the Nazi creed, Catholic leaders could not afford to remain passive without compromising the entire Catholic attitude toward the Nazi movement.[12] Thus the Catholic community formed a formidable barrier against the advancement of National Socialism in Holland; it has rightly been said that if the ecclesiastical and lay leaders in Germany had adopted the same uncompromising attitude in 1932 and 1933, Hitler would never have been able to rise to power.[13]

During the first half of 1940, the Christian communities had the support of their own daily newspapers and periodicals, which served to counteract the negative effects of German propaganda. However, it was not long before the Germans responded by censoring Christian newspapers. The papers most bitterly attacked by the German-controlled press were the Calvinist *Standaard* and the Catholic *Tijd*, both of Amsterdam, and the Catholic paper *Maasbode* of Rotterdam, three of the largest and most influential Christian newspapers in Holland. During the conflict in Rotterdam and the indiscriminate bombing that followed, the offices and printing plant of *Maasbode* were totally destroyed. It was reduced to a smaller paper after it was offered space by a sympathetic colleague, where it continued to uphold Christian principles of morality, and printed the Bishops' pastoral letters in full with favorable unambiguous editorial comment. In the spring of 1941, the paper was finally terminated by the Germans.[14]

On January 13, 1941, the Catholic Episcopate under the leadership of Dr. J. de Jong, Archbishop of Utrecht, issued a Catholic Action Pastoral Letter that reiterated the seven-year-old ban, which forbade its members from joining the Dutch National Socialist Party, and from participation in N.S.B. meetings, activities, parades, propaganda activity or in providing any forms of recognizable moral or financial support. Furthermore, if anyone violated any of these stipulations, such persons, after being warned personally according to the declaration, were to be refused the sacraments. Those who were openly members of the N.S.B., either by wearing its uniform or displaying its emblem, were to be refused access to the sacraments without any warning.[15]

There was an exception to this interdict for persons who might be given the choice of joining the N.S.B. immediately, or of losing their means of livelihood.

However, they were not at liberty to accept membership until they had obtained the permission of their priest-confessor, who was told to examine each case most carefully. But even if permission were given, such membership had to remain passive, while it was made clear beyond doubt that the person concerned became a member only *under duress*. This qualification reduced the "exceptions" of this kind to virtually naught.[16]

Marriages involving a member of the N.S.B. that took place in the church must occur in the same manner as a mixed marriage and without any announcements.

A religious funeral was to be refused if the deceased had not been converted or had not shown any signs of repentance, which would have to be made publicly.

In no circumstances would funeral processions be allowed to carry Nazi banners or flags or to allow N.S.B. members to take part officially in the funeral service or burial in N.S.B. uniforms.[17]

In early 1941, when the Germans began limiting the ways in which Jews were allowed to earn a living, the Catholic Church responded to these anti-Jewish decrees by establishing a Fund for Special Emergencies. It was originally intended to assist those Jewish converts to Catholicism, but after the dissolution of the Catholic Workers Union, it was decided to extend the Fund to all citizens who made sacrifices to aid others. A regular collection would be made at all church functions, but so as to avoid German countermeasures, the collections were targeted euphemistically for "the special needs of the archbishopric." The Fund grew beyond all expectations. Some, who sacrificed for the sake of Christian principles, even resigned from their jobs or gave up social security benefits. The Dutch Reformed Church also established a Special Fund, which disbursed hundreds of thousands of guilders to persecuted victims of the German regime.[18] This was but the opening wedge in a struggle that Protestant and Catholic Churches were to wage in Holland against Nazi efforts to rend the fabric of Christianity throughout the Netherlands. The pulpit became the national rostrum that prepared the people for a nation-wide resistance based on Christian ethics, in the name of justice and charity.

Throughout the year, various denominations protested jointly and repeatedly in letters and telegrams to the German Occupational authorities concerning the "complete lawlessness" that was the ongoing order of the day. In an effort to discourage the drafting and circulation of all such messages, a leading Protestant church leader, Dr. K.H.E. Gravemeyer, Secretary of the Synod of the Reformed Church, was arrested and imprisoned for reportedly drafting one of the many Synodal messages refusing cooperation with the Occupying Power.[19] But instead of daunting the efforts of the church members, their repeated protests became more urgent and vehement—words that stood out in high relief against a darkening background of crisis with the country.

This was followed by a persistent German effort to curtail the influence of denominational schools. The Catholic teachers were foremost amongst those whose aim it was to obstruct the introduction of National Socialist education. Whenever the Nazified Department of Education issued a circular that the Catholics considered contrary to their principles, it was immediately referred to the waste basket; and when a member of the National Socialist Bond was made a delegate of a Catholic teachers' organization, not a single member remained.[20] In the spring of 1941, priests in charge of Catholic schools were peremptorily dismissed, and in May at The Hague, the Jesuit college *Huize Katwijk* was seized. Teachers' salaries were severely reduced and many citadels of instruction were forced to close down.[21]

In June 1941, when Hitler invaded the Soviet Union, the German regime saw this as an opportunity to win the backing of the Dutch people in support of a "holy crusade" against a godless Bolshevist onslaught that the vast majority of Hollanders had always viewed as inherently evil and vehemently opposed by all the Christian churches. Assuming the role of "protector" of the Western World, Germany had hoped that the people of Holland would look upon the conflict with Soviet Russia as a "just war" in the true interest of Europe and human civilization. The German Propaganda Ministry took the occasion to condemn Great Britain for not only being a Russian ally, but also an accomplice of Bolshevism.[22] But Britain, and especially the prowess of the British people, had won the respect of the Dutch population; and moreover, whatever their political persuasions, the Hollanders admired the sense of reality, courage and military skill shown by the Russian armies, all of which had nothing to do with their support or opposition to Communist beliefs.

Even closer to home, the Dutch Queen, in a broadcast to her subjects over Radio Oranje from London, was harshly derided by the German regime for her whole-hearted support of Russia as a welcomed ally with whom the Dutch would one day fight the German invaders.[23] Her address served to clarify any confusion that might have existed in the minds of many Dutch Christians over a Nazi vis-à-vis Bolshevist dichotomy. A further effect of the Queen's remarks was a reaffirmation of Christian church opposition to Nazification, especially by the Dutch Hierarchy.

The Christian Church Reaction

By November, the German-controlled newspapers, enraged by the opposition of the Catholic bishops and their indifference to the "fight against Bolshevism," violently attacked those church leaders who continued to engage in anti-Nazi activity. Archbishop de Jong was sentenced to pay a fine of five hundred guilders for refusing to participate in a Nazi-sponsored propaganda campaign against Bolshevism as a "battle for Christianity." As soon as the news was made public, money from all over the country, from Catholics and non-Catholics alike, was sent to the undaunted Utrecht prelate to help pay the German levy.[24]

It was not long before the Dutch people recognized the German allegations as a propaganda ploy to establish an intensive recruiting drive throughout the country to enroll Dutch volunteers in the German army in its war against Russia. Hardly had the invasion begun than Hollanders between the ages of 17 and 40 were urged to enlist in the *Standarte Westland*, the Dutch section of the German *Waffen SS*. Yet despite the propagandized call to arms, only about one-third of the eligible members of the N.S.B. volunteered to aid the German war effort.[25]

In the summer of 1942, when the deportation of Dutch Jews to extermination camps officially began, the Catholic and all Protestant churches were compelled to express their emphatic and most serious objections. A fierce protest was sent to *Reichskommisar* Seyss-Inquart by the Catholic bishops informing him that the protest was to be read from all the pulpits. In retaliation, some 700 Catholics of Jewish origin were arrested and deported to the extermination camp at Auschwitz in Poland, where they were murdered. Among them was the internationally famous philosopher, Edith Stein.[26] This was one of the most glaring cases of Nazi reprisals in Holland, but others were to follow.

The pulpit became the national rostrum that prepared their flocks for resistance and its accompanying sacrifices. And despite repeated efforts by the Germans to prevent anti-Nazi sermons and Pastoral Letters from being read and published, the Letters were not only sent to the presbyteries, but also to some responsible parishioner, whose duty it was to transmit them to the local priest. Despite the personal risk involved, the system worked well.[27]

In the Dutch Reformed Church a prayer for Queen Wilhelmina was a traditional custom at all Sunday services. When attempts were made by Seyss-Inquart to stop this practice, the church refused to submit. Consequently, the prayer for the Queen was continued throughout the occupation, but a prayer for the Occupying Power was added. In Catholic chapels, the Latin hymn *Domine, salvam fac reginam nostrum* (Lord safeguard our Queen) was sung regularly.[28] Doubtless, the priests and ministers would not have been true to their mission had they not had the courage and perseverance to publicly identify fully with the hopes, aspirations and the agonies of their congregations.

Church leaders also had a strong influence on institutions of higher learning, especially those that had religious affiliations. Yet for their strong and uncompromising attitude, many courageous priests and ministers paid an exacting price. When German authorities demanded a loyalty pledge from students at the Catholic University at Nijmegen, the faculty advised them not to sign. As only two students signed, the rector, chancellor and a professor were imprisoned and forced to pay an exorbitant sum for the "privilege" of continuing to teach, which they were only allowed to do under strict German supervision.

Similarly, several leading theologians and laymen, among them the well-known Professor Hendrik Kraemer of Leyden University, a leading Dutch Reformed Church member, were incarcerated. By the end of the third year of occupation, conditions went from bad to worse. Dr. Hein Hoeben, a Dutch journalist from Breda in North Brabant and leader of the largest Catholic Press Bureau, died in a Berlin jail after suffering from wounds inflicted during more than ten months of torture. His organization had been the chief means of informing the outside world of religious persecution and atrocities against members of the clergy within the Reich. Toward the closing of the third year of the occupation conditions worsened even more. Books and pamphlets written by recognized theologians were destroyed. At least fifty Protestant churchmen were being held in German camps or jails. More Catholic institutions were taken over by the German military, and their occupants told to find lodging elsewhere. One order of priests was forced to find refuge in a derelict brewery. And when they attempted to take some of their own furniture with them to make their new surrounding "more livable," they were criticized by a local German commander as being "selfish and un-Christian."[29] Yet despite the efforts to paralyze the influence of Holland's churches, they were adamant in their refusal to yield.

In early 1943, one of the most vital issues in which the Christian churches gave leadership was support for the Dutch physicians in what one author aptly described as "the fight against moral perversion." The issue involved a German-sponsored "Physicians Chamber" in which membership was made compulsory. However, because it was considered incompatible with the precepts of Christian ethics, Christian doctors found it impossible to join. It was founded on Nazi doctrines that interfered with the relationship between physician and patient, a relationship that Christian as well as professional ethics demanded should be maintained. The practice, imposed by the Germans upon doctors, of diminishing the chances of life for the mentally deranged, the incurably ill, even to the extent of killing, was in conflict with both divine and natural law. The same view was advanced regarding sterilization of the unfit.[30]

According to one Dutch Underground newspaper, "the demand that Dutch doctors collaborate in measures to secure racial purity—for example by sterilizing fellow citizens against their will—must be refused by Netherlands physicians on human, scientific, and religious grounds, because the demand originates in a creed which, in its definition of race, blood, and soil, must appear to doctors as the purest paganism."[31]

Of all the medical associations in countries under Nazi domination, only the Dutch physicians as a national medical body stood up against the Nazi attempt to transform doctors into instruments of the state for malevolent purposes. When they learned of the Nazi plan to impose draconic regulations that radically compromised their personal and professional integrity, they resigned from the Dutch Medical Society.[32] When Seyss-Inquart threatened the doctors with revocation of their licenses, they returned their licenses, removed their shingles and continued seeing their patients secretly. The High Commissioner tried to cajole them, but the doctors would not give in. As a result, one hundred doctors were arrested and sent to concentration camps. Nonetheless, not one single euthanasia or sterilization was recommended or participated in by any Dutch physician.[33]

This defiant stand of the medical profession was staunchly supported by the Christian churches in a joint statement condemning sterilization: "Sterilization means dishonoring the divine commandments as well as the rights of man; it is the ultimate consequence of an anti-Christian and destructive racial theory, of boundless self-overrating, which undermines true Christian and human life, and finally renders it impossible."[34] Eventually, Seyss-Inquart forbade the sterilization of Jews in mixed marriages.[35]

In May 1943, the bishops issued a new Pastoral Letter to the clergy and the faithful, in which they reiterated their protest against the unjustifiable tyranny of the German invaders:

> *The people of the Netherlands will never turn Nazi provided we remain true to the faith of our fathers. There is strength only in faith. Yet, dear brethren, though our faith makes us fearless, we are full of deep anxiety and compassion in view of the calamities which have stricken our people and because of the even worse calamities with which they are threatened. We do not even think of the privations which many of you have got to suffer, and which in certain cases threaten to assume the nature of profound misery. Worse is the suffering entailed by deportation and forced labor abroad. Many families have been broken up and are thereby*

> *suffering spiritual distress. Tens of thousands are exposed to many dangers. Many people who, after years of effort, had established their own enterprises, are now threatened with destruction and see the joy of life departed from them.*
>
> *Now the limit has been reached. All able-bodied men who are available will be deported, a deportation on a scale such as the Christian world has never known. To find something comparable one has to go back to the time of the Babylonian Captivity, when God's people were taken into exile, which moved the prophet Jeremiah to exclaim: "A voice has been heard on the heights; a voice of lamentation, of mourning and of tears, which is the voice of Rachel, weeping for her children" (Jeremiah xxxi 15).*[36]

Throughout the course of the Occupation, 43 Dutch ministers of the two major Protestant denominations and 49 Catholic priests paid with their lives in resistance to the Nazis.[37] Additionally, hundreds of ministers and priests, as well as prominent Protestant and Catholic laymen, were arrested and confined in concentration camps, while others were heavily fined for obstructionist activities.

Nevertheless, despite the theological differences and the ecclesiastic disunion that existed between the several denominations in Holland before the occupation, the five years of Nazi rule fostered a cooperation and consultation that many believed was impossible to achieve. However, unified opposition created a coming together that, for the people of Holland, was a deep-seated denunciation of Nazification and a determination to thwart the efforts of the German and N.S.B. authorities.

8

The Conscience of the Nation

There are only two powers in the world, the sword and the pen; and in the end the former is always conquered by the latter.
   —*Napoleon Bonaparte (1769-1821) Emperor of France*

The unified opposition to Nazification by the Christian churches was intensified to an even greater extent by an underground press that might well be called the "conscience of the nation." As the catalyst for Underground activity it existed in all of the countries of Occupied Europe; in Holland, public opinion hardly needed mobilization. With the exception of Poland, nowhere else was there a broader distribution of manifestos, political pamphlets, news sheets and regular newspapers than in Holland, where nearly twelve hundred different illegal newspapers were published between May 1940 and May 1945.[1] (The term "illegal" refers to those publications in conflict with the German directives, not with Dutch law, and is synonymous with the term "Underground" press.)

According to the Dutch Institute of War Documentation, between one and two hundred people read each copy; many people read more than one newspaper.[2] Many of the papers had nationwide circulation, with a profound effect on the morale of the people. To highlight the vital role that the Underground press played in the overall Resistance movement in Holland, Herman Friedhoff, a former member of the Resistance, holder of the Dutch Resistance Cross and retired publisher, stated that the vast majority of the Dutch read the illegal press and "most acted upon its guidelines, silently, passively, actively or otherwise."

And in comparing the French readership at its apex of two million with the Dutch at four million, when Holland's population was one-fifth of the French population, the Dutch Underground press not only informed the populace, but also "inspired them to action."[3] Their propagation constituted a deliberate act of defiance against the Teutonic invaders.

Various papers had only a short lifespan, while still others were issued throughout the five years of the Occupation, and often with diverse editors; additionally, newspapers sometimes merged with one another. It was preferable to publish at irregular intervals; that is, once every two weeks or once a month, but never on the same day of the week. This made surveillance by the Gestapo much more difficult. During the last months of the war illegal newspapers were more widely read than the regular press;[4] a few were handwritten, but most were duplicated, and some were actually printed. The majority of the illegal papers appeared in print runs of a few hundred, but some achieved a circulation in the tens of thousands. By the end of 1940, over sixty clandestine periodicals were distributed, but some for just a short duration. In December of that year the total circulation of the Underground press was close to 57,000 copies.[5]

Those who were associated with clandestine publications could be found among various groups of the population. Social status, religion, age or gender was unimportant. All worked toward the same goal. As an integral part of the Resistance, the overriding purpose of the Underground press was to warn the Dutch people not to submit to the Germans and to promote the Resistance in whatever way they could.[6]

Throughout the 1930s, Dutch newspapers were perceptively free of governmental interference. There were a few incidents involving a Communist, a National Socialist and an anti-Semitic weekly that received reprimands and occasionally were even banned for a short time. Generally speaking, however, those newspapers that were not directly associated with the extreme Left (Communist) or the extreme Right (National Socialist), maintained a more restrained tone, even though they had their own opinions on national and international affairs. In the second half of the decade, and especially after the German invasion of Poland, when a state of general mobilization in Holland was proclaimed, there was a general mood of self-imposed neutrality in the press in which all military and strategic information was kept out of the newspapers.[7]

After the Dutch capitulation the first phase of the German Occupation was marked by a policy of "gentle persuasion." The various administrative structures of Holland, the political parties and departments and civil service grades were allowed to exist so as to give the Dutch people an opportunity to reach a *modus vivendi* with National Socialism and the "New Order."⁸ Two days after the signed surrender, German General Friedrich Christiansen, the Commander of the German Armed Forces in Holland, issued a decree stating that so long as responsible publishers and editors demonstrated their complete loyalty to the German regime, the Dutch press would not be subject to prohibitive censorship. The announcement was published in all of the Dutch newspapers.

What was also a part of the decree, but purposely omitted in the newspapers were forbidden topics that could not be published. Listed were information and news from English, French and other hostile sources; reports, editorials or news features detrimental or critical of Germany—including unseemly pictures of high-ranking German officials; even advertisements for Churchill cigars, Chamberlain umbrellas and Eden hats; and all international affairs, which included detailed weather reports that could be useful to enemy intelligence. All news from outside the country would be supplied by the German authorities, including the compulsory publication of a daily army press report. Offenses against these instructions were punishable by suspension or suppression of the paper. There were few restrictions on domestic matters, as long as they did not involve the Germans.⁹

Further directives and information were given to members of the press at daily press conferences by German press-attaches in The Hague. They continued throughout the course of the war, by which they became mere formalities.⁸ All matters relating to the press and propaganda were the exclusive province of Joseph Goebbels, the German Minister of Propaganda. Throughout all the occupied countries he established special propaganda units—*Propaganda-Staffeln*—that had a military status, but the personnel, equipment and instructions were provided by the Ministry of Propaganda.¹⁰

During the first two years of the war—1939–1941—when German expansionism was flourishing throughout Europe, the only news that was reported in the Nazified press were war bulletins of German successes that the Dutch people least of all wished to read. Listening to radio stations outside of Germany and its occupied territories was also *verboten*, and stiff penalties for violations of this regulation were imposed. Much of the populace turned to the Dutch-Exile-Government-sponsored Radio Oranje broadcasts and also to British radio news broadcasts that were transmitted in the Dutch language. Approximately 75 percent of the Dutch households had wireless sets;¹¹ and technically it was easy to tune in to the British Broadcasting Corporation (B.B.C.) for a far different perspective on the news. It was not until the May strike in 1943 that the confiscation of all radios was ordered, except those belonging to members of the N.S.B., who could obtain permits for keeping their sets. Generally speaking, however, for details and background information, newspapers were essential and remained the principal source for analyzing the issues of the day. After the confiscation of radios the number of clandestine news bulletins and other publications rose significantly.

In Holland nothing literary was free from German control, and to obtain permission to do any publishing one had first to belong to the Nazi-controlled press guild. The Germans were fully aware that they were promoting the development of an Underground press by their imposition of strict censorship. To discourage all such activity, for anyone who was actively involved in the writing or production of clandestine newspapers the penalty was death; for distributing, or failing to report the receipt of a newspaper, imprisonment. These were no idle threats!

Furthermore, ink was rationed and the unauthorized use of paper was forbidden; a ban on the use of duplicating machines was also put into effect.[12] Nevertheless, printing was one of Holland's largest light industries and there were thousands of small presses and skilled compositors and plenty of paper. Clandestine publishers managed to acquire paper from a variety of sources, some of which came from remainders of pre-war stock, some from stocks officially supplied for printing non-controversial matter for which paper had been authorized, but requested largely in excess of the amount needed for the proposed edition. Some of the paper was brown paper for packaging and not meant for printing at all. Much of the paper was stolen from warehouses of certain wholesalers or from known Nazi collaborators among printers.[13]

Publishing operations were set up wherever there was space for a person to operate a duplicating machine or a typewriter. Private apartments, cellars, churches and attics were desirable locations, but far more unconventional places were used as well. The editor of the Dutch paper *Voor Waarheid, Vrijheid en Recht* (For Truth, Liberty and Right) was situated among chickens in a barn hayloft. The editor of the *Amsterdam Scout* had his office in the boiler room of a hospital. An Amsterdam newspaper team worked in a meat factory; another from a hollowed-out haystack with radio, typewriter and mimeograph machine, from the attic of the International Court of Justice in The Hague, the editor of *Je Maintiendrai*, whose motto was "I will stand fast," turned out 40,000 small mimeographed sheets each month and later on a weekly basis.[14]

The first illegal bulletins and newspapers were hand-written sheets or typed messages placed in neighborhood mailboxes; copied and passed on in chain-letter fashion and known as snowball letters. The person who received the message was expected to pass it on as quickly as possible to friends and then to others for further distribution.

The earliest news messages were written by Bernard Ijzerdraat, a teacher and a confirmed opponent of National Socialism living in a neighboring community not far from Rotterdam, who was organizing a small Underground group the day after the bombing of that city. The group was called the *Geuzenactie*—the Beggars' Action. "Beggars" was a pejorative term given to Dutch partisans during the Spanish occupation of the Netherlands in the 16th century, but now out of defiance, it was adopted and converted into an honorable title.

On May 18, 1940, four days after the bombardment of Rotterdam, amidst a mixture of grief and anger, the second hand-written secret newsletter was composed and circulated; given the name *Geuzenactie*, after the name of the Resistance group, it was a clairvoyant message accurately predicting many of the coming disasters in Holland. The second of these bulletins is the earliest surviving example of Underground writing. It is possible that the second message was actually the first such bulletin distributed, even though it was listed as message number two. If such was the case, it was in the hope of misleading the Germans into believing that the bulletin was published elsewhere and more widely circulated than it actually was, and that the group was more firmly established than it was. This was a tactic used by other illegal publications such as the *Bulletin*, which numbered its first issue as number three.[15]

The *Geuzen* message drew an analogy between the Eighty Years War of liberation against Spain and the present struggle against Germany. It read as follows:

Geuzenactie Message No. 2.

The Geuzenaction was started on 15 May 1940 in Amsterdam. Our first message has already reached Nijmegen. The Netherlands will not stand for the loss of their freedom nor be easily misled. We know what awaits us. All our supplies will be taken away, food, clothing, shoes. Soon we will have the system of rationing for everything and then some; and after that we won't even be able to get the coupons. Our young people will be forced to work elsewhere for the oppressor.

Then the writer pointed to a well-known character, the cruel governor appointed by Philip II of Spain.

We'll soon be getting a new Duke of Alva with Council of Blood [i.e., executions] and the inquisition (or a Quisling). But the Geuzenaction shall gradually bring an organization into being, and one day we will recapture our liberty, just as we did in the eighty years war. Courage and trust. OUR COUNTRY SHALL NOT BE PART OF GERMANY!

This is the earliest specimen of the bond between Underground journalism and militant resistance; and to make clear that Underground activity must always do what it can to confuse and mislead the enemy, the message continued:

The Geuzenactie consists of the following:

Copy every message 2 or more times completely with twisted hand [i.e.,camouflaged handwriting]. Pass these papers (including this copy) unnoticed on to trustworthy Dutchmen, who shall do the same as you. Never interrupt this bulletin service even if you may sometimes get a message for a second time! We are appointing secret agents everywhere. Soon you will hear more. Let everyone do his duty as a Geuzen!

One for all, all for one![16]

On May 29 a typed message was sent out by Ijzerdraat as a forewarning to the Dutch people to guard against betrayal by German deception. Message No. 5 reads as follows:

*Now the second Alva with his spies (the Gestapo) is in our country to lure us out of our tents [a **Dutch expression meaning 'to provoke us.'**] Every Dutchman has to be extremely careful. Temporarily we shall be treated with treasonous friendship. At first one will not notice the Gestapo. But every casual remark that any of those spies may overhear will be carefully written down; and later you could be arrested, and perhaps even executed. SO KEEP YOUR MOUTH CLOSED. EVERYWHERE. Our Message No. 3 gave the times when London broadcasts in Dutch; (namely at 14 hours, 19 hours, and 24.07 hours on wavelength 373 meters.) Our secret Geuzen agents from all over our country have informed us that Message No. 3 was known everywhere within six days. Help us spread this message even faster. It could save many a Dutchman.*

Take note: The Geuzenaction consists of the following:

Copy every message 2 or more times completely. Pass these papers (including this copy) unnoticed on to TRUSTWORTHY Dutchmen who shall do the same as you. COPY THE MESSAGES WITH TWISTED HAND [camouflaged handwriting]

AND ANY POSSIBLE SPELLING MISTAKES, then no Seyss-Inquart spy will catch you. But still our entire people (N.S.B members excluded) can count on each other. One day we shall get rid of the traitor of Austria, just like our ancestors made Alva disappear. But don't do anything now. Wait for further messages. Appear to be calm and tame. The Geuzenaction was started in Amsterdam 15 May 1940. Never interrupt this bulletin service. Do your duty and do it fast. Think of your country. GEUZENACTION FOR A FREE NETHERLANDS.[17]

The *Geuzenactie* bulletins were hand-written or typed one to three times a week until August, 1940. The small group was terminated three months later when Ijzerdraat and most of the members of his organization were arrested. The story of its growth, development and demise is related in the following chapter.

The first clandestine newspaper to survive over a year was the monthly *Het Bulletin*. From June 1940 until August 1941, it circulated throughout the province of Utrecht, and was distributed mainly to warn the readers not to compromise with the Germans and to avoid all contact with them. It focused chiefly on domestic issues made available by patriotic government officials. It was considered the most important publication during the first year of the Occupation and had a circulation of 1,200 copies.[18]

On July 25, 1940, Frans J. Goedhart, a Socialist journalist from Amsterdam who took the pseudonym Pieter 't Hoen, produced a typed or mimeographed newsletter called *Nieuwsbrief van Pieter 't Hoen*, after an 18th century Dutch publicist. Goedhart was well aware of the fascist threat to Western European democracy as early as 1933 and the danger to Dutch independence posed by Germany, which is clearly reflected in his writing. The primary aim of the *Nieuwsbrief* was like that of the *Geuzenactie*, to incite his readers to Resistance.[19] He believed that any form of politics other than that practiced in the Underground was an act of collaboration with the enemy. This is attested to in the *Nieuwsbrief No.1*:

> *The five days that decided the fate of our army are now more than two months behind us. In the first place the question is what stance should now be taken. The large majority of our population has already answered this question. They have done this by ignoring the occupier. From left to right the only possible posture is no contact with the conqueror. The country and the entire world are facing a series of burning issues, but cannot be solved as long as non-German territory is still controlled by the Germans. Any cooperation with the occupier that goes beyond the minimum required by international law is collaboration with the enemy and is treason.*
>
> *There are already people who are not ashamed to be guilty of that. These are mainly the N.S.B. and the prostitutes. The N.S.B. has been the German party for some time. Several of its members have volunteered*

for all sorts of German espionage. They helped smuggle Dutch uniforms into Germany and they tried to infiltrate all sorts of positions to get state, army, fleet and air force secrets. A few days before the German invasion, the leader, Anton Mussert, declared that if Germany would invade, he would stand and watch with his arms crossed. This downturn was probably inspired by Berlin to increase the nervousness in this country on the evening of the invasion. But some of his followers went even further. These vagrants assisted the conquerors, and after our capitulation stood with raised hands on the side of the road to welcome them with their "Heils" shouting with flowers, fruit, cigarettes and chocolates. When Mussert crawled out of his hiding place after our defeat, he rushed to a meeting that ended with the war cry from the German intruder, "Heil Hitler!" And now this Mussert and his companions Rost van Tonningen and Woudenberg, are following orders from their German masters, and pulling the teeth, and cutting off the testicles from all sorts of Dutch associations, institutions and organizations, so that they will no longer be of any danger to the occupier.

With sneaky parrot-talk these German agents try to sweet talk our people, but luckily the great masses in this country aren't so numbed that they can't see through these flirtations. That there are a handful of women and prostitutes who like to be seen with the conqueror is saddening, but nevertheless normal. It is the normal state of affairs in a country occupied by a foreign power. From 1914–1918 you could see the same phenomenon in Belgium. After the German retreat these women had to face the consequences of their behavior. That too is normal.

Astonishing, meanwhile, is the attitude the largest part of the Dutch press has adopted. With hanging ears and wagging its tail, the newspaper editors report daily to the German Press Commissar, who tells them what to write. The enemy's decisions and speeches made by enemy leaders, and the portraits of enemy officers, politicians and bosses are printed with lots of respect and humble, German and un-Dutch cowardice and selfishness. The newspaper owners, who used to be the defenders of Public Opinion, are behaving themselves as quivering little businessmen, willing to make any concession to the occupier as long as he lets them keep their dirty jobs. Because of the profits on the investments they made in their companies they are selling our national honor. If they are confronted, all they can do is hide behind their business interests. Have our boys, who took up arms against the intruder, asked themselves what would

> *happen to them, their families, and their businesses? They put their lives on the line for the future of their country and people. But the newspaper owners apparently haven't learned anything from this. Profiting from their business apparently is their highest ideal. Now we see the immense danger of anyone with enough money being able to run a newspaper under the existing laws of freedom of the press.*
>
> *All these people who in one way or another cooperate with the occupier are collaborating with the enemy. They will have to pay for that as soon as the country will be free again because the day will come when the German intruder will have to leave the country. The day will come that the Dutch people will decide for themselves how to run their own lives. The era of democracy, with its most important characteristic being that it enabled rich merchants, bankers, and patricians to mould the country to their wishes, is over. The time of German domination, of the suicides, the treason by German henchmen, the looting of our storages and the measures taken against our population, shall pass as well. Don't bow, don't bend, and don't cooperate with the enemy! Courage and trust! The future belongs to a free Dutch people in a free people community.*[20]

The *Nieuwsbrief* soon reached a circulation of 7,000 readers. However, it was Goedhart's ambition to turn the paper into a national Underground newspaper. In February 1941, with the help of a larger editorial team, it was later transformed into one of the most widely distributed papers throughout the Netherlands and was called *Het Parool* (The Watchword). It was first mimeographed, but within six months it was being produced on the printing press, the first Underground paper to be so recognized.

One especially careful supporter of *Het Parool*, an unnamed civil servant, wrote enthusiastically to the paper in April 1942:

> *"The new issue, in a word: priceless! It is impossible to overestimate the value of these grey and undistinguished leaflets in this total war. How many waverers are given solid backing, how much confidence to faint hearts, how much rapture and insight and awareness. My hat off to you, anonymous editors: God's blessing be upon your work. I have to force myself to pass the issues on. One would like to read them again and again. But that is not right, for they must be handed on and quickly while still topical."*[21]

The editor of the paper might well have responded to the letter writer who obviously had a collector's instinct, to resist the temptation to hoard newspaper copies, and instead, try collecting German revolvers.

Het Parool flourished continuously until the liberation. Over the next four years, albeit left-leaning, the paper was loyal to the House of Orange and reprinted speeches of the Queen, counteracted Nazi propaganda, challenged the effectiveness of Nazi measures, warned against traitors and reported B.B.C. news. The paper grew steadily before reaching its maximum print run of 60,000 before the end of the war.[22]

In the autumn of 1941 a number of the paper's distributors were arrested in Amsterdam and The Hague. Goedhart was one of twenty-three brought to trial in December 1942. Seventeen death sentences were pronounced, and thirteen *Parool* workers were executed by firing squad. Goedhart, thanks to the help of a Dutch policeman to whom he had secretly disclosed his identity, escaped 18 months later in September 1943 after having been sentenced to die. He then returned to assume his position on the editorial board of *Het Parool*.[23]

Vrij Nederland (Free Netherlands) was another of the major highly respected Underground publications. It was started less than four months after the invasion by a group of young Calvinists. It appeared approximately once a month on a regular basis in mimeographed form until December 1941, when it then began to be printed; it managing to last throughout the Occupation. By September 1944, the circulation grew to 100,000 copies.[24] *Vrij Nederland* kept in close contact with *Het Parool*, even though the former publication was somewhat to the right of its sister paper, and tended to reflect a liberal Protestant bias that promoted social responsibility and broadly conceived Christian ideals. It also served as a link between the Socialists and orthodox Protestants active in the Resistance.

In March 1941, the Germans arrested most of the paper's staff members, but within six months the paper was organized under new management. Additional losses occurred in 1942, when a number of collaborators were arrested; this required reorganization once again. The group of younger Calvinists who were responsible for the production and distribution of the paper were concerned over the way the editorial direction was now veering more and more to the left. They wanted to separate the management and production and distribution from the editorial responsibilities. Additionally, the younger group, which was closely allied to the Reformed Churches, found the existing policies too secular and Socialistic.

A stricter Calvinist policy favored by the younger colleagues on the paper resulted in their resignation and formation of a new publication, which politically came to represent the right wing of the Underground press. Led by Wim Speelman, a former university student who had been the head of distribution for

Vrij Nederland, the paper sought a return to pre-war traditions, a strong colonial policy and in particular stressed loyalty to the Royal Family as opposed to a campaign for a new regime once the Occupation was over.[25] The first issue appeared in January 1943, and was called *Oranjebode* (Message of Orange) in honor of the birth of the Queen's youngest granddaughter, Margriet. Later that year the name of the paper was changed to *Trouw* (Loyalty). It also represented all orthodox Protestants and was closely associated with the conservative Anti-Revolutionary Party and those National Action Groups who sought ration books and identity cards for *onderduikers* in hiding.

Trouw became one of the most highly respected illegal newspapers in Holland, whose editorial analysis was highly regarded throughout the country; in just the first eight months of production, with approximately sixty local and regional editions, 60,000 copies were published. *Trouw* was also one of the most attractively printed Underground papers. Its masthead shows a rectangular link of chain, which enshrines a profile of the Queen appearing beside the Royal Crown against a background of the dawn of a new day, and three oranges representing the three young granddaughters of the Royal Family.

In the summer of 1944, the Germans offered to spare the lives of 23 *Trouw* workers who had been arrested on condition that the directors stopped publication of the paper. The offer was refused and the workers were executed summarily. Later Speelman was also caught and executed.[26] The executions not only failed to discourage the further publication of *Trouw*; they obviously provided the incentive to enhance its circulation. After September, *Trouw* groups published local editions of the national paper and news bulletins on an extraordinary large scale; and by January 1945, the total weekly circulation amounted to approximately two million copies.[27]

The courage and determination to continue publication of illegal newspapers were, not unnaturally, accompanied by the deepest psychological feelings that this perilous work entailed. Cases of torture and death inflicted by the Gestapo on the human body of those who refused to conform to the German decrees and directives were widely known to those in the Underground press. One such description was of *human beings who forced their victims into very narrow pillboxes, where the poor creatures had to stand for 24 hours, bent down, their feet in cold water. And the next morning they had to dance with their unfeeling, strengthless body, before the amused eyes of sadistic guards. Lunatics bellowed at the nearly fainting prisoners to close their eyes and open their mouths. Then a gun was put between the lips, squeezed against the weak gums. And if the man dared to tremble, he was stripped naked and had to creep forward on his elbows as fast as he could.*[28]

Publishers, editors and distributors alike were forced to control their imagination to keep from collapsing under the strain of nights without sleep and periods of living fear. Every decision taken and every move could mean that small mistake which could result in the arrest and execution of numerous people.

Equally perilous was the work assigned to couriers whose responsibilities involved the distribution of newspapers to subscribers, most often in public, right under the Germans' noses. Early in the Occupation, many newssheets were sent by regular mail with bogus return addresses, but with increased circulation, this became far more expensive and dangerous. Most of the couriers were women who were able to conceal copies of illegal material in handbags, shopping bags, false-bottomed suitcases or in their children's clothing. One such courier was the well-known film actress, Audrey Hepburn, who at the age of 16, besides serving as a volunteer nurse in a Dutch hospital and performing in Underground concerts to raise funds, ran messages for the Resistance.

Deliveries were also made directly to readers by milkmen or mailmen who were members of the Resistance. Because gasoline was only available to the Occupation forces, distribution was usually carried out on bicycle or foot. Sometimes canal barges were used to transport Underground news material, as was even the less conspicuous street cleaner's handcart, which could convey thousands of copies at a time. Several legal newspapers would be placed at the top and bottom of each stack so that if a superficial police investigation were made the bundle was not likely to be discovered.[29]

An additional aspect of the courier's life that was fraught with danger was the delivery of type from the typesetter to the printer, which involved carrying lead, which was quite heavy. To overcome this problem at *Trouw*, the production manager put a special unit composed of Indonesian students through a course in weightlifting so that larger loads of type could be carried without apparent effort. To avoid being stopped by the Gestapo, whose very nature was to be suspicious, it was always advisable to keep off of main thoroughfares and on back streets, which entailed considerable backtracking and circumvention.[30]

In May 1943, capital punishment was extended to include anyone found reading a clandestine paper. This prompted many of the illegal papers' editors to find ways of reducing the risk of detection by means of camouflage and stealth. One method involved smuggling the molding material and printing plate of the evening heading of a pro-Nazi newspaper from the printing plant, which would then be used in the production of a bogus Underground edition. Bundles of the bogus paper would then be delivered by Resistance couriers to several kiosks. From the title of the publication displayed on the top of the front page of the paper when picked up, the reader had the initial impression that he was picking up the authentic German version. One such distributor described how his hoax was rewarded: He was able to walk about the streets watching people. "They would start reading their copy normally and then, incredulously, as they realized what had happened. Finally they would look around to see if anyone was watching before stuffing their copies furtively inside their coats to enjoy later in private."[31] The same idea for distribution was carried out slightly differently by delivering the hoax edition of *Haarlem Daily* to kiosks throughout the city after the authentic version of the paper was delivered, and then explaining that there was a censorship problem and giving the falsified editions in exchange.[32]

Underground workers in Schoonhoven in the province of South Holland undertook a somewhat less subtle approach to both production and distribution. They raided the *Schoonhovense Courant* plant, held up the production staff at gunpoint and forced the plant personnel to print the hoax Underground edition on their own presses. To guarantee successful delivery of the bogus edition, the papers were then delivered in vans under Underground armed guard. The group then escaped with not a single participant being caught.[33]

Besides promoting Resistance activity, many of the Underground papers were devoted to full-scale news-gathering that provided readers with uncensored domestic and foreign news. News was obtained from sympathetic contacts in government agencies and police departments, from tapped official telephone and teletype lines and from the editorial staffs of Nazi-backed newspapers who leaked news they dare not publish, and from foreign broadcasts, mainly the B.B.C. For example, there was *Je Maintiendrai* (I Maintain), a major publication that drew the attention of a more educated readership. It was composed of a diverse group of Catholics, Protestants and humanists who seemed to work well together. As one of the more conservative Underground newspapers, *Je Maintiendrai* strived to publish news coverage from the various theatres of war as well as offering guidance and discussion in political affairs. It supported a strong government and a strong monarchy as the expression of national unity and provided up-to-date information on the Royal Family. It favored maintaining control of overseas Dutch colonial possessions and the armed forces necessary in defending them. Much of the paper was devoted to commentary regarding post-war reconstruction.[34]

The fifth major Underground periodical that had a large nationwide impact on the populace was *De Waarheid* (The Truth), after the Soviet daily, *Pravda*. In the late fall of 1940, it became the main publication of the Communist Party and criticized the war as an imperialist conflict, claiming that a victory of the

DAWN OF COURAGE

Allies would only result in the return of a capitalist government detrimental to the working classes. Ironically, it supported a re-establishment of the monarchy after the war. In 1941, after the German invasion of Russia, it reversed its description of the Allied cause, calling it a "war of liberation." Nevertheless, *De Waarheid* was unrelenting in its attack upon National Socialism even before the German invasion, and especially its policy of anti-Semitism. It was a major factor in fomenting the February strike of 1941, in which thousands of leaflets were mimeographed and circulated, urging a work stoppage.[35] Throughout the course of the Occupation, *De Waarheid's* wide readership was enhanced because of fly sheets, which were easily pasted on kiosks among legal outdoor postings, and in factories, universities and other well-populated areas where copies passed from hand to hand.

After the confiscation of all unauthorized radios in 1943, except for those that were kept hidden from the Germans, the illegal press concentrated more and more on war news from the fronts; in the several months prior to the final liberation, postwar problems became major topics of discussion, and all the papers welcomed the decision of the Queen to consult the Resistance on the formation of a new cabinet.

Besides the clandestine newspapers, periodicals and political pamphlets that circulated throughout Holland during the Occupation, a variety of books and literary works made their way into the lives of the Dutch populace. Dutch publishers chose books that inspired patriotic feelings by retelling the history of past sufferings and triumphs, especially those that told of the Dutch war of independence fought against Spain. In addition to numerous Dutch works of poetry, ballads, novels and stories, works by international authors were smuggled into the Netherlands, translated and secretly reprinted by various publishers under the noses of the Occupying Power. Editions included works by Emily Dickinson, Franz Kafka, Alexander Pushkin, Guy de Maupassant, Dante Gabriel Rossetti, Edgar Allan Poe, William Blake and Andre Gide, to name but a few.[36]

In January 1943, the publishing house *De Bezige Bij* (The Busy Bee) was formed by two law students from Utrecht University, both of whom had been active in the Resistance, who left the institution after refusing to sign a loyalty oath for the German regime. One of the students, Geertjan Lubberhuizen, earned the nickname "Busy Bee" because of his tireless zeal in working against the Nazis. The press published poems, stories and songbooks that expressed the struggle for dignity and freedom against the foreign oppression. It also published caricatures that satirized the German forces and described the misery and deprivation of the Occupation in an ironic, if not humorous fashion.

But publishers and printers also provided the people with resolve and words of hope. Two books by foreign authors were particularly noteworthy in Holland and elsewhere on the Continent, not only because they accurately described ordinary life in Occupied Europe, but also because they had the power to inspire the ordinary people of those countries to hold fast to that sense of national pride and remain implacable in the face of a harsh and merciless enemy. Those books were John Steinbeck's novel, *The Moon is Down* (1942), and *Le silence de la mer* (The Silence of the Sea) (1941), a short novel published clandestinely in France by Jean Bruller under the pseudonym Vercors. Both books were covertly translated and published by Underground organizations in Holland. These were just two of numerous works that helped to foster those virtues of resilience and boldness for millions of victims of Nazi oppression during those dark years when the lights went out all over Europe.

In any evaluation of the influence that the Underground press had on the hearts and minds of the people of Holland, it must be borne in mind that the clandestine press was not in itself a Resistance movement, even if it could function as a galvanizing force for one, as it did in the case of the *Geuzenactie*. What it did was uplift morale and sustain the notion that patriotism was still very much alive in Holland while promoting the belief that collaboration with totalitarianism was nothing less than reprehensible and irreconcilable with the Dutch national character. Moreover, the Underground press never tired of reminding the people that Holland was at war with Germany and exhorted the ordinary citizenry to resist in whatever ways they could; thereby undermining enemy morale by making life for the Occupying Power as uncomfortable as possible.

The men and women in the Underground press, the writers, editors, publishers, printers, couriers and distributors served as a constant reminder that freedom of the press was not free; that the power of the pen came at a very high price. This was attested to by the thousands of those in the clandestine press, not only in Holland, but throughout all of Occupied Europe who were caught and executed for having the courage to keep the minds of men free from tyrannical rule.

9

Resistance Initiatives

*Indignation fertilized the soil in which the people's
Resistance would eventually grow.*
   —*Herman Friedhoff, member of the Dutch Resistance*

In Holland during the early years of the Occupation, after a brief albeit unwarranted period of optimism that the war was simply a passing phase that would soon be ended by a quick liberation by the Allies, there was a dampening of hopes and expectations of an earlier end to the war. Despite the defeat of the German air offensive in the Battle of Britain in the fall of 1940, the following year continued to witness dazzling German exploits. Far-reaching successes of General Erwin Rommel's famed Afrika Korps in the Western Desert, the further eclipsing of practically all of Continental Europe by the overrunning of the Balkans and Crete and the ongoing destruction of British shipping by German U-boats in the North Atlantic drove Allied fortunes to their lowest ebb.

And while the vast majority of the Dutch population was growing increasingly embittered toward the Germans, intensified by the patriotic fervor and anti-Nazi rhetoric that emerged from the Underground press, few people were willing to actively participate in dangerous clandestine operations. As a result of its longstanding, uninterrupted period of peace and its tradition of neutrality, there was in Holland no experience of Underground activity as there had been in France and Belgium. Like Norway, few had any idea of how to organize Underground procedures and tactics. Everything had to be learned by trial and error in the hard experience of the Occupation.

Moreover, no geographical or logistical area was less suited for an organized Resistance movement than the Netherlands. Small, flat, highly cultivated and intensely populated, the country offered few natural hiding places. Conditions grew more serious in the spring of 1941, when the North Sea coast of Holland, which was already closely guarded, was in addition isolated from the rest of the country. The Frisian Islands, a chain off the northwest coast, the provinces of South Holland below Rotterdam and the whole province of Zeeland were off-limits for all but the local population. The coastal area, consisting of dunes and beaches, was well-guarded by the Germans both on land and at sea by patrol boats.

Those intrepid souls who attempted to escape to Britain had to be prepared to sacrifice all that they loved, including their own lives, for the privilege of getting to England to join the Allied forces. Throughout the course of the war, no more than 150 to 200 Hollanders succeeded in reaching England in small boats by crossing the treacherous North Sea, a distance of one hundred miles due west.[1]

Nevertheless, despite the numerous conditions inhibiting Underground activity, there were resolute individuals who began to form small clandestine groups, most of whom had no more than a vague idea of how to establish a Resistance organization. It was only after four men who were sitting together in a small town near Rotterdam on the evening of May 14, 1940, and witnessing the devastation of that city, that they sought the help of Bernard Ijzerdraat: a man for whom the bombardment and capitulation of Holland was a rallying cry for Resistance. It was his bulletins, which have previously been described, that were a clarion call to awaken the patriotic spirit of the Dutch people. Filled with loathing at what was taking place in their country, it was at this time that the Rotterdam teacher and his small group formed the Beggars' Action Resistance group. The aim was to launch a campaign to establish an Underground network that would undertake, *inter alia*, espionage and sabotage activity.

Ijzerdraat traveled throughout the country to provide leadership and to expand his organization. Most members came from the Rotterdam area, but others were in The Hague, Leyden, Amsterdam and surrounding areas. He made it appear as if a connection with England had been established to motivate the members of his group. His unrelenting optimism prompted him to write that *"the whole world already knows that Germany must quickly give up this war."*

Later issues of the *Geuzenactie* bulletin were replaced by mini-newspapers, which encouraged readers to engage in sabotage, spying and the recruitment of new members. They provided plans and instructions for Resistance activity. Lists were drawn up of N.S.B. members, collaborators and *Moffenmeiden*—women who consorted with the Germans. Drawings were made of searchlight sites and the location of anti-aircraft guns; minor acts of sabotage were committed against German ships that lay in dry dock for maintenance and reconstruction, German telephone lines were cut; on one occasion, the cable of a German searchlight was cut so as to safeguard British aircraft at night.[3]

Every member took the Beggar's Oath of Secrecy: *I promise in these serious times to be a good Dutch Beggar, to obey the Beggar's Law and the rules of the commanders. If I in any way violate my promise, all my property shall fall to the Beggar's Army or, if it no longer exists, to the Dutch State.*[4] But the lack of experience on the part of those engaged in Underground work resulted in underestimating the years of experience of German counter-espionage. This led to mistakes that ultimately resulted in the death of numerous members of the organization, mainly because much of the Beggars' Action was talked about in public.

In November 1940, through the careless neglect of certain security measures, or as one writer put it, the "proud indiscretions" of a newly admitted member of the group, information about a secret weapons cache in the town of Schiedam was overheard by an N.S.B. leader in Arnhem, which resulted in the arrest of more than 200 members of the Beggars' Action throughout South Holland. They were taken to the SS prison for political prisoners in Scheveningen, adjacent to The Hague, and commonly referred to by the Dutch as the "Oranje Hotel." After harsh interrogation in which he was severely beaten, Ijzerdraat refused to divulge the name of other members of the group still at-large.

On March 13, 1941, Ijzerdraat, fourteen of his associates and three Communist members of the February strike were executed by a firing squad as the result of sabotage activity at a Rotterdam shipyard.[5]

The group of the eighteen executed resisters was memorialized by the popular single-sheet illustrated Resistance poem, *De Achttien Dooden* (The Eighteen Dead), by the Dutch poet Jan Campert, who was later captured in 1943 while trying to get a Jewish journalist across the Belgian frontier. He later died in a concentration camp:[6]

A cell is just two meters long
And scarce two meters wide;
smaller will be that plot of ground
which I have not yet tried,
where nameless I will lie at rest,

Resistance Initiatives

my cellmates at my side;
none of us eighteen gathered here
will see the eventide.

Beloved, charming air and land
when Holland once was free!
But when our foes had conquered us,
there was no rest for me.
What can a man upright and true,
attempt in such a plight?
Just kiss his child, and kiss his wife,
and fight the useless fight.

I knew the task I had begun,
the burdens I would bear,
but hearts that are afire ignore
the dangers everywhere;
they know how once in this small land
we all were proud and free
before the cursed raper's hand
planned all things differently;

before the ones who break all oaths
performed this act of shame:
invaded Holland's low green land
and threatened us with flame;
before the ones who pride themselves
with Germany's purity
forced a whole land beneath their rule
and plundered shamelessly.

> *The fierce pied piper of Berlin*
> *now pipes his melody!*
> *As sure as I will soon be dead*
> *and never get to see*
> *my love and never break the bread*
> *or sleep again with her,*
> *you must reject all that he bids'*
> *that wily murderer!*
>
> *Remember, you who read these words,*
> *my comrades in distress*
> *and also all their dear ones in*
> *their deep unhappiness.*
> *Remember, just as we have thought*
> *of our own land and friends'*
> *day always follows after night,*
> *and darkness always ends.*
>
> *I see how the first morning light*
> *peeps through the small, high pane;*
> *my God, please make my dying light;*
> *if I committed sin*
> *as everyone can sometimes fail,*
> *grant me your grace, O God,*
> *so that I walk out like a man*
> *to face the firing squad.*[7]

In January 1943, in an effort to raise money for hidden Jewish children, the *De Bezige Bij* (The Busy Bee) Underground publishing house printed copies of the poem. Within a week, 500 stenciled copies of the poem were sold. By the end of the war, 15,000 copies had circulated throughout Holland. Many people taped the poem to the inside of their kitchen cupboard so it could be read daily while remaining hidden from random searches and Nazi sympathizers. Surplus proceeds were donated to the Resistance.[8]

During 1940–41, other Underground groups sprang up in Holland, and members came chiefly from Social Democrat and Catholic youth leagues. The Communists organized an Underground party organization in July 1940, but it was not until June 1941, after the German invasion of Russia, that they advocated cooperation among other Resistance groups, always being careful to maintain their own identity. There were several incidents of sabotage, but popular dissatisfaction was mainly expressed by demonstrations in the winter of 1941 caused by the rapid rise in the price of food and new, harsher rationing regulations. This led to attacks on trains carrying industrial goods and food from Holland to Germany.

One member of the Dutch Underground described the Underground atmosphere during those first two years as having the outward appearance of normalcy; however,

> *Holland's secret struggle took place in cafes full of people, quiet board rooms, cellars, busy shipyards, dark city streets, and always under the only cover available: everyday life… Every member of the Resistance led a double life. And once in trouble, you were on your own. The coast stretched straight and bare as a speedway. The land lay open and observed. No improvised airstrips marked with flashlights for fast pickups by RAF planes, as in France. The only two-way contact with the free world existed via secret wireless set, a deadly short cut to the firing squad.*[9]

In the summer of 1940, the Order Service, *Orde Dienst* or (*O.D.*), was the first nationwide Underground organization to be established. Members were mainly conservative commissioned and non-commissioned officers of the Dutch armed forces. Its main mission was to gather intelligence and to develop plans for the maintenance of law and order after the German defeat and until the arrival of the legal Dutch government from England. Closely associated with this aim were efforts to hasten the collapse of the Occupying Power by military espionage.

It is to be recalled that after the Venlo incident in November 1939, in which the Anglo-Dutch listening post in The Hague was destroyed (see Chapter Two), there was no longer any clandestine communication between Holland and England. Furthermore, at the time of the invasion, in a rush to leave the country, one of the important Dutch intelligence leaders failed to take a suitcase that contained a list of all of his contact addresses in Holland which, in turn, was found by the Germans.[10] Thus the entire intelligence network had to be rebuilt.

On July 19, 1940, the Dutch intelligence service in exile, the Central Intelligence Service, *Centrale Inlichtingen Dienst* (*C.I.D.*), was organized in London. Francois Van't Sant, the former police commissioner at The Hague, was put in charge and selected to work in conjunction with Colonel Euan Rabagliatti, the head of the British S.I.S. Holland section.

On the night of August 28, 1940, the *C.I.D.* dispatched the first covert agent to Holland. Lodo van Hamel, a Dutch naval officer, was dropped by parachute into a bulb field behind the dunes near Leyden to arrange for the establishment of secret independent listening posts, which were to be equipped with radio transmitters. Many of those he contacted refused to cooperate; however, after six weeks of tireless effort, he did manage to set up four wireless stations. He brought one transmitter with him; three others were built in Holland and tuned to a London receiving station. Van Hamel kept all of his transmissions to less than three minutes and never twice in a row from the same location. This was because of the ubiquitous German radio detection vans used for intercepting and plotting the location of wireless transmissions.

The German direction-finding network was highly efficient in tracking down wireless operators. Messages were first intercepted from a fixed location once the transmitting frequency was established; then by cross-bearings, a "snifter" van was dispatched that localized the position of the transmitter by registering the maximum and minimum strengths of the signal through a rotating aerial. Once the van arrived at the proximate location, the transmitting site was gradually pinpointed.

Even by reducing time on the air to a minimum, some agents were caught in the act of transmitting and killed while operating the telegraph. Others who were captured and unable to endure torture had ready access to a cyanide pill. The loss of an operator was a tragedy, but disclosure under torture was a disaster, since it usually led to a chain-reaction of arrests. This occurred quite frequently.

Van Hamel was accompanied by Professor Baas Becking, a leading member of the *Orde Dienst* and two couriers. After completing their mission, they were instructed by London to go to Zurig, a small village in the province of Friesland near the Tjeuke Lake. They were to rendezvous as close as possible to midnight on October 13, when a Fokker T8 Royal Netherlands Navy seaplane would pick them up on the lake and return them to England. In the event of bad weather, it would try again on either of the following two nights. The two men were able to collect valuable information, including codes, microfilm maps of German newly erected coastal defenses and photographs of great value to British intelligence.

On October 13, van Hamel, joined by two couriers of the *Orde Dienst*, awaited the arrival of the plane, but it failed to appear. On the following night, shortly after midnight, the plane made three passes at three different altitudes, but because of the heavy ground fog and water vapor, it was impossible to see the surface of the lake. The aircraft circled for twenty minutes in the moonlight above the heavy mist, and then headed back to England.

The following morning the agents were apprehended by the Dutch police at a farm where they had stopped for a drink of water. That night at midnight October 15, under clear skies and a bright moon, the plane landed on the surface of the water, but after the arrest of the four agents earlier that morning, a German patrol boat was on the water awaiting the arrival of the plane. The two vessels exchanged gunfire and the seaplane, although damaged by machine gun fire from the patrol boat, was able to lift off and make it back to England.[11] After some harsh police interrogation by the SS, the prisoners were taken to The Hague, where van Hamel convinced the Germans that his accomplice and the two couriers were in no way involved in the Resistance. Van Hamel, however, was confined to prison, but at no time did he divulge the names of his collaborators. Eight months later in June 1941, he was executed. Despite the tragic consequences of the mission for van Hamel, the wireless telegraphy (W/T) link with London was established. Three of the groups he organized continued operating throughout 1941, and one of these into 1942, when it was discovered and destroyed by the Germans.[12]

One of the groups was led by a young Rotterdam lawyer, Dr. Johan Stijkel. For several months, with the help of a skilled radio operator, the Stijkel group exchanged radio messages with the British S.I.S. In March 1941, Dr. Stijkel offered to come to London in a small cutter with three of his aides with some important information that had been obtained after the capture of van Hamel. Although the small group was warned by both Dutch and British intelligence of the difficulty of arranging a pickup in coastal waters, they nonetheless agreed. Dr. Stijkel enlisted the help of two harbor policemen who had secretly helped the Resistance. What Stijkel did not know was that the two policemen were Gestapo V-men (Dutch informers), and when they realized that the group was not going fishing, they were reported to the local Gestapo chief. During the night of April 2, as they were boarding the cutter, Stijkel and his helpers were apprehended by a detachment of SS men in motorboats that had suddenly appeared out of the darkness. The group was captured, taken to Gestapo headquarters in The Hague and then to Berlin where they were later executed by a firing squad.[13]

Between November 1940 and June 1941 only three agents were sent into Holland from England. Two were apprehended by the Gestapo; the third was able to continue covert activity for a year. Although there were a few cases of sabotage, the Resistance groups that did exist were still preoccupied with problems of organization.

During the first two years of the war, British strategists, and particularly Prime Minister Winston Churchill, had high hopes that the occupied countries on the Continent could be liberated by comparatively small, highly trained invading armies supported by uprisings of an indigenous armed resistance from within those countries. In July of 1940, in preparation for this final assault, with bulldog tenacity, the British leader established a secret "Department of Ungentlemanly Warfare" called the Special Operations Executive (S.O.E.). Its purpose was, in Churchill's words, to "set Europe ablaze" by local acts of subversion and sabotage activities—derailing trains, blowing up bridges, cutting telephone and telegraph cables, attacking aerodromes and sinking ships in harbor—all of which were designed to force the enemy to guard vulnerable points, thereby keeping the enemy preoccupied by immobilizing thousands of troops who might otherwise be employed in some other theater of operations.

On December 20, 1940, when the S.O.E. Dutch Section was started, the British insisted that all agents be approved, trained and dispatched by S.O.E. officials.[14]

Some who were recruited and eager to actively engage the enemy were soldiers evacuated out of Holland after the Five Day War in May 1940; some attempted to cross the dangerous North Sea in fishing boats and other creative types of watercraft; some survived the journey, but many drowned on the way or were forced to turn back. Thirty-one Dutchmen, including several university students, escaped to England by way of New York on a Swiss freighter—numerically the single largest escape from Occupied Holland during the war.[15] Others who sought an active role traveled from their empire in the Dutch East Indies where they were living before the war—later to be overrun by the Japanese; still others had been studying or working in Great Britain at the outbreak of hostilities.

From the British point of view, between 1940 and 1942, the Dutch Central Intelligence Service (*C.I.D.*) was far from satisfactory. The intelligence received from inside Holland was disorganized, slow in arriving and inadequate. Neither the Dutch Exile Government nor the British received basic knowledge concerning such things as the proper form of identity cards to be printed—an absolute necessity for agents entering Holland or for those *onderduikers* on the run—or information concerning the withdrawal of prewar silver coins in Holland or clothing essentials, details that would affect whether agents being sent to Holland were properly equipped.[16]

The Dutch had little control over the selection of agents to be dispatched to Holland, and were shown only those messages that the S.I.S. chose to pass on to them. This prompted the Dutch Exile Government to establish a new department in London called the Bureau for the Military Preparation for the Return—*Bureau Militaire Voorbereiding Terugkeer (M.V.T.)*—headed by Colonel M.R. de Bruyne, a Dutch Royal Marine officer. Its purpose was to come to a better understanding with the British concerning the selection and dispatch of agents and to render advice to British intelligence, because Colonel de Bruyne believed that he was being kept in the dark by British S.I.S. officials. This was perhaps understandable in view of the fact that de Bruyne, a marine, had just returned from the Far East and had no direct experience himself of the German occupation of his country. In short, he was viewed by the British as unsuitable for carrying out intelligence operations.[17]

Even amongst Dutch ministers themselves there was criticism over leadership of the Central Intelligence Service. Of approximately a dozen agents dispatched to Holland by the *C.I.D.* before the summer of 1942, all but two were caught by the Germans. Its head, Francois Van't Sant resigned in the summer of 1941 after criticism from within Dutch exile circles for combining his intelligence work with his work as Queen Wilhelmina's private secretary. The government's official view was that this combination might one day seriously embarrass the Queen.[18]

Disputes among the Dutch intelligence officials and ministers continued until November 1942, when by a formal pronouncement, Queen Wilhelmina ordered the complete reorganization of the Dutch intelligence network in London.[19]

In mid-June 1941, Hans Zomer, a twenty-year-old Dutch wireless operator controlled by the Dutch section of S.I.S., arrived in Holland by parachute. On August 31, after having exchanged one hundred messages with London since his arrival, a German direction-finding van cruising through Bilthoven near Utrecht narrowed its search to the vicinity of a villa where Zomer was staying. The villa was raided and the Dutch agent arrested. Under torture by the Gestapo he refused to disclose any information. He did manage to play his transmitter back for the Germans in such a way that London concluded he was in enemy hands. However, signal codes used for his transmissions were found in his possession. These proved invaluable to *Sicherheitsdienst* (*SD*) counterintelligence head, SS Major Schreieder, who referred them to an expert in secret wireless techniques, Sgt. Ernst May, who discovered that the code contained a "security check"[20]—*a code word or phrase that would normally be inserted into every message transmitted as a sign that the message was genuine. Omitting the security check or sending it incorrectly would signal London that the agent was operating under duress.* May's discovery combined with information obtained later from Willem van der Reyden, another captured agent, eventually led to the blunder that resulted in the collapse of the S.O.E. in Holland.

Meanwhile, during the course of both the intra- and inter-services disputes between the several intelligence services, the Exile Prime Minister Pieter Gerbrandy, who had a strong hatred of the Nazis, formed a separate secret service at his own office. Discouraged by the lack of cooperation within Dutch governmental circles, the cabinet minister made independent arrangements with British intelligence officials, and it was from these arrangements that the first agents were sent from Britain to Holland.[21]

In June 1941, a daring undertaking that received the backing of Gerbrandy was begun by a group of students from Leyden University who had escaped to London on a Swiss-piloted Panamanian freighter. Led by Erik Hazelhoff Roelfzema, the resolute young stalwarts established a small intelligence unit called *Contact Holland*. Its tasks were to establish radio communications with London from within Holland, and to ferry agents and wireless sets across the North Sea by motor gunboat in conjunction with the British S.I.S. Once established, an intelligence-gathering network would be organized to provide Anglo-Dutch intelligence with reports, maps, photographs and other items that were not transmittable along with selected persons to be landed and picked up via the sea by members of *Contact Holland*.[22]

Roelfzema was instructed to ferry an agent into Holland with new codes to be given to another agent who had been working in Holland, but whose code had been compromised after the capture of an agent sent by the Dutch section of S.I.S. The plan was to put ashore at Scheviningen, a beach resort and fishing village not far from The Hague where, on Friday evenings, the Germans held a boisterous party with guests on the hotel promenade just up from the beach. The scheme was to land an agent between the curfew hours of midnight and 4:00 AM in a wet suit that concealed formal evening wear to convey the appearance of an intoxicated guest from the hotel. He would walk from the beach and along the promenade well supplied with, and smelling of brandy. In keeping with the partygoer's charade, if challenged, he would appear as a guest from the hotel to get past the German sentry post and to a prearranged address.

The work proved far more difficult than anticipated. Six times the motor gunboat had to turn back because of severe weather conditions, and on the seventh attempt, some thirty miles from the Dutch coast, a motor and the steering system conked out. Using a hand rudder on the stern, they were forced to turn back to England. On November 21, as they approached the shore on the eighth attempt, wireless operator Willem van der Reyden, recruited from the Dutch merchant marine, was tossed overboard after the dinghy was seized by a breaker and capsized, resulting in the loss of the transmitter in the surf.[23] Van der Reyden managed to swim ashore and somehow made his way to a safe house in Wassenaar near Leyden. This was the home of a Dr. Krediet, who was at the time harboring another Dutch agent, Johannes ter Laak, *Contact Holland's* first wireless agent dropped by parachute more than two months earlier, and whose transmitter was badly damaged in the drop. Van der Reyden, a skilled radio operator and mechanic, was able to repair ter Laak's transmitter, which enabled them to exchange signals with London.

Shortly thereafter, the house was raided by German security agents. Van der Reyden and ter Laak were arrested; the transmitter and codes now in the possession of the German counter-intelligence service. When the *SD* chief, Major Schreieder, gave to van der Reyden the choice of working for him or of dealing with the Gestapo, the Dutch agent did not betray his trust. He did provide Schreieder with a good deal of information concerning the codes, but he did not reveal his "security check." When van der Reyden communicated with London the omitted security check was noted and no reply was given. The Dutch agent explained to Sgt. May, an expert in secret wireless techniques, the reason there was no reply was because he did not have a complete knowledge of the code. The Germans accepted van der Reyden's explanation. However, "in the course of several long talks with May he expounded the whole of S.I.S.'s systems for coding messages."[24] This enabled the German wireless expert to gain considerable insight into the British code system. Van der Reyden spent three years in Nazi prisons and was later liberated by the Russians from the Sachsenhausen concentration camp. Ter Laak was murdered at the Mauthausen extermination camp in 1944.[25]

Meanwhile, Prime Minister Gerbrandy called upon Roelfzema to arrange a pickup of two politicians, Dr. Wiardi Beckman and Frans J. Goedhart to be taken to London where they would be given seats in the Dutch Exile Government cabinet. On November 23, agent Pieter Tazelaar was put ashore by the Roelfzema ferry at Scheveningen where, in keeping with the partygoer's charade, he managed to get past the German sentry post to a prearranged address.

Arrangements were made with agent Tazelaar to have the two politicians on the beach at a specific time for the rendezvous. After two failed attempts to arrive because of severe weather, Pieter requested an additional sign of the boat's approach. Radio Oranje was called upon to provide the signal. Normally the nightly program opened with the singing of the Dutch national anthem. However, it was arranged that on the night that the rendezvous was to take place, the anthem would be spoken instead of sung, thereby informing Tazelaar that the boat was coming to pick up the passengers. On the night in question the gunboat made a successful approach to the rendezvous, but when the Radio Oranje evening broadcast opened earlier that evening someone at the station blundered because the anthem was sung rather than spoken. Unfortunately, after waiting in sub-zero temperature an hour beyond the 4:25 AM agreed-upon time for the passenger pickup, naturally, no one showed up.[26]

Finally, on January 17, 1942, Radio Oranje began its evening program with the spoken stanza of the national anthem—the signal to Tazelaar to have the two politicians on the beach at 4:30 AM for pickup and delivery to London. But what *Contact Holland* did not know was that a Dutch informer had somehow learned of the planned pickup and the Radio Oranje signal. This was reported to the *Abwehr* head of German army counter-intelligence in Holland, Major Hermann Giskes, who arranged to have the two politicians arrested at the beach landing rendezvous. Tazelaar was apprehended by The Hague Municipal Police, but shortly thereafter, managed to escape into the night.[27] He returned to England by way of Belgium, occupied and unoccupied France, Spain and Portugal escape route.

After this last failed rendezvous, Scheveningen was abandoned as a landing site for the delivery and pickup of agents and equipment. Henceforth, a succession of alternate locations on the Dutch coast became the objectives of *Contact Holland*, and from which a steadily rising number of agents and transmitters were landed successfully.

In September 1942, Queen Wilhelmina secretly asked the Belgian government-in-exile to establish a new underground organization in Holland. Dutch intelligence was still so fraught with political squabbling and factionalism that neither the Dutch *C.I.D.* nor the British S.O.E. was to know about it. A twenty-one-year-old innovative Belgian agent, Gaston Vandermeersche (code name: Rinus or Raymond), was put in charge of the network, which was named "WIM," in deference to the Queen's name. Gaston had no difficulty in recruiting

Resistance Initiatives

agents. Within a month, through contacts in Holland, Gaston recruited over 200 Dutch agents. It was not long before a considerable amount of raw intelligence came pouring in. Reports were prepared and sent to London, but most of them pertained to detailed accounts of political squabbling between various Dutch political factions. Moreover, Gaston was having trouble getting his special messages broadcast to agents over the B.B.C. And when he requested a radio operator be sent from London he got no reply.[28]

Nevertheless, the WIM intelligence group continued to grow. By the first part of January 1943, there were more than 1,200 agents operating in every province and major city in Holland.[29] Moreover, the organization was sending London numerous microfilmed pages of intelligence material including maps, detailed locations of German anti-aircraft installations, the names of Dutch officials collaborating with the Nazis and providing WIM agents with identity cards, ration coupons, etc. Additionally, WIM's system of coast watchers kept London informed of German bunkers and heavy artillery. Nonetheless, despite numerous requests, London failed to acknowledge publicly that Gaston was a bona fide representative in Holland.[30]

In May 1943, Gaston went to Perpignan, France, to check on some microfilm shipments where he was arrested at another agent's apartment. He was taken to the prison at Fresnes, a drab Paris suburb, and later to Gestapo headquarters at Avenue Foch where he was subjected to weeks of continuous beatings. Through it all, he refused to disclose any information concerning WIM or any of its agents. However, within two months the network was destroyed and about 80 members of the organization in Holland and in Belgium were rounded up by the Germans. In June of 1944, 48 of the prisoners were tried by special court martial in Haaren and sentenced to death.[31] Gaston miraculously survived the war and was repatriated by the Allies at war's end from the Gestapo prison at Luttringhausen, a small town near Dusseldorf, Germany.[32]

The questions concerning the unresponsiveness of both the Dutch and British intelligence chiefs, even to the point of being hostile to the efforts of WIM, still remain unanswered. The Dutch historian Louis de Jong noted that "it is sad to relate that the reports gathered dust on the shelves of the Belgian Intelligence Service in London until, about a year later, they were discovered there by the Dutch."[33]

In summation, the intelligence activities carried out in Holland during the years 1940–1942, despite the efforts of dedicated Dutch patriots, had but few and scattered results mainly because of political and personal differences within the British and Dutch intelligence services as well as extremely difficult conditions that interfered with effective work.

Further difficulties arose when S.O.E. met with a series of disasters that were unique in the history of wartime espionage. This was the German counter-intelligence penetration of the S.O.E. Dutch section, which paralyzed British and Dutch intelligence operations from March 1942 to the autumn of 1943. It is to this tragic and still unsolved failure of Allied espionage that we now turn.

10

A Dutch Calamity

Falsehood, like poison, will generally be rejected when administered alone; but when blended with wholesome ingredients, may be swallowed unperceived.
—*Richard Whately (1787-1863), Archbishop of Dublin*

As early as July 1941, the Dutch Section of the Special Operations Executive (S.O.E.), acting in collaboration with Dutch intelligence and with the full cooperation of their Exiled Government in London, conceived a plan to establish a sabotage network in the Netherlands that envisaged 1,000 saboteurs and the creation and arming of a secret army of 5,000 men to assist in an Allied invasion of Holland.[1] In its preparatory stage, Plan Holland, as it was labeled, involved the insertion of S.O.E. agents into the country by parachute. The agents would serve as liaison officers with organized units of the Dutch Resistance and as wireless operators to keep an open line of communication with London regarding, *inter alia*, the timing and location of suitable reception sites for the dropping of weapons and other sabotage material by parachute.

Once the preparatory stage was in place, the plan set out to disrupt enemy communications on or soon after D-Day, the main invasion of the Continent. It would also prevent, by this disruption, the removal of Dutch locomotives and rolling stock to Germany. After D-Day, the plan anticipated providing for direct support of armies in the field and the prevention of the demolition of bridges, power-stations, dock facilities, etc. and other objectives constituting a scorched earth policy.[2] The overall plan was well-conceived since it involved the application of general principles of irregular "ungentlemanly warfare" conjoined with the specific needs of Holland.

On November 7, 1941, two S.O.E. Dutch agents, Hubertus Lauwers, a wireless operator, and Thijs Taconis, a sabotage organizer, were dropped by parachute in East Holland not far from the German border. Lauwers was one of many agents who knew why this mission was so important to the liberation of Holland. During their first four months, Taconis traveled throughout the country contacting *Orde Dienst* Resistance commanders while Lauwers transmitted to London information received from agent Taconis. Radio transmissions were made at the home of former army Lieutenant Teller and family at 678 Fahrenheitstraat in The Hague.

At about this same time, a Dutch informer (V-man), Georges Ridderhof, a professional criminal, smuggler in opium and diamonds and a gun-runner, in the employ of Major Hermann Giskes, the *Abwehr* counter-intelligence chief in Holland, penetrated an *Orde Dienst* Resistance group. He succeeded in locating a number of wireless operators and gained the confidence of Resistance leaders, even to the extent of being asked to take charge of the reception of arms dropped by parachute. One such report that Ridderhof received was information that spelled out in detail early preparations for Plan Holland. The report indicated that a British agent was looking for suitable landing sites for the dropping of weapons and other sabotage materials. Additionally, it stated that a secret army was being planned that would be "systematically trained and armed."[3] Giskes, however, considered the report so incredulous that he told the V-man to "take stories like that to the North Pole." Thus the *Abwehr* codenamed what was soon to become "Operation North Pole," in memory of that remark. The parallel SS codename was *Englandspiel*, which means the "game against England."[4] Giskes believed that Ridderhof's reports were mere fabrications so that the informer could earn his pay as a traitor.

However, a further report by Ridderhof, that three Dutch escapees were to be picked up by a British motor torpedo boat and taken to England, was verified when, on the night in question, the three men were arrested on the spot described by Ridderhof. This was enough to convince Giskes of the V-man's credibility. Additionally, a Lieutenant Heinrich in charge of the radio detection and interception service of the Gestapo informed Giskes that his direction finding (DF) station had picked up a series of radio signals that clearly indicated a communication link between London and Holland.

Furthermore, the Germans were also monitoring broadcasts by the B.B.C.'s Radio Oranje to various Resistance groups in Holland in the form of personal messages. The broadcasts consisted of information that made no sense to anyone other than to the message recipient. For example, "The little white rabbit has returned to his hutch" might mean that an agent and his wireless operator will be dropped at a particular field on such and such a night. Ridderhof informed Giskes that the Resistance group he had infiltrated was expecting an arms drop on a certain date and that the signal would be given by Radio Oranje. Again, the informer's information proved accurate. The dropped container was filled with explosives, fuses, revolvers and ammunition. Giskes also learned that the arms reception had been directed by a man whom Ridderhof believed to be an S.O.E. instructor. After Giskes consulted with SS counter-intelligence Lieutenant Colonel Shreieder, further information that came from another informer who had infiltrated the *Orde Dienst* group disclosed the name of agent Thijs Taconis, and that he was operating in The Hague.

On March 6, 1942, after prolonged mobile direction-finding in The Hague, a German detection van was able to narrow the search to a block of flats on Fahrenheitstraat. Shortly before 6:30 PM, the prearranged time for Lauwers to contact London, and as snow was beginning to fall, Teller, who was standing watch by the window, noticed three suspicious police cars parked down the street. Wireless operator Lauwers immediately stopped transmitting, rightly presuming that this was a direction-finding team, and instructed Mrs. Teller to drop the transmitter out of the window into a rose bed below. The two agents left the house and proceeded down the street away from the parked cars, but—as Ridderhof had provided the Germans with a detailed description of Lauwers—were soon apprehended by German security police, who took them back to Teller's flat. The transmitter could be seen in the darkening gloom caught on the laundry-lines of the flat below.[5]

At the *Abwehr* headquarters in Scheveningen, Schreieder gave instruction that when Lauwers was interrogated by the Gestapo he was not to be tortured. Major Giskes not only treated the agent humanely; he also treated him with respect, and complimented him for his courage and his patriotic duty. After acknowledging the agent's duty to obey orders, Giskes set to work to disarm him by pointing out the futility of starting a war by providing arms and explosives to a civilian population. He asserted, "In a country as civilized and as thickly populated as Holland, I personally consider such methods to be highly dubious. The possible advantages of this kind of warfare can never bear comparison with the consequences of reprisals by the Occupation authorities as justified by the laws of war. Any army of occupation, irrespective of its nationality, will crush such attempts by means of the shooting of hostages and the terrorizing of the population." He then told Lauwers that it was his intention to prevent the Allied Secret Service, "by every means at my disposal, from supplying tons of arms and explosives to irresponsible fanatics in this country, the use of which can only mean a blood-bath for the civil population."[6]

Giskes believed that Lauwer's vulnerable point was his blind confidence in the S.O.E. and that by pointing to its failures, he could break him down. The *Abwehr* head spoke of Dutch agent van der Reyden and how he had divulged a good deal of information concerning not only the system for coding messages, but also details relating to his own particular case, and how the Germans obtained his notebook containing the names and addresses of Resistance men and details of several dropping grounds. But van der Reyden never revealed his security check. Giskes also went on about agents who had been caught before Lauwers and who had agreed (which was not true) to transmit to London under German control.[7]

Lauwers denied and disputed everything that Giskes had said. He knew nothing of the agents who were mentioned, nor did he know van der Reyden (which was true). Giskes then suggested striking a bargain with Lauwers. Confronted with Lieutenant Heinrich and Sgt. May, who had a flair for deciphering, Giskes proposed to the agent that if one of the three coded messages that were found on Lauwers could be deciphered he would surrender his own code and agree to work with the Germans. Lauwers agreed because he remembered what he had been told at the S.O.E. training school: he could disclose everything, even his code, but he would die before revealing his security check—the code word or phrase that let London know that he was operating freely and not under duress from the Germans.

What Lauwers did not know was that one of the messages found on him—which happened to be false naval intelligence information; namely, that the German cruiser *Prinz Eugen* was damaged a fortnight earlier off Norway and was in dock at Schiedam—was planted on him through the traitor Ridderhof, who fed it to agent Taconis, who gave it to Lauwers for transmitting to London. Lauwers had not had time to send the message before he was arrested. Heinrich, who had the message, turned to Giskes and said, "I've just discovered that the *Prinz Eugen* is at Schiedam!" At that moment a shocked and despondent Lauwers suddenly realized that what Giskes had told him was true: for weeks, Ridderhof had been feeding false information to Taconis, which Lauwers was unknowingly sending to London; thereby unwittingly working for the Germans. Consequently, the bargain Giskes proposed was all for naught.[8]

The *Abwehr* Major, sensing that Lauwers was still wavering and unnerved by what he had just been told, reminded the agent that as a spy caught in the act, his life was of short duration, but if he agreed to transmit to London under German control, his life as well as that of Taconis would be spared.⁹ Lauwers still believed that he held the advantage: by omitting his security check he would automatically warn London that he was transmitting under German control and they would stop sending agents into Holland.

Lauwers began transmitting for the Germans on March 12, 1942. Yet just before going on the air, Giskes hastened to remind the agent not to forget his security check. (It is to be recalled that the *Abwehr* learned of "security checks" in the course of several long talks that Sgt. May had with Dutch agent van der Reyden, who revealed, among other things, special security measures.) Fortunately for Lauwers (codename "Ebenezer"), he was able to concoct a false security check that Giskes, after some hesitation, believed. Between groups of Morse, instead of the word "stop" he would send "stip" or "stap" or "step." His real security check was quite different: he was required to make a spelling mistake every sixteenth letter. He was also required to insert three dummy letters at the end of each message.¹⁰

From the outset Giskes took special precautions to ensure that he was not being duped. Lt. Heinrich put the headphones on and was listening in with Lauwers, who was tapping out his call sign—RLS—three times to London. He then received the acknowledgement to start sending. The message he was told to send contained falsified information of a most detailed nature: troop movements in northern Brabant, the strength of the *Luftwaffe* squadrons stationed at Eindhoven, and the construction of a U-boat base south of Rotterdam.¹¹

Lauwers was still beset with anxiety. It was possible that London would not reply at all, since he omitted his real security check. Lt. Heinrich, who still had his headphones on, suddenly heard a reply from London: "Message received and understood." A new message that came from London concerned approval of a dropping zone for S.O.E. agents south of Zoutkamp near the banks of the Reitdeip Canal, a reception area that was found earlier by Taconis. Lieutenant Arnold Baatsen (codename "Watercress") was scheduled to drop by parachute during the forthcoming moon period on March 25 along with several arms containers. The Germans considered the Reitdeip dropping ground too isolated (presumably because of genuine Resistance groups in the area who would be able to either identify or capture the Dutch traitor reception committee) and had Ebenezer propose another dropping zone in northeast Holland, in the moorlands north of Steenwijk, to which London agreed. Ebenezer was told to prepare to receive Lieutenant Baatsen within 48 hours.

Lauwers was now thoroughly confused. He knew that his messages to London had been understood. But he was certain that he had not given his real security check. He deliberately refrained from making any spelling mistakes every sixteenth letter during his transmission. So why then, had London then given Giskes more information than he could have dragged out of the worst of traitors? Lauwers pondered the grim and awful truth that London was still unaware of the fact that he was now being used as a tool of the *Abwehr*.

Matters were made even worse for Lauwers by other prisoners who believed that he was willingly working for the Germans—that he was a traitor. He tried to get word to Taconis by tapping out in Morse code on the pipes along the floor in his cell a relay message that he was not using his security check, but who, apart from Taconis would even know what a security check was?[12]

On March 27/28, shortly before midnight, a string of cars led by Giskes left Steenwijk with dimmed lights across the moorlands in the direction of the dropping ground and into a small wooded area. Lights in the shape of a triangle illuminated the drop zone for the R.A.F. twin engine bomber that circled the area several times before dropping the agent and four heavy containers filled with revolvers, Sten guns, ammunition and explosives. Baatsen was met on the ground by the traitor and Resistance imposter Ridderhof and two other V-men.

After stepping into the car, Baatsen was arrested and taken to The Hague and then to *Abwehr* headquarters in Scheveningen. This was the beginning of the so-called "radio game," the *Englandspiel* or "Operation North Pole," one of the most ingenious and perplexing counterintelligence coups of the war that resulted in a series of S.O.E. parachute drops that were followed in most cases by arrests upon landing or soon afterwards.

According to Giskes, Baatsen's capture had little influence on further developments of "Operation North Pole." He was to have been met by Ebenezer and from that time on was simply to make his way independently as an agent.[13] After his arrest, his interrogator tricked him into believing that he was betrayed by a German agent in London, after which Baatsen behaved as if everyone in that city was his enemy and disclosed a great deal of information about where he had been trained, and how and by whom. This knowledge enabled both SS Lt. Colonel Shreieder and Giskes to facilitate later interrogations of other agents who were caught; many of whom were unnerved by the extent of detail that the Germans already had.[14]

On March 29 Giskes had Ebenezer report to London that Baatsen had been dropped safely with four containers. In that same transmission London queried Ebenezer and instructed him to find out what had happened to two agents who had been dropped on March 10, but London had received no confirmation of their arrival. The agents, Leonard Andringa (codenamed "Turnip") and Jan

Molenaar (codenamed "Turnip II") dropped blind (without benefit of a reception team to greet them) near Holten. *Abwehr* knew nothing about this drop, but knew that a convincing reply had to be sent if their deception was not to be discovered.

The problem was solved when Giskes receive a report from German field police that the body of an enemy parachutist had been found near Holten whose forged papers identified him as agent Molenaar. He had apparently fractured his skull upon landing. On April 4 Ebenezer replied that the one agent had been killed and that he was trying to establish contact with the missing agent, Andringa, who managed to get to Amsterdam and then to a safe house in Haarlem, where he was looking for someone to replace his dead wireless operator. At the safe house, a cigar shop that served as a go-between, he met Gerard Ras (codenamed "Lettuce") and wireless operator Lieutenant Hendrik Jordaan (codenamed "Trumpet"). Jordaan informed London that he had just met Andringa and that the latter's wireless operator was killed upon landing. Jordaan agreed to transmit for Andringa until London could send a replacement.[15]

On April 5/6, two more S.O.E. agents, Barend Kloos (codenamed "Leek") and Hendrik Sebes (codenamed "Leek II"), were dropped by parachute in Overijssel. Their assignment was to sabotage engineering firms in the town of Hengelo.[16]

On April 18/19, yet another agent, Lieutenant Hendrik Jan de Haas (codenamed "Potato"), was landed by motor torpedo boat in North Holland at Castricum on the Dutch coast. He was the first Dutch agent to be equipped with an "Eureka," a device that enabled an agent to guide an aircraft to a dropping ground without the use of lights or flares, no matter how dark the night. Its built-in transmitter was tuned to the wavelength of the aircraft's receiver, which was called a "Rebecca," and was capable of picking up a continuous high-frequency signal. The "Eureka" provided a radio beam in the form of a blip on the receiving screen. This enabled the pilot to navigate with greater accuracy.

De Haas was to link up with Andringa, who would pass his messages to Ebenezer. His task was to organize a sea ferry for S.O.E. agents if at all possible. It was well known that agents who boarded a plane for a parachute drop might several times be brought back to base without being dropped, either because there was no reception committee, or none that the pilot could find when one was expected; or because bad weather occurred on the way to the dropping zone; or, less frequently, because the aircraft developed a problem that made continuing on too risky. In fact, de Haas was the only instance of an S.O.E. Dutch section agent put in by sea. He had attempted two previous attempts to put ashore, the first on April 11/12, but because of worsening weather he had to turn back;

and on April 16/17 when the boat encountered an enemy convoy, and lost too much time evading it.[17]

On April 28, de Haas was arrested at the cigar shop safe house in Haarlem by a V-man who posed as a member of the Resistance. Like Baatsen before them, both Andringa and de Haas were told that they were betrayed by London; they too believed it. Andringa made matters worse by telling his captors that on May 1 he was scheduled to meet four other agents in Utrecht at a bar at the Terminus Hotel: Ras, Kloos, Jordaan and Sebes. The agents were sitting two and two at separate tables. As the two former agents were being arrested, Jordaan and Sebes got away. But in Ras's pocket the Germans found Jordaan's telephone number, through which they reached him. He was arrested on May 3, after he revealed to a presumed friend where he was to meet Sebes, who was arrested six days later.[18] Nevertheless, on May 11, London, unaware of de Haas's capture, sent a message to him via Ebenezer's transmitter, instructing him to find suitable points along the coast where agents and equipment could be landed at night.[19]

The parachute drops continued. On May 28, London told Ebenezer to prepare for the arrival of two more saboteurs, Herman Parlevliet (codenamed "Beetroot") and his wireless operator, Antonius van Steen (codenamed "Swede"), on May 29/30. They were to organize sabotage groups in Limburg. Initially, they were instructed to blow up the Juliana canal locks. They were equipped with two "Eureka" transmitters, and S-phones, which enabled them to have ground-to-aircraft conversations. They were dropped to a reception committee of Germans who were waiting for them on the Steenwijk moors.[20]

On June 22/23, S.O.E.'s next pair of agents, saboteur Jan van Rietschoten (codenamed "Parsnip") and his wireless operator Johannes Buizer (codenamed "Spinach"), parachuted to the Assen dropping ground which Ebenezer/Giskes had selected and which London approved. They were to organize a sabotage group in Overijssel.[21] Like the other agents, they were arrested by a German reception committee as soon as they landed.

Members of the Dutch Exile Government in London and the British chiefs of staff had high expectations for the Underground organization *Orde Dienst* despite the fact that it had been penetrated. Allied intelligence estimated that most of the O.D. cells were still loyal and could be depended on to provide assistance during the liberation of Holland. But they also realized that there was no centralized body of Resistance leadership in connection with the establishment of the "secret army," a key element in the implementation of Plan Holland. Therefore, it was decided to send an official representative of the National Resistance Council in London who would act as the liaison between the Dutch government-in-exile and the *Orde Dienst*.

A Dutch Calamity

The man selected for the job was George Louis Jambroes, a Dutch Reserve officer who before the war was a highly respected Professor of Physics at Utrecht University. He had escaped to England in 1941. He was originally asked to assist British scientists on the development of radar, but chose instead to work in the S.O.E. as a secret agent. He was to take command of the Dutch secret army and prepare it for Plan Holland. He was also to meet the leaders of the various Dutch Resistance groups and coordinate them under a National Committee of Resistance. Their mission was to destroy all German facilities in the provinces of Limburg, Brabant and Gelderland. The plan had the full backing of the Allied High Command.[22]

On the night of June 26/27, 1942, shortly before midnight, Jambroes (codenamed "Marrow") and his wireless operator, Lieutenant Joseph Jan Bukkens, equipped with one of the new and smaller transmitters that the S.O.E. was now supplying their agents, took off from an R.A.F. aerodrome in southeast England in a large four-engined Halifax bomber converted for parachuting agents. S.O.E. was so concerned for Jambroes's safety that five different dropping grounds were suggested to Ebenezer before finally agreeing on the Apeldoorn zone in Gelderland.[23] Upon landing the two-man team was greeted immediately by a group of Resistance imposters who first posed as a welcoming committee for the new Dutch chief organizer. Moments later, they were handcuffed and put in a waiting car where they were greeted by both Giskes and Schreieder before being taken to Gestapo headquarters and later to the prison at Haaren for S.O.E. agents.

The capture of Dr. Jambroes put an abrupt end to Plan Holland. The inability to implement and coordinate Allied and Resistance military actions marked a turning point in the *Englandspiel*. At this point the Germans had taken over Plan Holland, and Giskes was to make sure it did not turn out as intended by London.

It soon became obvious that Giskes could not tell London what Jambroes had discussed with the *Orde Dienst* leaders since the *Abwehr* major did not know who the leaders were, and since Jambroes himself had not met with the leaders since he was at the time under arrest. Consequently, to maintain the German deception and to solve the problem of pretending contact with the *Orde Dienst*, London had to be made to believe that Jambroes's assignment was impracticable. Giskes then proceeded to have Ebenezer send London several messages describing the "demoralization" among the various *O.D.* groups he had contacted. He also said that the leadership was so penetrated by German informers that any direct contact with its members as ordered by London would certainly attract the attention of the Germans. He emphasized to London that it was essential for Jambroes's security that he travel from place to place and that he would no longer be in contact with London on a day-to-day basis. When London began to show signs of uncertainty, and instructed Jambroes to be careful, Giskes proposed that the agent make contact with reliable leaders from the *O.D.* area groups so as to form the sixteen groups planned by consultation with the Resistance leadership. Naturally at no time were links established with the *O.D.* groups or with their leaders.[24]

London was now no longer satisfied simply with consultation with the Resistance groups; it was now expecting action from them. On July 5, Ebenezer was instructed by London to investigate the possibility of blowing up the Kootwijk radar station, a major detection center that was able to observe all Allied air and naval activities in the North Sea. Further instructions were that the attack was to be led by Taconis, assisted by a team of demolition experts.[25]

Taconis, for the past four months, had literally not seen the light of day, as he was placed in solitary confinement after he attacked a guard in his prison cell. He was of no use to the Germans since he was not a wireless operator, and so could not be "turned." He had stopped wondering who had betrayed him and had fallen into a state of lethargy, silently heading into oblivion. Nevertheless, Lauwers tried to get a message through to him that he had omitted his security check, but the other prisoners refused to cooperate, still believing him to be a traitor. And besides, Taconis, as described by one writer, "having committed psychological suicide, no longer knew about the Germans, the British, or even that there was a war on."[26]

Between July 8 and 20, Giskes had Ebenezer send a number of messages to London giving full details of the layout of the Kootwijk transmitter and claiming that it was lightly guarded.[27] On July 23/24, one more wireless operator, G.J. van Hemert (codenamed "Leek A"), was dropped, supposedly to Taconis with an urgent message to prepare an attack at Kootwijk from which German U-boats waging the battle of the Atlantic were receiving their orders. He of course was arrested upon landing.

Then on July 28, Giskes told London that the attack had been a disaster as some of Taconis's men had run into a minefield. The explosions had alerted the guards and the operation had been abandoned. Three of the attacking party had been killed and five were still missing. Taconis himself was safe and unwounded. Giskes had Ebenezer stress that the Kootwijk transmitter and other similar installations were now heavily guarded. The Dutch section in London replied to Ebenezer that they regretted the loss of life and warned him to suspend all operational activities for the time being. Two weeks later, Ebenezer received a congratulatory message from London to all members of the raiding party on their heroic attempt, and stated that Taconis would receive a British military decoration for his leadership.[28] So even though the operation ended in complete failure, London, still unaware that Lauwers was a prisoner and sending messages prepared by the Germans, was pleased that Plan Holland had gotten underway.

Throughout the late spring and summer months, Lauwers had informed London on at least four separate occasions in quick succession that he had been captured by repeatedly omitting his security check. The missions of van Steen, Parlevliet, van Hemert and Jambroes had all been forewarned, but to no avail.

By the middle of August, long silences and Jambroes's apparent lack of progress created an increasing unease in London, which sent repeated messages urging him to return home for consultations. Ebenezer replied for Jambroes that he was too busy to return; that a pick-up by sea or air would be too dangerous and that it was not the right moment for him to leave Holland. The Dutch section of S.O.E. replied that he should use S.O.E.'s Spanish escape route and offered to put him in touch with a group of agents in Paris who operated the escape line. Jambroes agreed and promised to use it at the earliest moment.

By now the *Englandspiel* wireless network had been greatly expanded. Before Jambroes's capture, Giskes had a radio link with five S.O.E. transmission posts from captured transmitters located at The Hague, Rotterdam, Amsterdam, Gouda, and Noordwijk—cities where S.O.E. operators were to have set up their communication stations. Additional locations for keeping in contact with London were Eindhoven, Utrecht, Hilversum, Arnhem, Driebergen and Hertogenbosch.[29]

Giskes was given additional help from the *Luftwaffe*, whose Fieseler Storch light aircraft were able to locate suitable dropping ground sites that numbered about 30 in all. It was into these zones that unsuspecting S.O.E. agents and hundreds of containers with arms and supplies landed into the arms of the Gestapo. Of particular concern to Giskes and to Schreieder were the German anti-aircraft batteries and airplanes, especially the night fighters that targeted British and American bombers on flights to or from dropping zones. Throughout the period of *Englandspiel*, according to Giskes's records, twelve four-engine Allied bombers were intercepted and shot down after dropping their load of agents and containers. The proportion of twelve bombers lost to a total of about 200 organized supply flights was not very high. The number was increased, however, due to other factors, which resulted in the halting of R.A.F. "specialist" flights over Holland by the middle of 1943.[30] Giskes frequently requested the *Luftwaffe* refrain from attacking certain enemy aircraft on specific moonlit nights when he knew that an air drop was scheduled to arrive. The *Abwehr* major knew that many more S.O.E. agents would be sent into Holland now that Plan Holland was in operation, and he wanted them caught alive to assist him in his ongoing *Englandspiel* "radio game."

The number of Allied agents who dropped into the hands of the Germans had become so commonplace, Giskes later stated:

> *The reception preparations were arranged in accordance with a fixed programme. It developed into an all-day and all-night affair which held neither romance nor excitement... The Reception Committee and all others concerned at once knew their meeting point and which dropping area would be used. For example, a code message which read "Visit No. 17 this evening with two ladies" signified that two agents would be dropped that night at dropping area No. 17.*[31]

Resistance historian Professor Michael Foot has aptly described the typical reaction of an agent who managed a successful parachute drop into a dark strange field and was received by a German Reception Committee.

> *This is an achievement in itself, which brings a great surge of joy; to do it secretly and then be greeted by the correct codename in one's own language by one's reception committee brings another great surge of joy; and anybody with an ounce of patriotic feeling is delighted to be back in the homeland; further surge of joy. Then, just as he is about to set out on the work of liberation, someone on the reception committee says that there's a rather awkward control near by, and it would be as well for the newcomer to hand his pistol over, so that it can be smuggled past by those who already know how. So one holds one's pistol out by the muzzle—and is thereupon handcuffed. In a moment one is surrounded by men in Wehrmacht helmets and being questioned by an elegant officer in Gestapo uniform. The shock is bound to overwhelm anyone.*[32]

Sturmbann-Fuhrer Schreieder recorded in his diary that the continuous capture of S.O.E. agents also created a great deal of work for him and his men. After the reception and interrogation of the captured agents and their incarceration in the Haaren Prison, their transmitters had to be played back to reply to the numerous queries and instructions from London. "We had to compose replies and reports of imaginary sabotage actions and activities of the prisoners... and put into the S.O.E. code... and all this meant to compose the messages in phrases which the individual captured agents were likely to use. Some were intelligent and well-educated men, others were former sailors and artisans, and would express themselves differently from their colleagues."[33]

By mid-September, presumably because of the long delay in receiving a report on the progress of Plan Holland, London notified Ebenezer to expect the arrival of an important new mission, codenamed "Operation Erica," headed by Christian Jongelie (code named "Parsley"), the personal emissary of Dutch Prime Minister Gerbrandy. Jongelie was to carry a message from the prime minister to the leaders of all the political parties in Holland urging them to form a coalition under a National Council of Resistance. He was accompanied by Captain Carl Beukema (codenamed "Kale"), Jongelie's liaison with the *Orde Dienst*.

"Erica" was dropped on September 25 to a reception committee arranged by Ebenezer/Giskes and received by Schreieder's V-men. During the course of his interrogation, Jongelie told Giskes that in order to confirm his safe arrival he was to send a message to London; the message was to read: "The express left on time." Giskes took this to mean that if confirmation of his arrival was not made at 11:00, he was in German hands. The *Abwehr* seemed to think this was a trick with a true meaning that the agent had been caught. So at 11:00 Giskes had Ebenezer report to London that an accident occurred during the drop and that Jongelie was suffering from a severe concussion and was still unconscious. Three days later Ebenezer reported to London that Jongelie had regained consciousness for a short period and that the doctor hoped for an improvement. The next day London was told that the agent died and would be buried on the moor.[34]

Between October and November, London received a number of messages purportedly from agent Beukema, who had now taken over the "Erica" mission. Giskes had Beukema praise the progress which Jambroes was making. In mid-October, the S.O.E. Dutch section ordered Beukema back to London for consultation and arranged with Ebenezer that he be picked up by motor torpedo boat. To deal with this situation, Giskes staged another accident. He had Ebenezer advise London that the agent drowned while waiting to be picked up on the coast.[35] Like the other cases of deception, London accepted another of Giskes's hoaxes and sent another message appointing agent Cornelius Fortuyn (codenamed "Mangold"), one of the two remaining survivors, to act as the S.O.E. political coordinator in the overall Plan Holland operation. He too was arrested and sent to the Gestapo prison in Haaren.

By mid-September 1942, Jambroes/Ebenezer began reporting to London the excellent progress he was making with the sixteen new Resistance groups he was forming. As a result of this apparent progress, within the next two months London sent seventeen agents into Holland to help the build-up of the secret army for Plan Holland. The air drops continued in successive operations. So did the arrests. On October 21/22, three agents and a W/T operator, codenamed "Tomato," were landed, followed two nights later by four more including W/T operators code named "Chive," "Celery," and "Broccoli." On October 27/28, two more agents landed, including W/T operator "Cucumber." Each of these five wireless operators gave dropping sites to London, all of which were approved and supplied continuously with materials. In December, Ebenezer sent a progress report to London that about 1,500 men were in training and attached to eight resistance groups. Giskes requested articles such as clothing, underwear, footwear, bicycle tires, tobacco and tea to meet the needs of these detachments and to which London responded by sending a consignment of 32 containers dropped in four different areas in the course of one night.[36]

In late December, Jambroes's long delay in making arrangements to return to London for consultations prompted the S.O.E. Dutch section to send a special four-man team into Holland to assist him in his journey. The operation was given the code name "Golf." Meanwhile, messages continued to arrive from Holland reporting the steady progress of Jambroes's organization and the build-up of the secret army.

On February 18/19, 1943, the "Golf" team consisting of Jan Kist (codenamed "Hockey"), who was to work with the intelligence branch of the *Orde Dienst* groups, Gerard van Os (codenamed "Broadbean"), sabotage instructor, and the brothers Pieter and Willem van der Wilden (codenamed "Tennis" and "Golf"), both trained wireless operators, parachuted into the arms of the waiting German reception committee. The four man "Golf" team had been provided with escape-route maps and compasses, and what was needed to guide Professor Jambroes through Belgium and France to the Spanish frontier. Soon after their capture, Ebenezer/Giskes informed London that preparations for Jambroes's journey were going ahead, but that it might be several weeks before he could leave Holland.

While the S.O.E. Dutch section was anxiously awaiting the departure of Jambroes from Holland, Joseph Schreieder was informed by one of his most trusted double agents that an *O.D.* Resistance group leader, Hendrikus Knoppers, was being sought by the Gestapo. For this reason the National Committee of the Resistance wanted him in London. Schreieder saw this as an opportunity to placate the S.O.E., who were growing impatient over the delay of Jambroes's return to London. For greater reassurance London was told that Knoppers—who knew nothing of Jambroes's arrest—was being aided by the "Golf" team. The Dutch agent was accompanied to Brussels by double agent Ridderhof, and on to Paris by another double agent, Richard Christmann, a German who had earlier come to Holland to infiltrate the Dutch and Belgian Resistance as an *agent provocateur*. The escape route was by now controlled by the *Abwehr* and the Gestapo. Knoppers then traveled down the escape line—codenamed "Vic"—from Paris through Lyon, Perpignan, over the Pyrenees and into Barcelona, Spain. He reached London on September 9, 1943.

S.O.E. commended the "Golf" team for arranging Knopper's escape, but also considered Jambroes too important to be sent across Belgium and France. "Golf" leader Captain Kist was ordered by London to go to Paris and make arrangements with members of the S.O.E. network there for a Lysander pickup of Jambroes to London.[37]

Because Kist was in the custody of the Gestapo, Giskes had to find someone to impersonate the "Golf" agent, who was unknown to members of the Paris network. The *Abwehr* sent one of its own, Sergeant Boden, who spoke fluent Dutch, to become Captain Kist. He was accompanied by the German double agent Christmann, who was less likely to be recognized in Paris. He had frequently traveled to Belgium, where he had penetrated several of the Resistance groups there and was highly regarded by the S.O.E. in London as a successful member of the Resistance. Christmann was so successful as a double agent that he even organized his own escape line; to prove to London just how successful it was he even sent V-men and members of the *Abwehr* as "escapees" to Spain. Knoppers, of course, was one legitimate escapee who was successfully passed down the Christmann escape line.[38]

In Paris, Christmann arranged a fake arrest of the bogus Captain Kist at a café by German field police. This enabled the German provocateur to convince London that ushering Professor Jambroes through the escape line was now far too dangerous. Nevertheless, the S.O.E. was still determined to retrieve their agent. But by now Giskes, who was losing patience with the whole Jambroes affair, was running out of excuses and devices to postpone the agent's return to London. To dispose of the case, Giske and Colonel Schreieder sent the same *Abwehr* Sergeant Boden, who had acted the role of Captain Kist, to assume the identity of the Dutch professor. While in Toulouse, France, allegedly making their way to Spain, Boden and another V-man staged a fake accident in which the German police put out an announcement that a "Dutch national suspected of illicit activities and attempting an escape to Spain had died in a car accident." London soon received messages from the Resistance in Toulouse that Jambroes was dead.[39]

Throughout the course of *Englandspiel* there was one man who had uncomfortable suspicions about the deceptive radio game that by midwinter, 1942–43, were hardening into certainty.[40] The man was Leo Marks, the head of S.O.E.'s deciphering section. As the one in charge of agents' codes and as the chief coding problem solver, he was ultimately responsible for dealing with the "indecipherable" codes. These were garbled messages that were transmitted by the agents in the field. They could be the result of bad atmospheric conditions, deliberate interference by the Germans, or distortions by the agent himself.[41]

Because agents didn't usually transmit for more than ten minutes at a time, and typically from a different location so as to avoid being pinpointed by a German direction-finding van, a shaky hand or a hurried and perhaps frightened transmission could cause a mistake with the code. These garbled communiqués were handled by decoders, usually women who were trained to deal with these problems, and who would work for hours at S.O.E.'s listening post struggling to decode messages.

Patricia Jones, a decoder whose cousin was already working on indecipherables, gave this description of what life for a decoder was like.

> *You could go over their messages because you roughly knew who the agent was, how he wrote, but some were very, very difficult to decipher. Veronica would work all through the night on them, looking whiter and whiter. We chain-smoked, of course. It would go on for twenty-four hours. Veronica might hop into bed for a couple of hours and back she'd go again, until I presume Leo Marks came to the conclusion that it wasn't decipherable, but I think those occasions were very rare.*[42]

Usually there was a time factor involved in the transmission, which meant that if these messages were indecipherable, they had to be broken before the next scheduled transmission or "sked" (as they were called), which could be within the next forty-eight hours.[43]

Barbara O'Connell, another listening post decoder described the peril and anxiety that the wireless operator experienced in the field.

> *We gathered from the messages that came in that they were in sabotage of some kind and it was extremely dangerous work, and therefore the quicker we got on with the message, the better it would be for them. We knew that the agent must be under considerable stress, because from time to time they just disappeared or they'd be sending a message and would break off in the middle. You knew that the DF's (direction finders) had homed in on them and they'd had to stop.*[44]

A Dutch Calamity

There was no greater failure in the code room than to know that an agent had risked his or her life coming on the air to send a message that a coder could not read, and that the agent had to come on the air again. Coming on the air any more than was necessary made it more likely a detection-finder van could target the agent.

As the S.O.E.'s chief codebreaker, Marks was under considerable pressure from the various Country Sections (of which Holland was only one) to know what the agents were sending back to London. But for reasons he could not quite apprehend, Marks had a feeling of uneasiness about the traffic from Holland. "There was a cataract over my mind's eye and I didn't know how to remove it. There were so many conscious reasons for worrying about the Dutch traffic that this elusive anxiety could have been triggered by any or all of them."[45] His concerns fell into three main areas.

His initial concern was "Ebenezer," who had been dropped in November 1941, and whose security check involved making a deliberate mistake every sixteenth letter. He had transmitted his security check correctly until April 1942, after which he suddenly began introducing variations of his own, such as spelling "stop" as "stip," "stap" and "step" in places which were not multiples of sixteen. He had also stopped using his second check altogether. But in the opinion of the Dutch section heads, these irregularities were due to "Morse mutilation and bad training."[46]

Another area of concern was a traffic snarl-up between two wireless agents and London that lasted from August 3 until November 12 and resulted in thirteen indecipherable messages, all of which had to be repeated both from Holland to London and vice-versa. These repeated messages had totally compromised the security of the agent's codes. "*The Dutch section attributed the snarl-up to the natural hazards of clandestine communication.*" From November 12 onwards, traffic proceeded to flow smoothly in both directions.[47]

A third cause of Marks' disquiet was that London had never received an indecipherable message from Holland due to mistakes in coding. Why were they so good? All of the groups of agents who were dropped into Holland to help in the establishment of Plan Holland knew that if any of them were caught, there could be repercussions all the way up to the Committee of Resistance and to Plan Holland itself. This was an additional pressure under which the agents were working beyond just the normal dangers and feelings of anxiety that came from being a wireless operator in an enemy-occupied territory—all of which Marks was all too consciously aware. And yet, "despite deaths by drowning, by exploding minefields, by dropping accidents, despite every kind of difficulty, setback and frustration, not a single Dutch agent had been so overwrought that he'd made a mistake in his coding."[48] Given these considerations, there was no doubt in Marks' mind that the vast number of messages had been sent by the Germans. The main concern was not which agents had been caught, but which were still free.

But the chief of the Dutch Directorate, Major Charles Blizard, his deputy, Captain Bingham and others in the section were all too quick to dismiss Marks' doubts. There was still no positive proof that any agents had been caught. Nevertheless, in support of his contentions to the contrary, Marks devised a plan. Without informing anyone in S.O.E., he sent a deliberately indecipherable message to one of his agents in Holland that could not possibly be decoded without the help of a trained cryptographer. If received by an agent, he would have to ask London to repeat it. If it was answered without a request to repeat, the only explanation was that it was unscrambled by a trained expert. And that expert had to be a German. There was no request to repeat the message and London did receive an answer.[49] This proved that the wireless operator to whom the message was sent was being controlled by the Germans. To this there could be no doubt.

Marks' report to the S.O.E. Dutch section now raised enough questions to warrant an independent investigation into the Dutch agents' security. Particularly disturbing was the interlocking of so many wireless circuits, which was potentially extremely dangerous.[50] Yet the parachute drops of agents and arrests upon landing continued.

Meanwhile, throughout the spring and summer of 1943, the Dutch section had ordered its agents to attack enemy installations, though the security of their wireless links must be preserved at all costs. Targets included U-boats, coal harbors, railway sidings, supply trains, electrical repair shops and factories producing spare parts for night fighters. Additionally, information about *Luftwaffe* divisions in Amsterdam was urgently needed to know at what times night fighters were lined up on the tarmac at certain Dutch airfields for take-off.

Giskes was quick to comply as numerous messages from the German-controlled Ebenezer, Parsley and Cucumber listening posts conveyed reports of "successful" sabotage operations against patrol boats, barges and railway cars in Rotterdam, Amsterdam and Delft, as well as minesweepers, factories and storage depots, while at the same time suffering very few freedom-fighter casualties. Yet despite all of the wireless traffic, there was still not a single mistake in the agents' coding[51]—which served to give further credence to Marks' reasoning.

A Dutch Calamity

From the end of November 1942 until the middle of February 1943, few S.O.E. agents were sent to Holland, partly because of bad weather and partly because London was apparently satisfied with the creation of a radio link with the National Committee of Resistance, so it was believed unnecessary to dispatch more agents for a while. Dropping operations resumed in mid-February and were finally stopped in May due to a significant number of arrests of leading members of the Resistance that were discovered from other sources in Holland and also because of the suspicious increase of losses of aircraft involved in special operation flights.

Other suspicions were also beginning to surface. Towards the end of June, a London chief signal master at one of the listening posts had become wary of wireless agent F.W. Rouwerd's (code named "Netball") operating ever since the agent had been transmitting two weeks ago. Netball had previously been arrested upon landing in April. At the end of one of his scheduled transmissions with Netball, the London operator set a trap for him. He knew that German wireless operators often signaled "HH" (Heil Hitler), the habitual automatic Nazi signal clerk's farewell, when they were about to conclude a transmission. So the operator ended his sign-off to Netball with "HH," to which Netball replied "HH" without a moment's hesitation. This convinced the signal master that Netball's set was being operated by the Germans.[52]

Throughout the course of *Englandspiel*, the captured S.O.E. agents were held in a four-story building, a former theological college in Haaren in the province of North Brabant, which had been converted into a prison. Well-guarded by sentries, the agents were confined to twenty large cells on the second floor, two or three to a cell, but they could talk to one another inside the building as well as during the daily exercise period. Although escape was seen by most as an exercise in futility, at least two prisoners believed otherwise.

In adjacent cells, agents Pieter Dourlein (code named "Sprout") and Johan Ubbink (code named "Chive") worked out an escape plan that was executed the evening of July 31. While a noisy food trolley was passing their cells in the prison corridor, the two agents managed to loosen the bars of the little fanlight above their cell doors and crawl through a small gap. The gap was less than a foot in diameter, but being of slight build, they both managed to squeeze through. Once out of their cells, they tiptoed around a corner into a lavatory. After dark, they lowered themselves some 45 feet out of an unbarred corridor window into the yard, using strips of sacking from mattresses as rope. According to Giskes, the prison sentries, Dutch SS men unfit for war service and of uncertain reliability, were not to be wholly trusted.[53] The agents managed to crawl through the barbed wire, avoid a sentry and walk several miles to Tilburg to an address they had previously been given. The address turned out to be a closed chemist's shop. They then walked to a Catholic church where a priest put them in touch with a local Resistance leader who took them to a farmhouse in a nearby village where they remained hidden for two weeks while inquiries concerning an escape route were made.

Meanwhile, *SS Sturmbann-Fuhrer* Schreieder and heads of the prison administration vacillated between hope and fear. If the escaped agents could be recaptured quickly there would be no reason for further concern. If not, those responsible would be severely reprimanded. Consequently, an intense manhunt was ordered involving roadblocks and SS search parties with dogs. Both the *Abwehr* and the Gestapo were in a state of frenzy. But being unable to track the escapees down, Giskes realized that the *Englandspiel* was now at an end. Whether their escape led them back to London or not, it was presumed that the Dutch Resistance would receive word of the German penetration.

In a last-ditch effort to maintain the deception, however, Schreieder and Giskes had Ebenezer signal to London that Ubbink and Dourlein were now "turned" German spies and would try to make their way to England in the employ of the Germans so as to cause confusion within the London intelligence services. But Giskes himself admitted that he did not take seriously this final hoax, as he was convinced that the scheme would be seen through in London.[54]

After remaining hidden in a nearby farm for several weeks and being within only a few miles of the prison, Ubbink and Dourlein managed to make their way across the Belgian border with the help of a member of the Resistance and some friendly policemen. They made their way to Antwerp by bus with money given them by the Resistance, and then on to Brussels by train where they made contact with a monk who saw them across into France; and then to Paris by express train where they shared a compartment with German soldiers passing themselves off as workers on their way to work on an airfield near Marseilles. After spending a night in hiding in a brothel, they made their way southward into Switzerland where, after almost three months since their escape, they reported to the British and Dutch military attaches in Berne.[55]

The hoax that the escapees were now working for the Germans was not immediately recognized as such in London. Both Ubbink and Dourlein were received with suspicion and incarcerated in a British prison for many months even though both the Dutch and British intelligence authorities suspected the truth about *Englandspiel*. The agents were finally cleared in 1947 after the Dutch

Parliamentary Inquiry Commission investigated the incredible German deception. Three years later they were belatedly awarded the Dutch Knight's Cross of the Military Order of William of Orange for gallantry.

On November 23/24, 1943, three other S.O.E. agents, Jan Rietschoten (code named "Parsnip"), Aat van der Giessen ("code named "Cabbage"), both of whom had organized sabotage operations in the South Holland province, and Anton Wegner (code named "Lacrosse"), a trained secret army organizer, escaped from Haaren. Both Parsnip and Cabbage managed to contact the Dutch Underground, but were later recaptured. Agent Lacrosse was also recaptured, but not before making contact with a Secret Intelligence Service agent to whom he entrusted a message for London that the entire Dutch section of S.O.E. was in the hands of the Germans and that all of the reception landings were controlled by the enemy. The note was dated December 10, 1943, but did not reach London until March 2, 1944.[56]

In that same month, Giskes proposed to Berlin that *Englandspiel* be ended by means of a final message to London. On All Fools' Day, Giskes dispatched a sarcastic telegram to London adding insult to injury that read:

> To Messrs. Blunt, Bingham & Co., Successors Ltd., London. We understand that you have been endeavoring for some time to do business in Holland without our assistance. We regret this the more since we have acted for so long as your sole representatives in this country, to our mutual satisfaction. Nevertheless we can assure you that, should you be thinking of paying us a visit on the Continent on any extensive scale, we shall give your emissaries the same attention as we have hitherto, and a similarly warm welcome. Hoping to see you.[57]

Englandspiel Afterthoughts

In the annals of Allied espionage, the German penetration of the S.O.E. Dutch section remains to this day an extraordinary phenomenon which, in the words of the post-war Dutch Parliamentary Commission of Inquiry, "assumed proportions far in excess of any failure in any of the other German-occupied countries in Western Europe."[58] From a tactical standpoint, *Englandspiel* prevented the realization of Plan Holland by halting armed Allied sabotage that could have crippled German defenses throughout the Netherlands. And as Giskes pointed out in his treatment of this tragic episode, "The complete deception of the enemy [i.e., the Allied Secret Services] about the real state of affairs in Holland would have subjected him [the Allied forces] to the danger of a heavy defeat had he attempted to attack during 1942 or 1943."[59]

Certainly there were lessons to be learned from this disaster that lasted over eighteen months and took the lives of 47 of the 54 agents involved. Throughout that period, one of the principal faults within Allied intelligence was a failure of collaboration between S.O.E. and the S.I.S. The S.O.E.'s function was to organize sabotage and resistance; the function of the S.I.S. was restricted to the acquisition of intelligence, but the two were kept entirely separate. As Leo Marks later observed, "we used to talk to each other, but officially S.O.E. and S.I.S. hardly spoke."[60]

There were those in the higher circles of the S.O.E. Dutch section who were unwilling to listen to or consider the astonishing revelations of Marks, whose suspicions about the Dutch traffic were becoming more and more credible, but who "found the Dutch more difficult to approach than any other country section."[61] In his account of discussions he had with the chief of the S.O.E. Dutch section, Charles Blizard, his second-in-command, Seymour Bingham, and Signals Officer Captain John Killick in the fall of 1942, all had a "stock answer to every inquiry I made about the security of their agents: 'They're perfectly all right' they said; 'we have our own way of checking on them,' and I wasn't in a position to ask what they were."[62]

Unquestionably, if the success of the Dutch Resistance in Holland had been left entirely to the efforts of the S.O.E. Dutch section and the Dutch Secret Service in London, there would have been no workable Military Resistance Movement in the Netherlands. As one former Resistance leader and later a staff officer of the Dutch Intelligence Bureau in London observed, "the main reason that all the agents dispatched to Holland fell into German hands was that information other than S.O.E. communications was practically non-existent. This was obvious from the fact that between August 1942 and March 1943 very few reports about the situation in Holland were received in London. It was only in the spring 1943 that a little more information reached London which should have given some indication that doubts existed concerning the activities of S.O.E. agents."[63]

Patrick Howarth, himself a former member of the S.O.E. with an insider's knowledge of clandestine activity, claimed that the failure to expose the deception "stemmed from an initial oversight on the part of S.O.E., followed by a period of somewhat ingenuous trust." He cited the observation made by Giskes himself, who later pointed out that "a party dropped unannounced in the Netherlands with instructions to watch the next arranged drop could have destroyed at once, the whole of his exercise of deception."[64]

Conditions were made worse in Holland after the S.O.E. agents were captured upon landing or shortly afterwards, when leaders in the *Orde Dienst* organization were also captured. This critically weakened the one key element in the Plan Holland operation—sabotage. Although *Englandspiel* may have had no significant effect on the outcome of the war in Holland, the failure to implement the plan did prolong the fighting in Holland along with a continuation of the untold suffering, hardship and deprivation of the Dutch people until the German surrender.[65]

The study by the Inquiry Commission disclosed that grave mistakes were made in London attributable to "a lack of experience and utter inefficiency and disregard of elementary security rules, mistakes that led to catastrophic results and the loss of many lives."[66] Thus it is not surprising that such conduct led some in the Netherlands press and other Dutch public figures to allege treachery on the part of those within the London headquarters. Among the claims was the charge that Major Bingham, the head of the S.O.E. Dutch section, had acted as a double agent for the Germans. But according to the Commission there was no evidence to support this allegation. In fact, it was a Dutch V-man, Albert Brinkman, who betrayed a number of Resistance members while posing as Major Bingham.[67] Furthermore, Bingham was not in a position to decide policy until March 1943, when he took over as head of the Dutch section.

Nevertheless, a British Foreign Office statement issued to the Chairman of the Inquiry Commission two years after the Commission had been set up raises a number of unanswered questions. According to the statement "Bingham was opposed to the system of reception committees, and once he took charge he insisted on doing away with it and adopting the more secure system of the 'blind drop,' i.e., dropping without the benefit of a reception committee."[68] Yet if this were true, then why were the agents O.W. de Brey (code named "Croquet"), L.M. Punt (code named "Squash") and A.B. Mink (code named "Polo") dropped on May 21/22 into the hands of a German reception committee?[69]

There was also the admission by the Foreign Office that "investigations were held at various periods after the original penetration had begun, but in each case a decision was taken to continue the operation."[70] Yet no date was given in the report as to when the investigations were held or by whom. If investigations were indeed carried out, was it because they had strong suspicions, if not certain knowledge, that the agents who were captured were operating under German control? It should not have taken a particularly astute intelligence officer long to have realized that Taconis, Lauwers, Baatsen and Jambroes were captured.

The Foreign Office statement makes reference to "the original penetration [that] was due solely to the operations of the German counter-intelligence…" suggests an insinuation that at the beginning it was the Germans who were entirely responsible for the *Englanspiel*. Did that mean that later they were helped? And if so, by whom? Was this meant to incriminate Lauwers or possibly a traitor who was later discovered?[71] Marks dispels any such suggestion concerning the Dutch agent. "No agent in my experience—and I think I have met all of them—tried harder than Ebenezer to let us know that he was caught."[72] Any willful collaboration by the Dutch agent was also rebuffed by *Abwehr* chief Giskes himself, who said, "Lauwer's 'check deception' was successful. All of his signals transmitted from March 12 to the end of October 1942 were ciphered up,"—sent to London in such a way as to conceal their meaning to the Germans—"by him personally so he was able to confirm that each one of his messages contained a clear warning to London."[73]

After being liberated from a concentration camp in Germany, Lauwers returned to Holland, where he was denounced as a traitor, whereupon he returned to London where he sought official repudiation of these false allegations. The British not only failed to provide any help; he was accused of treason and turned back over to the Dutch authorities. Unfortunately, all the records relating to the *Englandspiel* were destroyed in a mysterious fire in 1946 so that only verbal evidence was presented to the Parliamentary Commission. Lauwers was saved from further legal entanglement by Major C. de Graaf, an officer active in the Dutch Resistance who gave evidence of the agent's innocence before the Commission Inquiry.

Moreover, in fairness to Lauwers, his own explanation of what went wrong is certainly worthy of serious consideration:

> *We had been given first-class training by efficient officers who had completely convinced us of the outstanding qualities of this Service and its leaders, both through their conduct and their complete mastery of the subject. How were we to know that the men who controlled our activities and our fate after we had gone into action would not be of the same efficient quality as those officers who had given us our training?*

In trying to understand responsibility in this very tragic affair, the historian has the somewhat dubious advantage of hindsight. But as the British General Sir John Hackett reminds the reader, one must try to look at the situation "from inside the wormhole, instead of from the peaks of Olympus."[74] Although those peaks can provide partial truths or hypothetical explanations to very difficult problems, they often fail to provide the whole truth, which, in the case of *Englandspiel*, will probably never be known.[75]

11

A Spirit of Defiance

The Resistance learnt how to select its objectives and adopt tactics to suit them; it gained experience by demonstrations, strikes, sabotage and assassinations. Then it blossomed into armed groups in town or country, frequently subordinate to a single headquarters.

—*Henri Michel, The Shadow War*

In the late fall of 1942, the American landings in Algeria and Morocco dampened Hitler's hope of an early end of the war. This led some to a more hopeful prospect for the opening of a Second Front by the Allies the following summer. Although this was an overly presumptuous expectation, 1943 saw the German defeat in North Africa and severe German setbacks at Stalingrad; the Allied invasion of Sicily, which was a stepping stone to the Italian mainland; American ship convoys that crossed the Atlantic in increasing numbers unchecked and largely unopposed by the U-boats, whose losses were numerous compared to few successes; and the extensive physical destruction of German war producing factories by American and R.A.F. bombers.[1]

This caused Hitler to shift to a more defensive strategy on the Western Front. The Germans controlled 3,000 miles of coastline in Western Europe, from Denmark down to the Spanish border. To protect the major portion of this vast area, Hitler ordered the construction of a line of coastal fortifications known as the Atlantic Wall. However, the zone of a possible Allied assault was narrowed to a 300-mile stretch along the western coast of France between Flushing and

Cherbourg, since this was the only sector that could be adequately covered by fighter aircraft based in Great Britain. However, the work in that area had not been done very systematically because the damage caused by the Allied air raids in the highly industrialized Ruhr Basin, the center of German steel and iron production, necessitated a shift in manpower to that region.[2]

Yet despite a developing optimistic global situation on the war front from an Allied perspective, the news was far less promising in Holland. The German defeat at Stalingrad resulted in the surrender of over 94,000 troops and the loss of over 200,000 men, including the complete destruction of two Rumanian, one Italian and one Hungarian army.[3]

As a result, those Germans who were working in the armament factories were now being mobilized to fight on the Eastern Front. Consequently, in all of the Occupied Countries under German rule, this meant an even greater exploitation of foreign workers to take the place of German workers in those same war-producing factories. The people of Holland were no exception. Dutch workers were called to meet the ever-growing demand for help on behalf of the German war effort.

Not long after the Occupation began, the Germans began a campaign to incite Dutch workers to leave Holland and come to work in German factories. They were promised good wages and good working conditions. Some went but the vast majority did not. Some refused because they did not want to be separated from their families and loved ones; others feared injury or even death from Allied air bombardment, since armament plants were prime targets in German cities; most simply refused to contribute to the German war effort. Consequently, the effort to draft Dutch workers became increasingly coercive.

On April 29, 1943, General Friedrich Christiansen issued a proclamation ordering Dutch army veterans to report for re-internment in Germany.[4] To the Dutch citizenry, the announcement was the catalyst for the beginning of a more vigorous public expression of open resistance. The following day, the Dutch Exile Government in London appealed to all involved to refrain from obeying the German orders, evade registration and go Underground.

For the rescuers and numerous other patriots as well, and many who had previously taken a more passive attitude toward the Occupation, the atmosphere was one of outright defiance. The time had come for a more active opposition. What was happening in their country strengthened their courage, clarified their understanding, sharpened their consciences, steeled their nerves and gave reassurance to their convictions. Under the cover of darkness, increased public antipathy was shown by new signs of anti-Nazi graffiti. *Vry Nederland!* (Free the Netherlands!)

A Spirit of Defiance

Lang leve de Koningen! (Long live the Queen!) *Verraders sullen hangen*! (Traitors will be hung!) *Dood oan de rotmoffen*! (Death to the Germans!)

In an atmosphere of increasing tension, the immediate reply was a spontaneous strike, or more properly, a series of strikes, which were probably the strongest demonstrations of popular unrest during the Occupation. Unlike the February strike of 1941 that was directed primarily against the N.S.B., the strikes of 1943 were aimed against the Nazi regime. Upon hearing the announcement at midday, Dutch citizens were enraged. War production workers in the eastern industrial city of Hengelo walked off their jobs immediately, and before long the entire province of Overijsel received the news, which was then transmitted to neighboring provinces by travelers on trains.

In Eindhoven in the southern province of North Brabant, the workers engaged in sit-down strikes; in Limburg more than 40,000 coal miners left their jobs; and in the northern province of Friesland, farmers refused to deliver milk and other dairy products; schools closed and buses and trams stopped running. In all, several thousand men took part in the strikes. Only in those larger cities in the western provinces and the heavily settled coastal regions did it remain relatively peaceful.[5]

As in the earlier strike of 1941, Seyss-Inquart was out of the country, and Nazi Security Chief Hanns Rauter was left to deal with the disorders. He immediately proclaimed a "police state of siege," whereupon, with the exception of the miners in Limburg and the Philips electrical firm factories in Eindhoven, who prolonged the strike several days longer, most of the strikers returned to work. As could be expected, Rauter exacted violent reprisals including firing by the SS and the police without warning on any assembled group. The strikes resulted in the execution of 80 Dutchmen and 95 people shot in the street and over 400 seriously wounded. Of the thousands arrested, 900 vanished into concentration camps in Holland and Germany.[6]

And although they lasted no more than three or four days in most urban areas and only a week after its inception in most rural areas, the events were a clear demonstration that the people of Holland had not lost their patriotic feelings of national identity nor had they fallen prey to Nazi propaganda. Moreover, the demonstrations fostered a far stronger feeling of unity that engendered a rapid expansion of the Resistance movement. According to the Underground publication *Het Parool*, the 1943 strikes were "the greatest event(s) since the capitulation… For a few moments the fear psychosis was broken and we did not feel like fear subjects of a terror regime, but like courageous and liberated people suddenly pushed on by an invisible mutual bond."[7]

On May 19, in a B.B.C. announcement from London, Dutch Prime Minister Gerbrandy sent a warning to the people of Holland to refrain from a premature revolt against the Germans, which could easily be suppressed; but encouragement was given to widespread passive Resistance.[8]

Organized Underground activity actually began in late 1942, when the National Organization for Assistance to Onderduikers (L.O.) was created to contact families who were willing to take the *onderduikers* in and, if necessary, to accompany them to their new address. Its purpose was to meet the need for proper coordination of both individuals and groups in helping those who were forced to hide. It also disseminated news, watched for collaborators and did whatever would help to maintain morale. It was started by Mrs. Helena Theodora Kuipers-Rietberg, a Dutch housewife and mother of five children, living in the southeast near the German border, and Rev. Frits Slomp, a Calvinist minister who was forced out of his ministry because of anti-Nazi preaching and activity. Within eight months, the L.O. expanded to include a number of Catholic groups working in the southern provinces, which joined forces with the more distant northeastern provinces of Friesland, Groningen and Drente, where additional branches were established. Its effectiveness lay mainly in individuals and local groups in the rural locations rather than urban areas.

Certain Resistance groups were able to coordinate their activities with Belgian Resistance groups by smuggling Dutch *onderduikers* and downed airmen to a crossing site on the Belgian border. Farther south in Limburg in the town of Roermond, some fifteen members of a small L.O. group had its headquarters in a vault in the local cemetery. The group maintained radio contact with the Belgian Resistance and was credited with saving the lives of 29 airmen whose aircraft had been shot down, by getting them across the border. (More will be said about the downed airmen and their helpers in the following chapter.)

By the end of the war, the L.O. had approximately 15,000 helpers. Roughly 1,100 of those who served paid the ultimate price, including Mrs. Kuipers-Rietberg, who was arrested and later perished in the Ravensberg concentration camp. The L.O. grew to be one of the largest organizations in the Resistance, and was responsible for arranging the placement of tens of thousands who needed shelter, false papers, ration books and food.[9]

One of the most remarkable escape and evasion experiences that was attributed to a local branch of the L.O. was that of British Brigadier and later General Sir John W. Hackett who, while recuperating from injuries sustained in the ill-fated airborne assault on Arnhem in September 1944, was being sheltered by a family at great risk to themselves. In a tribute to the heroism of the L.O., the family and other Dutch civilians, Hackett in his war memoir, *I Was a Stranger*, related the following procedure that was followed when visitors came to the home where he was living in a German-occupied section of Holland.

> *Searches were frequent in the town and were always possible in Torenstraat. We worked out and practiced a drill for my concealment, in a hiding place between the floor of the landing outside my bedroom and the ceiling of the hall below, and for the rapid removal of all traces of a compromising presence in the house. If a search happened at night one of the aunts would occupy my bed and act as a very sick woman. Another would help me to the hole, put the lid on after I was safely in and straighten up the carpet. A third would hold the enemy in conversation through the front door until all was ready. Everything that could knock a few seconds off our time for the whole maneuver was studied.*[10]

To carry on their operations successfully, the L.O. received generous contributions of financial aid from its individual members and from churches, but as the number of those who went into hiding increased, the amount being collected was only a small proportion of the money required to meet the growing need.

By mid-year 1943 the Jews who went into hiding were vastly outnumbered by tens of thousands of workers who were ordered to report for labor conscription in Germany. Those who went into hiding were often moved from place to place by the Dutch people. Aside from barns, livestock shelters and hay lofts, those who hid on farms were often concealed in Underground hiding places that had been dug for that purpose.

On one rather large fruit and vegetable farm near a village not far from Utrecht, James de Wit along with a number of other enterprising growers owned a nursery with rows of greenhouses that were particularly suitable during the summer for hiding the *onderduikers* who were otherwise destined for labor service. In the winter they were kept hidden in a room in the main house. The farm could only be reached by a narrow road about one mile long off the main road that led across a small bridge over a canal beyond which was the farmhouse. Just past the farm where the road reached a dead-end were four other growers, each with a plot of land and greenhouses; beyond those were fields of grain where holes had been dug for those in hiding. The family would take in three or four *onderduikers* who were kept hidden in the back of one of the greenhouses where sacks of straw served as mats for sleeping. Grass mats were hung up to serve as curtains to conceal the presence of the evaders.

In the yard near the family residence was an electric pump used to water the greenhouses from which an electric wire ran a connection to a bell in the greenhouse where the men were in hiding. When a raid by the German police or Gestapo appeared imminent, the bell was sounded and would alert the men in hiding to rush to the grain fields where they could lie flat, or in summer behind stacks of harvested grain or by the canal where they concealed themselves in tall reeds until it was safe to return. However, since the use of electricity was limited to only a few hours a week, when the pump was inoperable and a raid appeared immanent, a member of the household would have to run to the greenhouse to warn the men to go into the field.[11]

An increasing number of disparate groups sought covert refuge: members of the Resistance betrayed by Nazi collaborators and an overwhelming majority of students who refused to sign loyalty pledges toward the Nazi regime. Additionally, those forced to seek sanctuary included members of the Dutch armed forces who avoided the call-up to report for German military service. By the summer of 1944, the total number of those living underground was estimated at more than 300,000.[12]

In anticipation of that expanded number a National Support Fund (N.S.F.) was established in 1943. With the help of the former Director of the Netherlands Bank it provided financial aid to the growing number of those in hiding. In fact, the number of those in financial need grew so rapidly that the Dutch government in London guaranteed reimbursement to business firms for loans made to the Fund. By the beginning of January 1944, the government authorized the disbursement of 30,000,000 guilders. Henceforth the (N.S.F.) became the "Banker of the Resistance."[13]

Closely allied to the L.O. were networks of "National Action Groups," *Knokploegen*, or (L.K.P.) formed to establish a more aggressive policy by sabotaging population registers or by raiding government food offices to secure ration and identity cards on a much larger scale. Gradually, Amsterdam emerged as the center of these raids. In some cases, members wore German or N.S.B. uniforms to conceal their identities and break into government offices to destroy population records that might otherwise be used to locate men for the labor draft. The offices were closely guarded by the police. Often raids were conducted with fake revolvers made from wood, which, fortunately, did not have to be used.

An additional activity of the L.K.P. groups was supplying food to those in hiding—Jews and *onderduikers*—who were without ration cards. In Holland, as in all of Occupied Europe throughout the war, food shortages were commonplace occurrences, as was to be expected; so also were black marketers. It was illegal as well as unethical for farmers to hoard food, or to sell their foodstuffs for more than the ceiling price. Yet a certain percentage of farmers who grew food accumulated a surplus and sold their food at exorbitant prices. Consequently, black market farmers became a target of the Resistance.

Those farmers who were willing to surrender their stockpile to a church would be left alone. At other times members of the L.K.P. would call on known or suspected black marketers in police uniforms stating that they were acting on orders from the occupying authorities. They would provide the farmer with an official-looking fake receipt for the food that was taken so that when the Germans came for food they would be fooled by the fake dated receipt and leave empty-handed. Later, when food rationing was even more severely restricted and farmers became less cooperative, the L.K.P. used more forceful methods to obtain the needed food.[14]

In September 1944, the L.K.P. became a part of the Netherlands Forces of the Interior, the officially recognized Dutch Resistance force set up by the Netherlands Government-in-Exile under the command of Prince Bernhard. By then they were receiving arms and ammunitions dropped by the Allies and conducting outright sabotage against the Germans.

The nationwide Underground organization most clearly associated with sabotage was the Council of Resistance, *Raad van Verzet*, or *(R.v.V.)*. The Council was organized just prior to the April-May strikes of 1943, and although closely allied with the Dutch Communist Party, members came from a wide range of political backgrounds.

One of the most highly regarded members of the *Raad van Verzet* was Hannie Schaft, a twenty-year-old law student from Haarlem when the Occupation began. She left the University of Amsterdam rather than sign a German loyalty declaration. Her Resistance activity initially involved providing Jewish friends with stolen and falsified identity cards and stealing and transporting German weapons to the Resistance. In 1943, she joined the *R.v.V.* where her duties involved distributing illegal newspapers and pamphlets, gathering intelligence data for the Allies, various sabotage attacks and the assassinations of Dutch collaborators involved in the betrayal of their fellow countrymen. She was accidentally arrested at a checkpoint while distributing copies of the illegal Communist newspaper *de Warheid*. On March 21, 1945, she was taken to the dunes where she was shot and buried in a shallow grave. She was later reburied at Overveen near Haarlem, where an annual commemoration is performed in her honor.[15]

In addition to working closely with the L.O. and L.K.P. in matters concerning the protection of *onderduikers*, the Council operated wireless transmissions and an espionage service with the *Bureau Inlichtingen (BI)*, the Dutch Government-in-Exile bureau that provided London with political and economic information within the occupied territory. One of its principal objectives was to help unify or coordinate the numerous Resistance groups that came into being in 1943 when activities of the Resistance greatly increased. To maintain contact with local bodies, some 2,000 members functioned in small groups of three individuals for specific operations so as to avoid the loss of large numbers in case of capture.[16]

A good deal of the sabotage, much of which was ordered by the Allies, involved the destruction of German military installations. Supply depots were targeted, cables and telephone lines were cut and military traffic signs were destroyed, removed or displaced. One such explosive commonly used was the tire buster, a small device about the size of a shoe polish can with a rounded detonator cap and capable of bursting a truck tire. This was an effective means of slowing down troop convoys. Detonating railroad tracks and train derailment was performed by placing explosive charges on one of the inner rails fitted with a "pencil" time fuse. This pencil-like tube contained a glass cylinder filled with acid. Applying pressure on the knob broke the glass, spilled the acid, which then attacked a thin copper wire. When this was eaten through, it released a hammer, which struck the detonator and set it off igniting the charge. Charges would be laid out about 100 yards apart using one-hour time pencils. At a safe distance the saboteurs would witness a number of succeeding explosions, tracks being blown apart and twisted every which way.[17]

Although most of these acts continued to be a source of harassment to the enemy, the damage was repairable in most cases and created no serious restructuring delays. However, they did create a great deal of fear and anxiety in the lives of many of the ordinary citizens since it was not uncommon for the Germans to exact reprisals against civilians for sabotage and various kinds of anti-German activities.

In December 1941, High Commissioner Seyss-Inquart issued a directive stating that individuals, groups or municipalities could be held responsible for anti-German activities punishable by the imposition of heavy fines and compulsory services where such activities had occurred. Furthermore, for every attack on a German soldier a minimum of ten executions on civilians would be carried out. In January 1943, after a German soldier was shot in Haarlem, ten Dutch hostages were immediately taken and executed. All such acts of resistance were met with increasing German brutality. After an assault on a German officer near Putten, the entire male population of the town was deported to a concentration camp without trial.[18] German activities such as these only served to enhance and intensify a more determined and militant defiance throughout the Netherlands.

Despite a radio broadcast by the Dutch Government-in-Exile, which announced its disapproval of political assassinations, a surge of liquidations occurred throughout the country. Between February and September 1943, more than 40 members of the N.S.B. were shot by the Resistance.[19] A major Dutch collaborator and founder of the Dutch Nazi SS Netherlands Legion, Lieutenant-General Hendrik Seyffardt, was assassinated by an Amsterdam-based Resistance unit; the chiefs of police in Nijmegan and Utrecht were also liquidated. In the eastern provinces Dutch N.S.B. peasants were killed and their farms burned. In September after a number of prominent Dutch Nazis were assassinated, SS Security Chief Rauter authorized the secret killing of three Dutch patriots for every one N.S.B. member. The Security Police would carry out the slaying at night. The German police would then conceal the names of the Dutch assassins to prevent their discovery. In 1943 and 1944, 45 Dutch citizens were killed in this manner.[20]

On March 6, 1945, while traveling by car near Apeldoorn, Rauter was attacked by members of an Underground group. His aides were all killed and he was so badly wounded that he spent the remainder of the war in a hospital. As a result, the head of the German Security Police had more than 250 Resistance prisoners executed. This was the greatest number of persons executed in any one reprisal during the Occupation.[21]

Within certain patriotic groups, there was some disagreement about the justification of these assassinations. However, most of the Resistance groups and Underground newspapers supported the liquidation of German officials, Dutch Nazi policemen and informers, especially those traitors and spies who endangered the lives of the resisters by their deceptive activities. Advocates of these assassinations justified the killings on the grounds that the German authorities and the Dutch Nazis had declared war on the civilian population of Holland. Gradually the liquidations became accepted policy.

A number of Underground organizations were established by individuals who operated without any structured connection to any other group. In 1943, a photographic group called the Underground Camera was started in Amsterdam. It consisted of a number of like-minded photographers skilled in the use of cleverly concealed cameras in purses, shopping bags and canvas bicycle bags, who documented a number of German military subjects and other illegal scenes and conditions in Holland during the Occupation. Emmy Andriesse, a well known fashion photographer, illegally photographed the devastation to land and life in Amsterdam that occurred during the "hunger winter" between 1944–1945.[22]

In April 1943, when Dutch students were being sent to work in Germany, Hoynck van Papendrecht, a young engineering student at the Technical University in Delft, went into hiding and later moved to Eindhoven where he started a group known as the "Partisan Action Netherlands" (P.A.N.), which operated along the lines of the L.K.P.

P.A.N. established several small cells in other towns near Eindhoven consisting of between 80 and 100 young men and women.[22] The female members, who were primarily couriers, also collected valuable intelligence data. Two P.A.N. female Resistance members, Margarethe Kelder and her sister, were asked to go into the woods near Eindhoven to confirm the presence of a German anti-aircraft battery. Under the pretense of gathering mushrooms, they conducted their reconnaissance and when confronted by German sentries near the battery, were able to convince them of their innocence.[23]

Eventually the Resistance groups in the Eindhoven area grew to a total of several hundred members. One group of saboteurs hampered the transport of men and supplies by pouring salt in the gas and oil tanks of parked German military vehicles, and by blowing up railroad tracks using explosives provided by mining engineers.

In the Nijmegen area there were several Underground groups. Jules Jansen, an engineering professor at Saint Canisius College, was a leader of one of the local National Action (K.P.) groups. He set up a laboratory in his house for manufacturing explosives and an indoor firing range in his basement to teach members of the group the basics of marksmanship.[24]

Although there were numerous occurrences of minor sabotage activity in Holland during the war, there was no large-scale sabotage program or any actual uprisings other than those that took the form of general strikes. Most of the Resistance involved assisting Jews, Dutch workers summoned to work in Germany, the overwhelming number of students who refused to sign a loyalty declaration toward the German regime and members of the armed forces ordered to report for internment in the German army, all of whom went into hiding.

Aside from those publicized personal narratives, compared to the far larger number of unrecorded events in the history of the Resistance, it is impossible to accurately assess the sum total of Resistance activity. According to the foremost Dutch historian, Louis de Jong, whose monumental thirteen-volume history of the Netherlands in the Second World War is the definitive study of the Occupation period, "few of the (Resistance) groups saw to it that their activities were properly documented after the war; most of them did not."[25] However, he estimates that between 50,000 and 60,000 took part in the Resistance. And of those, more than 10,000 were either shot by the Germans or died in concentration camps.[26]

Unlike France, where the disparate Underground organizations merged into a single United Resistance Movement; or in Poland, where a complete Underground nation was created and in direct contact with its Government-in-Exile in London, a coordinated unity of action in Holland did not exist. Even though there was a general will to resist, the country was too flat, urban and densely populated for any sustained guerrilla fighting to succeed. Nevertheless, despite those limitations, by war's end, the total number of those who went into hiding was estimated at more than 300,000; and with 3,372 rescuers, Holland claimed more rescuers than any other occupied country in Europe.[27]

12

Brotherhood of Strangers

Many people ask with an air of self-justification: Why should I get involved in the lives of others? Because it is your Christian duty to get involved in their lives, in order to serve them. Because Christ has got involved in your life and mine.
—*Saint Josemaria Escriva (1902-1975)*
Founder of Opus Dei

By mid-1943, the American 8th Air Force and British Bomber Command were conducting massive daylight and night raids against the industrial heartland of Germany with ever-increasing frequency. The success of the D-Day invasion of northwest Europe depended in large measure on the destruction of German fighter aircraft production. These bombing missions were the precursor of that invasion. The "crescendo of bombing,"[1] as the combined air offensive was so aptly described by military analyst Liddell Hart, targeted those installations that made the component parts for German aircraft: ball-bearing plants at Schweinfurt, wing and tail assembly plants at Anklam for the Focke-Wulf 190, aircraft tire factories in Hanover, propeller works near Frankfurt, synthetic-rubber-producing plants at Huls, the high-grade aviation steel plant at Bochum and the railroad marshalling yards at Hamm. Additional raids were made on the major fighter assembly plants where the aircraft was assembled into the finished machine: Marienberg in East Prussia, Regensberg, Bremen, Oschersleben and Kassel.[2]

Holland straddled the main bomber route from England to the Ruhr in western Germany where on any given day as the Allied bombing campaign intensified, the skies above Holland witnessed upwards of 2,000 bombers and 1,000 fighters in any one maximum effort. In 1943 because of limited range capacity the fighter escorts could not continue much beyond the Dutch-German border in the vicinity of Aachen.[3] When they withdrew, the bombers were attacked by wave after wave of German fighters or assailed by anti-aircraft flak on the way to their target and then back as far as the Dutch or Belgian coast. As the Allied bombers and fighters made their way through German defenses, those airmen fortunate enough to complete their missions could be back in England within several hours. Those less fortunate who were shot down or severely damaged by flak had to risk forced landings or descend by parachute.

Many of those airmen who were shot down over Germany headed for Holland or Belgium from where they could travel south into France, which was the only practical way back to England. The numerous bridges that spanned the major rivers and waterways in Holland were well guarded and the fifteen-mile coastal defense zone that the Germans established was so heavily defended that it was virtually impossible to return home by sea. Those crew members who landed near the coast had to be especially vigilant since there was scarcely any form of concealment or cover that would be of any help as they worked their way inland. Many of those who bailed out were injured in the air or when they landed and possibly in various degrees of shock and needed medical attention.

A large percentage of the Dutch population were willing to assist the downed airmen and escaped prisoners of war, even though they knew that the penalty for aiding the evaders was torture or death. Many of those who helped could be found on isolated farms, at railway connections and by those who worked on river barges. These were considered good initial contacts. Most of those laudable rescuers, who sought no personal recognition for themselves, fought the war from within their own homes by risking their lives and those of their families by providing the food, shelter and civilian clothing that the evader needed until word could be sent to the Underground that an Allied serviceman was in the vicinity.

Many helpers were simply individuals who did not belong to any identifiable group or organization. They were the good Samaritans who had an intolerance of injustice, and an ability and willingness to put themselves in harm's way for the sake of those servicemen who were fighting a common enemy in a struggle for survival. Yet most of the evaders who managed to find their way back to their units did so by way of organized escape networks.

After the initial contact with a resistance organization was made, which was not always easy, a representative would interview the evader by asking him his name, his unit, where he had come from and where he landed. The information he gave would then be radioed to London to determine whether the evader was in fact the person he claimed to be. London would then respond in a coded B.B.C. message that might read, "There are no big birds in the Pyrenees," confirming that the evader was who he said he was. He would then be processed further through the Underground.

As a first link in the escape line he would be taken to a nondescript covert location such as the basement of a fish market where he would be further processed by the Resistance; and while being photographed and before false identity papers and travel documents were prepared from a secret printing press, he would be questioned in greater detail. A number of simple questions that an American or Englishman could easily answer, but that a German could not would be asked, such as "What is a bellyache?" or "What is a Texas leaguer?" or "What squadron is so-and-so in?" to enable the Resistance to determine whether the crash survivor or escapee was who he claimed to be, or a German spy. If the evader could not answer the questions, he would be shot without delay. If his *bona fides* were confirmed he would begin the first stage of a journey that would hopefully lead him back to England by an Underground escape line that would provide the potential to fight another day

The evader would then be escorted to a safe house, which was not always easy to find, as many of the local residents were fearful that if they were discovered by the German authorities their lives would be in serious jeopardy. Matters were made even more difficult in that people were needed who would share their ration of food, which was very hard to come by because the Dutch food supply was already severely rationed. In most cases it was almost at starvation level. The safe house was usually a private home or apartment where the evader would remain for several days and then be moved to another location so as not to arouse the suspicion of curious neighbors. Normally the evader would be led either by a member of the Resistance or a sympathizer who would walk some forty or fifty paces ahead of the airman so that if the latter was caught by the Germans the escort up ahead would not be associated with him. A prearranged signal would be known by the evader so that if there was an indication of proximate danger the escort up ahead would raise his or her coat collar or give some such sign so that he would know how to react. It was particularly difficult at the Belgian or French border crossings for those evaders who did not speak the native language.

Several guides would be involved in the escape process. The evader would be led to a rendezvous point where he would be met by another guide. After exchanging a prearranged password, the guide would lead the evader to the next rendezvous point. The guides were purposely unknown to each other so that if one was arrested and tortured, he or she could not betray the next guide. Contact was made either by public telephone, or by some prearranged signal; for example, a man seen standing outside a phone booth at a particular intersection of town at a designated time reading a copy of *Signal*[4] would indicate that it was safe for the guide to pick up an evader at a certain park bench; if the man was not at the phone booth at that time, it meant that the Gestapo was in the area; or perhaps a certain piece of clothing hanging from a certain apartment window might indicate that a certain rendezvous point was under surveillance. If there were no complications, the guide would then escort the evader on another leg of the journey that would take him by way of an escape network from Belgium, and by rail on into Paris staying overnight in one or more safe houses along the way, and then continuing by rail to Bordeaux or possibly Marseilles; then by bicycle or on foot with a guide into the foothills of the Pyrenees Mountains, a natural frontier that divided France from Spain. For the escape network it was the only corridor into neutral territory. The Germans made escape especially difficult by establishing a forbidden zone twenty kilometers from the border, which was patrolled by sentries and dogs. At the border the evader would be met by a Basque guide. Together they would cross the frontier at the River Bidassoa, which at certain times was bitterly cold and after heavy rains, so high that the evader would either have to wade at shoulder depth or be carried across or swim; failing that, it meant an extra five hours' march across a suspension bridge; then what was normally an eleven- or twelve-hour arduous trek through the Pyrenees into San Sebastian or Bilbao in neutral Spain where the evader would then be transferred to the British embassy in Madrid, then taken to Gibraltar and from there to England.

The first escape lines were established as early as 1940 by small groups of patriots without money or outside help to provide aid to those soldiers who survived, but were left behind after the evacuation from Dunkirk.[5] However, those earlier circuits proved unmanageable and the inexperience of too many people left them open to easy infiltration by the Gestapo. Shortly after the Allied defeat at Dunkirk, the British recognized the need for a more efficient organization to deal with the hundreds of troops cut off from their units behind enemy lines.

The urgency of the problem was met by MI9, an organization formed to train hundreds of thousands of airmen and soldiers in the art of escape and evasion, i.e., the avoidance of capture. Under the leadership of British Major Norman Crockatt, who had served with distinction in the First World War, MI9 was established shortly before the invasion of France and became fully operational by 1941.[6] Although there are no separate figures from France, Belgium and Holland, numbers based on reports from the main escape organizations estimated that over 4,000 British and American downed airmen and prisoners of war escapees reached England before the Allied landing in Normandy in June, 1944. The largest proportion of all Air Force evaders was American.[7] The majority of those who were not taken captive returned to England by two of the most successful and well-known Second World War escape networks: the "Pat" or O'Leary Line and the Belgian Comet Line.

The "Pat" Line was started by Captain Ian Garrow, a tall commanding Scotsman of the Seaforth Highlanders, who chose to remain behind in France after the British evacuation at Dunkirk in May 1940. Garrow soon recognized the need for a means of providing for the return of those numerous servicemen who had evaded capture and managed to avoid internment by the French police in Vichy, i.e. the French unoccupied or "free" zone.[8] Through sympathetic acquaintances and contacts in Marseilles where he finally settled, and with dogged persistence, he arranged a number of safe houses to accommodate the airmen. He also established a network of rendezvous centers in the north of France—Lille, Rouen and Amiens—and couriers that served as guides to Paris where the evaders would pass through safe houses as they headed south.

During the first ten months of 1941, Garrow established the model for future escape operations. He formed an escape line from Paris down across the demarcation line into Vichy to reception areas in Marseilles and Toulouse. From there the evaders would be assisted by guides over the Pyrenees Mountains to a way station in neutral Spain. In October 1941, Garrow was arrested and imprisoned by the Vichy police after keeping an appointment with a police officer thought to be a member of the escape organization. In early December 1942, Garrow managed an escape after being provided with the uniform of a gendarme that was smuggled into the prison and in the following month he reached London.

Meanwhile, the escape network was taken over by Albert-Marie Guerisse, a Belgian Army doctor under the *nom de guerre* of Patrick O'Leary. Guerisse, a member of the British Special Operations Executive (S.O.E.) had been captured by the French after having been left behind accidentally during a clandestine night operation on the French coast in April 1941. In the summer, Garrow received word of O'Leary's captivity in a French internment camp for British prisoners. When he learned of the agent's experience in Underground activity and his mastery of the French language, he seemed an excellent recruit for escape and evasion work, so Garrow arranged for his escape and employment. Once Garrow received confirmation of Guerisse's *bona fides* from MI9 and the British Admiralty, he was assigned as a courier and coordinator in the O'Leary network.[9]

After Garrow's arrest, O'Leary took charge of the "Pat" Line as it came to be known in Marseilles. Under his leadership the clandestine circuit spread a net of over 250 couriers and helpers throughout France. The personalities and occupations were highly diversified: a former well known Marseilles stockbroker who provided funds to support the escape line;[10] a devoted Abbeville priest who provided evaders with bogus identity cards and passes printed on his own press;[11] two elderly Scottish ladies who ran a tea shop in Monte Carlo and who provided shelter for numerous airmen on the run;[12] a Jewish tailor and his wife in Toulouse who fashioned civilian clothing and disguises for evaders;[13] a 60-year-old woman, the owner of a dress shop, who lived next to the Gestapo headquarters in Toulouse, who escorted numerous airmen into Spain;[14] a portly congenial chef on the Paris-Marseilles express train who served as O'Leary's courier between those cities.[15] These are but a few of the dedicated persons who risked their lives for the sake of the servicemen trying to get back to England.

In July 1942, O'Leary established a plan to evacuate downed airmen by sea from southern France to Gibraltar. A small villa was rented by O'Leary's agents at the seaside village of Canet-Plage, near Perpignan, for use as a safe house where evaders could wait undetected before being evacuated by British trawler. Over the next several months more than 100 servicemen were safely rescued by sea.[16]

In March 1943, the Pat Line faded out of existence after O'Leary was arrested by the Gestapo in Toulouse. After prolonged torture and the horrors of Mauthausen, Natzweiler and Dachau concentration camps, which he managed to survive, he was liberated in 1945; for over 100 courageous men and women who provided the help that facilitated the successful return to safety of over 600 airmen and soldiers who passed through the Pat Line, their fate was suffering and death in concentration camps.[17]

Unlike the O'Leary Line that sent evaders across the Spanish border from Vichy, the Belgian-based Comet Line ran completely through German-Occupied France where a chain of safe houses was planned in Brussels, Paris and the frontier zone. With border access to the two neutral countries of Switzerland and, mainly and more often, Spain, the Allied evaders with the proper forged credentials and guides were able to make their way back to their units in the British Isles to continue the fight.

DAWN OF COURAGE

The Comet chain was created in August 1941 by 25-year-old Andree ("Dedee") de Jongh, a commercial artist with some training as a nurse from Brussels who, with the aid of her father, Frederic de Jongh, had been helping British soldiers and airmen in Brussels since 1940. Fiercely independent, Dedee wanted no help from MI9 other than the funds that were necessary to feed and house the evaders on the way from Brussels, and the cost of the mountain guides who put themselves in jeopardy by taking Allied soldiers through occupied territory and across the Pyrenees.[18] Throughout the war the line was run by Belgian leaders along the journey from Brussels.

On the early morning of June 9, 1942, the first downed airman to land in Holland was Royal Canadian Air Force Flight-Lieutenant Angus MacLean. Flying from Yorkshire on a night raid to the heavily defended Krupp steel works at Essen in the Ruhr basin, his Halifax bomber was struck by a burst of anti-aircraft fire. He managed to maintain control of the aircraft and continue his mission. However, on the return run he was attacked by a Messerschmitt 110 night fighter. The aircraft was already badly damaged from the flak and now both port engines were lost. MacLean ordered his crew to bail out. When his turn came, the aircraft started rolling, causing him to be caught in the hatch and delaying his departure. He finally fell free and landed in an open field on a small island between the towns of Zaltbommel and Hertogenbosch, just north of the Meuse River, injuring his back in the fall.[19]

After disposing of his parachute in an irrigation ditch, he followed a road alongside a nearby canal. After passing through an orchard he made use of his farm experience in Canada by rounding up some cows and driving them ahead of him so as to cover up his footprints. He milked one of the cows, drank its milk and then went to sleep under a hedge in the orchard. He later met two girls picking strawberries in a nearby garden who were able to show him his position on a map. Later, their grandfather, a tall bearded farmer, arrived and led the airman through several miles of fields. McLean was later led to another orchard where he was told to stay until the following day when he would be brought food and some civilian clothing. However, when no one came, he set off on his own. As he was walking along a path into a wheat field he met another farmer who provided him with hot milk, a rye bread sandwich and civilian clothes.[20]

He then set off on a main road, but was met by a woman who eyed him suspiciously and queried him where he was going. MacLean sensed danger in the air. He soon hid in some thick bushes for several hours, during which time two German officers on motorcycles and a truckload of soldiers arrived in the area, presumably searching for him.

He later managed to cross a bridge with a crowd of people and after walking a short distance up a road by the river he observed a woman washing clothes in a tub on a houseboat tied up by the shore. The Canadian airman was immediately welcomed by the woman, her husband, three daughters, ages 11, 18 and 21 and a son of 15, the Pagie family, who provided him sanctuary in their floating domicile. He remained sheltered with the family from June 10 to July 18, spending the days in his room, playing solitaire, reading an occasional German newspaper or reciting to himself every poem he could remember, since the houseboat was situated close to the road near a German checkpoint. Occasionally at night he would take the family's small rowboat out into the stream to break the monotony.[21]

During his stay with those on the houseboat, MacLean made contact with the Dutch Underground. He soon made his way through Belgium and then into France. His identity was not questioned until he arrived in Paris. While staying with an engineer in a safe house who was a member of the Comet Line, he was rigorously interrogated. Fortunately, he provided the right answers, was given an identity card and then introduced to his guide, Frederic de Jongh. From Paris, MacLean was taken by train to the foothills of the Pyrenees and then into Spain where he was released into the custody of the British Consul.

Upon his return to England by boat, he was questioned by Airey Neave, the chief staff officer of MI9 responsible for escape operations in the Low Countries who had a particular interest in his escape since he was the first evader to have spent any time in Holland before making his way back to England.[22]

The Germans were aware that there was an escape line and made numerous efforts to uncover it by infiltrating agents posing as shot-down British airmen. Numerous arrests were made, but most of those arrested kept silent. Dedee wanted no radio operators from England who could give the Germans a fix on her position. It was not until 1943 that MI9 provided radio links and trained agents to strengthen the escape line. Dauntless and defiant, between July and October 1942, the young Belgian leader and her Basque guide, Florentino Giocoechea, personally escorted 54 members of the Royal Air Force over the Pyrenees.

On January 15, 1943, Dedee was arrested in a police raid at a farm that served as a safe house near St-Jean-de-Luz, along with the woman who ran the place and three young airmen who she was preparing to escort across into Spain. By her own admission, Dedee acknowledged to the Germans that she was the organizer of the Comet Line, but for several weeks they refused to believe her. She was held in the Fresnes Prison in Paris and spent the next two years in the Ravensbruck concentration camp, surviving its horrors, and although suffering in health, after the war she resumed her nursing profession and spent many years in a leper colony in the Belgian Congo and later in Ethiopia.

Dedee de Jongh was undoubtedly one of the most courageous women of World War II. Since her arrival at San Sebastian in 1941, in sixteen back-and-forth journeys across the Pyrenees Mountains, she escorted 118 airmen to safety.[23]

In February 1943, the Comet Line was broken when the Gestapo in Brussels arrested about 100 members. Dedee's father, Frederic, evaded capture and returned to Paris to reorganize the line. Throughout the spring he was guiding evaders traveling on the circuit across Paris. They were pleased with the new successes on the line. On June 7, he left his flat for the last time and went to a train platform where he was scheduled to meet five British airmen and an American. What he did not know was that the man who arranged the meeting was a Gestapo agent, a traitor posing as a member of the group. As the party was shaking hands they were apprehended by a dozen German policemen and taken to Gestapo headquarters. Frederic was shot on March 28, 1944, along with other members of the line.

Early in 1943, the local head of the Comet Line in Brussels wanted a link on which he could rely for a system of guides from The Hague and Amsterdam that would send shot-down aircrews safely southward through the Netherlands.[24] Airey Neave was granted authorization to organize a Dutch connection. Neave himself was highly experienced in the art of escape and evasion. Having been wounded at Calais and captured at Dunkirk in May 1940, he was later put in the infamous German prison at Colditz Castle from where numerous successful escapes were made by British officers. From within the prison he made a masterful escape dressed in a German officer's overcoat made from a Dutch Home Army uniform. Later, disguised as a Dutch foreign worker and with forged papers, he eventually made his way into neutral Switzerland.[25]

Neave believed that he had found the ideal agent to coordinate the Dutch escape link in a modest and attractive 27-year-old Dutch KLM air stewardess, Beatrix Terwindt, whose personal experience was aptly demonstrated by her own successful escape from Holland in March 1942 and who, with another Dutch student, maneuvered through Belgium, France, Switzerland and Lisbon; soon after arriving in London she volunteered to return to Holland. Trix, as she was called, was fluent in both English and French and also knew some German. She also seemed to possess the self-assurance and composure required of a successful agent.

Although she was an agent belonging to MI9, Trix (codenamed "Chicory") underwent extensive and strenuous training at S.O.E. paramilitary schools until

A cardinal axiom of Resistance activity was that anything clandestine was temporary. Duplicating machines could not produce as many copies as a printing press but they were quiet and easier to move.

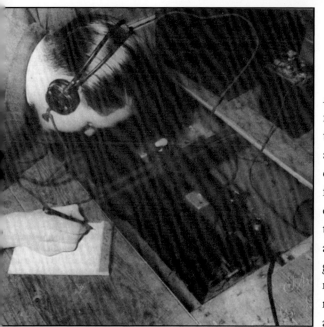

An illegal news gatherer receiving war news from the BBC in London from a radio receiving set concealed from beneath the floorboards. In the midst of defeat and by their tireless efforts the men and women in the underground press were largely responsible for upholding morale under the most adverse conditions.

Geuzenactie Bericht no 2.

De Geuzenactie is ingezet op 15 Mei 1940 te Amsterdam. Ons eerste bericht heeft nu al zelfs Nijmegen bereikt. Nederland zal zijn vrijheidsberoving niet voor zoete koek opeten! We ~~weten~~ moeten weten wat ons te wachten staat. Al onze voorraden zullen worden weggehaald, voedsel, kleding, schoeisel. Spoedig krijgen we het bonnenstelsel voor alles en nog wat en daarna kunnen we zelfs op de bonnen niet meer krijgen. Onze jonge mannen zullen worden gedwongen elders te gaan werken voor den overweldiger! We krijgen stellig spoedig een nieuwen Alva met bloedraad en inquisitie (of een Quisling). Maar de Geuzenactie zal ons geleidelijk organiseren en eenmaal zullen we, evenals in de tachtigjarige oorlog onze vrijheid heroveren. Moed en vertrouwen. Ons land zal geen onderdeel van Duitsland worden!

De Geuzenactie bestaat uit het volgende: Schrijf elk bericht twee of meer keer volledig over met verdraaide hand. Doe ongemerkt elk papiertje (ook dit exemplaar) toekomen dan een betrouwbaar Nederlander, die weer hetzelfde doet als gij. Onderbreek deze actie nooit, ook al krijgt gij soms een bericht voor de tweede maal. Overal stellen we geheime agenten aan. Spoedig hoort ge meer. Laat ieder deze Geuzenplicht doen!
Wij voor allen, allen één!
Dit ~~bericht~~ is uitgezonden op 18 Mei 1940.

Opposite: The first illegal news sheet to appear in Holland after the German invasion was *Geuzenactie*, a hand-written bulletin composed on May 18, 1940. It was to be passed on in chain-letter fashion to friends and others for further distribution.

Right: Two members of an Underground group of covert photographers using a camera concealed in a handbag to photograph German military objects.

Trouw was one of the most highly respected clandestine newspapers in Holland. By January 1945 the total weekly circulation was approximately 2 million copies.

Canadian troops marching through the Netherlands on April 9, 1945.

German prisoners being escorted out of Holland.

Dutch civilians celebrate the liberation of Utrecht by the Canadian army May 7, 1945.

Eighteen members of the Dutch Resistance executed by firing squad in March 1941 as the result of sabatage activity at a Rotterdam shipyard are memorialized at this monument at the Emmaus Cemetary in Vlaardingen, Netherlands which reads: "For your freedom they fell."

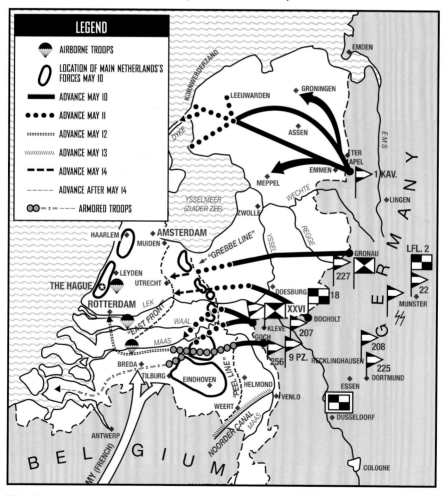

The German conquest of the Netherlands, May 10-15, 1940.

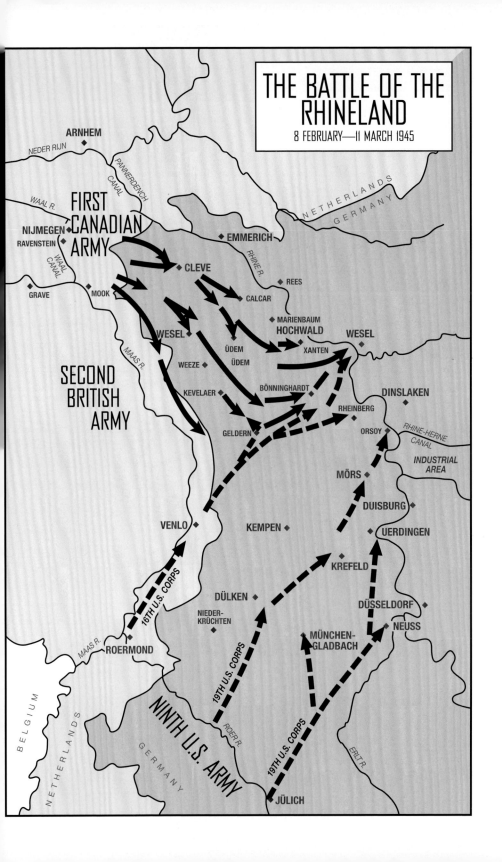

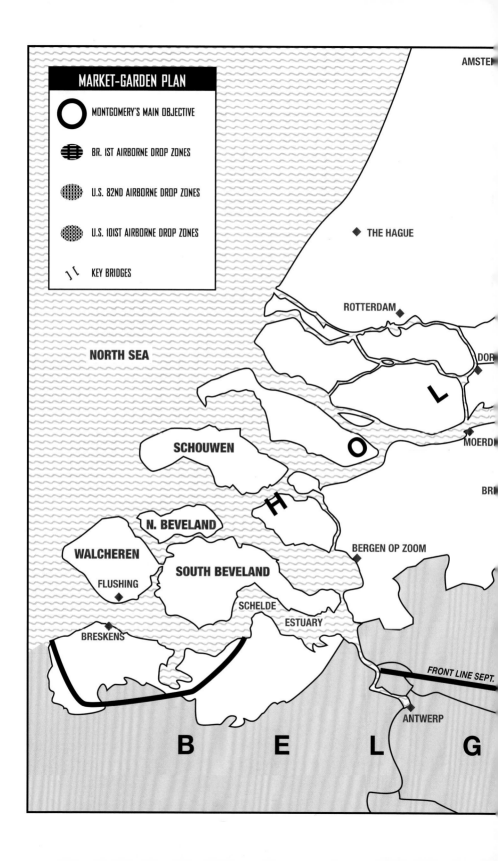

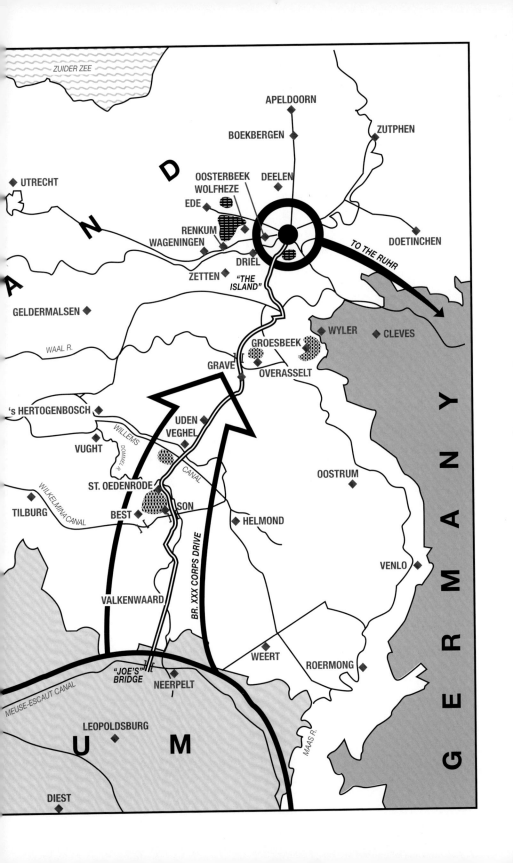

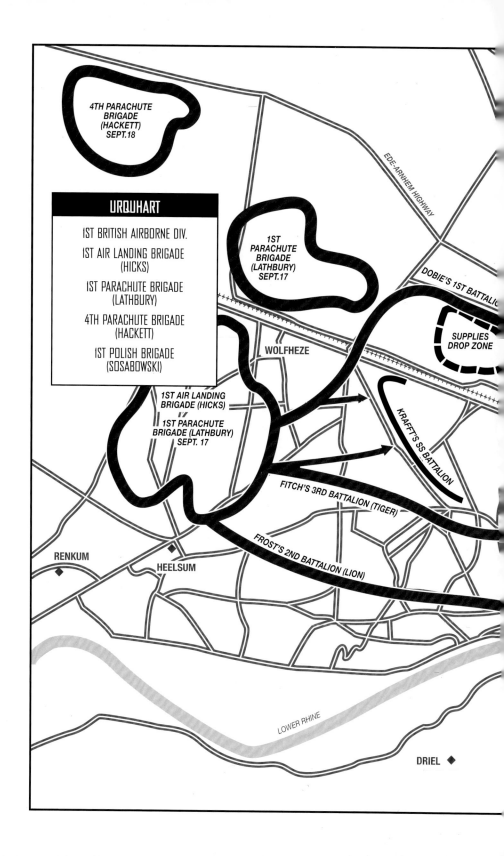

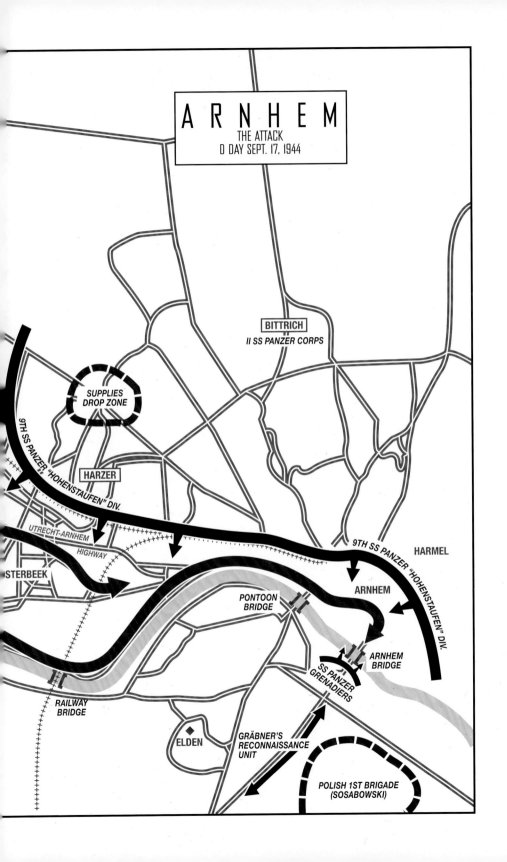

1939
Wer hat den Blitzkrieg gewollt?

Deutschland 1937

ENGLAND
das bis zum Sommer 1939 keine allgeme[ine] Wehrpflicht besass?

das sich 1935 mit Deutschland im Fl[ot]tenabkommen auf U-Bootparität einigt[e]

das bei Kriegsausbruch keine 100 Ta[nks] besass?

dessen Hauptstadt noch 1940 in 57 Näch[ten] hintereinander mit Bomben belegt werd[en] konnte?

POLEN
das nicht einmal voll mobilisiert war, [als] die deutschen Armeen seine Grenze üb[er]schritten?

das so gut wie keine Luftwaffe und Lu[ft]verteidigung besass?

dessen Armeen mit Kavallerie geg[en] Panzer kämpfen mussten?

dessen Widerstand nach drei Wochen [zu] Ende war?

FRANKREICH
das 1936 die 40-Stundenwoche einführt[e]

dessen Flugzeugproduktion 1938 [im] Monatsdurchschnitt 39 Maschinen betru[g]

dessen Armeen zum Teil mit Waffen a[us] dem vorigen Krieg ausgerüstet waren?

dessen Widerstand nach sechs Wochen [zu] Ende war?

ODER

DEUTSCHLAND
das 1934 „die Aufrüstung im grösst[en] Maasstabe begann" (Hitler),

das 1935 die Parole "Kanonen st[att] Butter" ausgab,

das laut Hitler in sechs Jahren 90 M[il]liarden Reichsmark für Rüstungen a[uf]wandte,

das von März 1938 an pünktlich alle [paar] Monate unter Kriegsdrohung ein neu[es] Gebiet annektierte?

1939

Who wanted the Blitzkrieg?

ENGLAND
- which until the summer of 1939 did not have general conscription?
- that entered into a naval treaty on submarine-parity in 1935?
- that did not have one hundred tanks at the outbreak of war?
- whose capital as late as 1940 was subject to fifty-seven consecutive nights of air raids?

POLAND
- which was not even fully mobilized when German forces crossed its border?
- that had practically no air force nor air defenses?
- whose forces had to go into combat with horses against tanks?
- whose resistance was over in three weeks?

FRANCE
- that introduced the forty-hour (work) week in 1936?
- whose average monthly production of aircraft in 1938 was (only) thrity-nine?
- whose forces were in part equipped with weapons from the previous war?
- whose resistance was over in six weeks?

Or

GERMANY
- which (under Hitler's orders) began a program of massive rearmament in 1934?
- which issued the slogan "Guns instead of butter" in 1935?
- which, according to Hitler, has expended ninety million Reichsmarks for armaments over a period of six years?
- which, from March 1938, annexed a new area every six months by threat of war?

1943
Wer wird den Weltkrieg verlieren?

ENGLAND
das nicht einmal 1940, im Zustande seiner äussersten Schwäche, niedergerungen werden konnte?

das seitdem seine Kriegsproduktion versiebenfacht hat?

dessen Flotte nach dreieinhalb Jahren U-Bootkrieg mehr Schiffe hat als 1939?

dessen Luftwaffe heute stärker ist als die deutsche und italienische zusammen?

dessen Armee in den letzten drei Jahren aus der Armee von Dünkirchen zur Armee von Tunis geworden ist?

RUSSLAND
das über die Arbeitskraft von 170 Millionen verfügt?

das seine gesamte Kriegsindustrie in den Ural transferiert hat?

das jedes Jahr 2 Millionen neue Rekruten in seine Armee einstellen kann?

dessen „vernichtete" Armeen in diesem Winter der deutschen Armee die Niederlage vor Stalingrad zugefügt haben?

AMERIKA
das über die Arbeitskraft von 130 Millionen und die modernste technische Ausrüstung verfügt?

das heute schon mehr Flugzeuge produziert als Deutschland, Italien und Japan zusammen?

dessen Produktion „bombensicher" ist?

das in einem Jahr trotz der U-Boote bereits 1½ Millionen Soldaten mit voller Ausrüstung übersee geschickt hat?

ODER

DAS BLATT HAT SICH GEWENDET!

DEUTSCHLAND
das sich dreieinhalb Jahre lang verblutet hat, ohne eine Entscheidung zu erzwingen,

das heute Facharbeiter an die Front schicken und Ausländer an die Maschinen stellen muss,

das seine Industrien nicht mehr gegen Luftangriffe verteidigen kann, und das mit immer geringeren Kräften immer mehr Fronten halten muss?

1943

Who will lose the war?

ENGLAND
- which despite its extreme weakness, could not be brought to its knees in 1940?
- which has since then increased its war production seven-fold?
- whose navy has more ships than it did in 1939, despite three and one-half years of submarine warfare?
- whose airforce is stronger today than those of Germany and Italy combined?
- which in the last three years has turned the army of Dunkirk into the army of Tunis?

RUSSIA
- that has a work force of one hundred seventy million?
- that has moved its entire war industry to the Urals?
- that can enlist two million more recruits each year?
- whose "annihiliated" armies this winter defeated the German army of Stalingrad?

AMERICA
- that has at its disposal a work force of one hundred thirty million and the most up-to-date equipment?
- that is today producing more aircraft than Germany, Italy and Japan together?
- whose industry is "bomb-safe"?
- that in one year, despite the submarines, has shipped overseas more than one and one half million troops with full equipment?

Or

GERMANY
- that has been bleeding for three and one-half years without a decisive victory?
- that today has to send its work force to the front and have foreigners man the factories?
- that can no longer protect its industry from air raids and with fewer and fewer forces must defend more and more fronts?

This typed message was distributed by the Resistance as a forewarning to the Dutch people to guard against betrayal by German deception and treasonous friendship.

Headline: U.S. tanks cross the Elbe 120 Kilometers from Berlin. Below: Announcement of President Franklin D. Roosevelt's death April 12, 1945.

she was prepared to carry out her mission. On the night of February 13, 1943, she departed from the fog-obscured Tempsford Bomber Command aerodrome in a converted Halifax bomber and was dropped by parachute near Steenwijk into what she believed was a friendly Dutch reception committee. In fact she was but another agent dropped into the hands of Dutch traitors in the employ of Major Giskes's ingenious *Englandspiel* deception coup. Like all the other German replies to London, the *Abwehr* sent the following wireless message to S.O.E.: "Felix [her operational codename] has landed safely in spite of wind and rain."[26] Trix was taken to Haaren Prison where she was kept in total isolation for fifteen months and where she suffered dreadfully, both in mind and body. She was then moved to Germany at the Ravensbruck concentration camp for women and later to the camp at Mauthausen in Austria where her spirit continued to remain unbreakable until shortly before the end of the war when, with the help of the International Red Cross, she arrived in Switzerland.[27]

A Dutch escape link to Brussels was established in June 1943 by a Dutch agent, Dignus (Dick) Kragt, who was air dropped without benefit of a reception committee. Three earlier dropping attempts were made, but as the pilot was unable to find the dropping zone, the aircraft returned to base. On the third attempt the plane was struck by enemy anti-aircraft fire, but was able to crash-land back in England at the Tempsford aerodrome. On the fourth and final attempt, Kragt was accidentally air-dropped in the garden of a Dutch collaborator in suburban Vaasen near Apeldoorn, eight miles from the designated drop site in open country. Upon landing, his baggage parachute that included his wireless set, clothing and most of his money ended up in a tree beneath the traitor's window. However, he managed to get away and make contact with the Comet Line through a courier in a nearby village. Kragt was a resourceful, tenacious agent who was able to establish a successful conduit to Brussels. Over the next fourteen months, before the Allied airborne attack on Arnhem, he managed to send over 100 airmen across the border into Brussels.[28]

While it is impossible to accurately compile and assess all of the accomplishments of those who put their lives at risk to aid the Allied airmen who were forced down in Holland, one additional evasion and escape network is deserving of special mention. It is the courageous account of a dedicated Dutch businessman whose hatred of Nazism was matched by a passionate concern for those Dutch detainees being held in France as well as those aircrew members and other refugees in danger of death trying to make their way into neutral Spain or Switzerland. This brief chronicle deals with the men and women of an Underground organization that operated principally in what was initially the unoccupied "free zone" of France close to the Swiss border, but which later was totally under German control. What follows is their story.

13

The Dutch-Paris Underground Line

To live is not to live for one's self alone;let us help one another.
—Menander (342-291 B.C.) Greek dramatist and poet

Shortly after the French-German armistice was signed under the new government of Marshal Henri Petain in June 1940, John Weidner, a native of Holland residing in Paris, left the French capital to re-establish his textile business in Lyons in the unoccupied "free zone" of southern France. It was not long, however, before the new Petain Government, at the prodding of the Germans, severed diplomatic relations with the Dutch Exile Government in London. The Dutch Consulate could no longer provide needed help to its own countrymen. All matters relating to Dutch refugees in France were now being handled by the collaborationist Vichy government.

In 1941, the influx of new arrivals from Holland accelerated as the persecution of Jews in the Netherlands increased. As a result the Dutch Consulate in Lyons began to overcrowd with these poor homeless souls. They were in financial need and constantly in danger of being sent to detention camps.[1] All foreign aliens, many of whom had traveled long distances for days and even weeks to reach the relative safety of unoccupied France, were being put into detention camps in southern France. Before the armistice was signed, the refugees who came to the camps were treated with some care and given some shelter and a small food ration.

After the armistice was signed with Germany, many of the refugees were to be turned over to the Germans for deportation; within the camps the middling regard for the welfare of the aliens turned into something much worse. Many of the guards and camp officials were less than humane in their treatment of the prisoners and the slightest offense was met by severe physical reprimands. Besides the simple refugees, the camps housed aliens with criminal records and political "undesirables." Food, accommodation and hygiene were notoriously bad. According to one detainee, conditions at the camps were likened to Nazi concentration camps.[2]

To avoid this fate, aliens sought desperately to reach a safe country such as Switzerland and then England. Conditions for Dutch refugees were generally better than those from other countries. Accommodations and food were slightly better, but without valid travel papers, escape to a safe haven was all but impossible. Weidner, the son of a Seventh-day Adventist minister, had become involved in Christian relief work; after having witnessed first-hand the Nazi brutalities, he took a special interest in the Dutch detainees and their predicament.

As a social worker, he was able to obtain papers from French officials, which gave him access to the camps. He also made the acquaintance of families residing near the camps that were willing to hire certain "non-political" camp detainees who were allowed to live outside the camps to work as long as their employment was guaranteed. By working with community and provincial officials, Weidner helped to provide housing for "political" prisoners who might later be helped to escape.[3]

In 1942, Weidner came to the realization that finding housing for the prisoners and places for them to work and hide was but the initial stage of a plan to get them out of France where they could not be seized by the Gestapo and transported to Germany. The only safe place would be across the border into Switzerland or Spain. Having spent much of his childhood in Collonges, a small French border town at the foot of a mountain and not too far from neutral Switzerland, near Geneva, where his father taught school, he was very familiar with the area.[4]

He moved part of his business to Annecy, a small resort town in the border region where he was able to evade the travel restrictions at the border crossing. Through his work he built up contacts with influential church leaders. It was not long before Weidner was leading refugees with properly forged travel documents by train from Lyons to Annecy. There they would receive lodging at his store or in the rear of a gift shop operated by a small middle-aged woman who was always willing to help anyone in need. As the number of Jewish and other refugees increased, Weidner needed additional financial aid, which was provided by a close friend, the Secretary General of the World Council of Churches in Geneva. Additional funds were given by the Dutch Government-in-Exile.[5]

The Dutch-Paris Underground Line

During the first ten months of 1942, the French-Swiss frontier was patrolled by the French police, but Weidner relied upon numerous friends who could help get the refugees across into Switzerland. Farmers, teachers from the Adventist college at Collonges, local officials favorable to the Underground, storekeepers and others familiar with conditions at the border were of considerable help to the escapees. Those friends who lived in the vicinity of the immediate escape areas were able to observe any changes that might take place on the border such as whether new guards were assigned to the area, where patrols were located and whether they were being increased. Of particular importance, they also knew where along the border the barbed wire was electrically charged. Friends also provided wire cutters and ladders needed to get through or over the wire.[6]

The border crossings became increasingly more dangerous after the American invasion of North Africa in November 1942 as the southern French "free zone" was now being occupied by the Germans. At this juncture, the borders were being controlled by Italian and soon after, German, troops. The Italians were often careless and inattentive in their duties; the Germans were more conscientious and security was always tightened when inspectors were on hand. In addition there were French Government riot troops and the customs service, all of which indicated that security measures had increased sharply along the French-Swiss border. One could never be sure whether the guards could be trusted or whether they were working in collusion with the Germans; nor could a trustworthy guard know with certainty whether a refugee escapee might at the last moment reveal himself as a member of the Gestapo.

In Lyons Weidner met a Brussels businessman who proposed the establishment of an escape line running from Holland through Brussels to Paris, then to Lyons and Switzerland, or to Toulouse and Spain. After considering the feasibility of the escape line and the reliability of those he could count on to run it efficiently, plans were made to mobilize the operation. Since the plan dealt principally with the Dutch people, with Paris as the focal point through which all evaders would pass, the network was named the "Dutch-Paris" Line. The organization was comprised of all kinds of people: Catholics, Protestants, Jews and agnostics.[7] These were persons whose sole purpose was to rescue men and women caught in the web of Nazi oppression.

Weidner had numerous friends on whom he could rely. There were several young girls who would escort airmen arm-in-arm through the mountains near the border, appearing to the border guards simply as young lovers. But under cover of darkness the girls would return to a nearby farm or a waiting car near the border. Meanwhile, their "boyfriends" would cut their way through the barbed wire into Switzerland.⁸ The airmen who were being helped along the way back to England would frequently ask who the people were that were escorting them on their way and the name of the escape organization. They wanted London to know of the good work they were doing.

As the war progressed, Allied bombing of the occupied countries increased substantially; so also did the number of airmen whose planes had been shot down by the Germans. Weidner and members of the Dutch-Paris Line knew that if the evaders were to successfully pass through the occupied territories they would have to know how to conduct themselves as French civilians in public under the watchful eyes of German soldiers. Thus, once they successfully stood up to the stiff questioning by the Underground that established their *bona fides*, they were taught some local customs and proper etiquette that differed from their own forms of social behavior.

For example, both the American and Frenchman hold their fork in the left hand when cutting their meat with a knife; however, the American then passes the fork to the right hand after cutting the meat, but the Frenchman keeps the fork in the left hand and raises it up to the mouth; even the way in which the Americans smoked their cigarettes was distinct from the French. The former normally smoked their cigarette only halfway through before throwing the remainder away; whereas the latter used up practically the entire cigarette before discarding it. These eating and smoking habits of the American escapees could easily come under the meticulous scrutiny of the Gestapo or the SS; if observed, the consequences could be disastrous. The French customs had to be taught to the American airmen before they were given public exposure.

Like the other escape lines, the Weidner group was always in danger of being infiltrated by German spies disguised as Allied airmen seeking information about Underground activities. A particularly effective means of determining whether an airman was who he claimed to be was by putting two members of the Underground in Gestapo uniforms. The airman who was suspected of being a spy would be taken into a room where plans for his escape would be discussed. Then suddenly the two "Gestapo" agents would enter the room, arrest the Underground member and the airman and lead them outside for immediate execution. Once outside, if the airman was legitimate, he would protest and simply give his name, rank and service number. If he were a German spy, he would in all likelihood identify himself as such, disclose the name of his unit and ask the "Gestapo" officers to verify the information he was giving.⁹

Besides the difficulties involved in evading the border guards and customs authorities, finding homes for the refugees and airmen to stay as they were

The Dutch-Paris Underground Line

making their way back to England was another serious problem. Finding a willing sympathizer was not easy mainly because the penalty for hiding an evader or escapee was death. The penalty was the same for hotel owners, so to help alleviate this problem, and for extra money given to the proprietor, Weidner was able to find hotels in the French towns who supported the Resistance and who provided overnight accommodations for the evaders.

The Gestapo and the French police frequently checked the rooms against the hotel registry for the names of those persons they were hunting, but by not entering the name of the evader on the registry, and keeping their false names on a separate piece of paper that corresponded with their false travel papers, the hotel manager would have a ready explanation. The clerk would say that in order to get the newly arrived "guests" to their rooms quicker they were to write their names on a slip of paper and he would transcribe the information to the registry later. And if an arrest was made, the hotel clerk would simply say he had no way of knowing that false papers were involved. Several hotels in Paris, Toulouse and Lyons cooperated with Weidner's Underground group and numerous airmen were kept overnight as they made their way from one place to another.

On one occasion when Weidner was traveling by bus to Switzerland to make arrangements for the reception of a group of airmen, he was accosted by two French policemen. Despite the fact that his papers were in order and his textile business enabled him to evade travel restrictions, he was nonetheless arrested and taken into custody in the small country town of Cruseilles. After repeated explanations that he was simply a businessman who had an appointment in Collonges near the Swiss border, the police refused to believe him. Suspecting him of being a Dutch refugee attempting to escape the country, the interrogation soon evolved into a severe beating, kicking and striking him with fists and rifle butts and which, with increased brutality continued in the jail cell where he was finally left in a semi-conscious state. With the help of an outside contact, Weidner was able to get a hearing before a local judge who accepted his story and granted his release.[10]

After the Nazi occupation of southern France was complete in the late fall of 1942, Weidner knew that the movement of refugees and evaders would be far more difficult than when the only border guards and patrols were French, some of whom were willing to provide occasional protection. The situation had now changed dramatically. Throughout what was previously unoccupied France, new elements of Nazi-directed activity were very much in evidence. In addition to the French *gendarmerie*, German soldiers who seemed to be on every street corner, and the dreaded Gestapo who could turn up anywhere, there were now the German counter-intelligence *Abwehr*, the *Gardes Mobiles*, government riot troops and the despised *Milice*, the fanatical French fascist paramilitary police force whose brutal tactics matched those of the Gestapo. If the effort to save the lives of the Jews, evading Allied airmen and other Dutch refugees was to succeed, the Dutch-Paris Line would have to operate far more clandestinely than when the French were in control of the region.

The year 1943 saw a significant increase in the number of airmen in need of a safe escape route back to England. Weidner realized that by taking the evaders into Switzerland there was no way for them to reach England from there unless they returned to France by way of the Annecy-Avignon-Toulouse escape route. However, because the Dutch representative in Vichy had been arrested, and the French Consuls in Toulouse and Perpignan were also arrested by the Gestapo, diplomatic measures for obtaining transit visas for Dutch nationals in Switzerland who wanted to go through southeastern France into Spain to get to England were now impossible.[11] Henceforth, all escaping refugee activity would have to be carried out through the Underground. This would require the establishment of a new escape line.

In Toulouse, Weidner had a Dutch escapee who he was trying to get across the border. With the help of a French widow who had been married to a Dutchman that Weidner knew, he obtained the service of a French guide who had much experience in the Pyrenees. However, the border crossing into the mountains was not only heavily patrolled by the Germans, but was now a forbidden zone to all except those living there.

Fortunately, the guide had an idea for getting himself and the escapee across the frontier. He knew the bus driver in the town of Ax-les-Thermes, whose route ran south to the mountains. His plan was to put Weidner and the evader on top of the bus where they would conceal themselves among the baggage. According to the driver the baggage area on top was never checked by the Germans at the checkpoints. The trip took between eighteen and twenty hours through the mountains with little rest to reach the tiny, neutral country of Andorra separating France from Spain. From there, the refugee purchased a bus ticket to Barcelona where he would contact the Dutch Consul.[12]

Throughout the course of the day in Andorra, Weidner and a member of his organization studied the several roads and trails that led into Spain. Once back across the mountains and into France, the two Underground stalwarts made their way back to Ax-les-Thermes by putting themselves on top of the bus among the baggage and then by train into Toulouse where Weidner made arrangements with the necessary contacts to set up the new Pyrenees escape line.

The Dutch-Paris Underground Line

After Weidner returned to Lyons, he was unexpectedly arrested and taken to Gestapo headquarters, where he was accused of providing illegal aid to Dutch Jews. The Underground leader responded by saying that he was simply giving assistance to refugees because the Netherlands consulate was no longer allowed to provide the help that it had previously given to Dutch nationals.

After hours of endless accusations by the Gestapo that Weidner was actively involved in the Underground, and Weidner's repeated denials, he was taken to a room where his clothes were removed, his hands tied behind his back, and he was thrown into a tub of cold water. His head was held under water until he was about to drown, then he was raised up. When asked about the members of his Resistance organization, he denied knowing anything about it. Again his head was forced under water until he was about to drown and then jerked up. The process was repeated for three straight hours. This was followed by vicious kicking and beating amidst the repeated accusations and denials of Underground activity. He was then taken to another room where large steel rulers were set on edge. Weidner was then forced to kneel on the rulers where they pressed deeply into his legs just below the knees. The pain was unbearable. The questioning and the torture finally ended at 3:00 in the morning, but he still refused to provide any information about his Underground organization.[13] Satisfied that Weidner could disclose nothing further, he was released from the custody of the Gestapo.

It was not long after his release from the Gestapo that Weidner was rounded up with a number of other men under the age of 35 and marched into a German detention camp. The following morning they were all put aboard a slave labor train headed for Germany, where they were to be used as forced laborers in war munitions work. Uppermost in Weidner's mind was the need to return to his workers in the Dutch-Paris organization. The opportunity to escape came as the locomotive was nearing the Swiss-German border. The resolute Dutchman managed to jump from a coach platform and landed at the bottom of an embankment, losing consciousness for a time. When he awakened he managed to cut through barbed wire and across the border. After going a short distance he soon discovered that he was still in Germany, where he was re-arrested and put on another train headed east. Again, the Resistance leader managed to escape when the German guards left the train to enter a cafe on the station platform. He headed for Switzerland where the Rhine River forms the boundary that separates that country from Germany. After plunging into the water he was soon observed and fired upon by a German machine-gun positioned on the riverbank. After swimming frantically underwater and with the help of the rushing current, he managed to avoid being hit by the spray of bullets that punctuated the water all around him. After an effort that seemed endless, he made it out of machine-gun range; he then managed to reach the Swiss shore where, with the help of friends, he was able to make his way back to Annecy.

By the early winter of 1943, the German reign of terror—augmented by French collaborationist activity—created terrible fear in the hearts and minds of the civilian populace; nevertheless, the Dutch-Paris group continued to operate quite effectively. Weidner's organization had now grown to three hundred members. Financial aid was now being provided to the Dutch-Paris network through the Netherlands military attaché in Bern to escaping Dutch military personnel.

Although Weidner's headquarters was in Lyons, the Underground head traveled extensively throughout France, Belgium and to the Dutch border, keeping in close contact with the inner circle of the network's members. For the safety and continuous well being of the organization, Weidner emphasized the importance of agents working alone, of avoiding close contact with friends, and of not being seen in the same place too often or at the wrong time by a friend who might forget himself and reveal the work the agent was involved in.

One day, Weidner received a phone call in Annecy from an associate in Lyons informing him that the Gestapo was making inquiries about him and that they were certain to arrest him once they caught up with him. But before they arrived at his office in Annecy he hastened off to a ski resort in the French Alps, where he took the name of Jean Cartier, one of the several aliases he used during the German Occupation. He knew that he would have to return to Lyons covertly to continue the Resistance activity, but since he also knew that because the Gestapo office in Lyons would have a rather extensive file on him he could no longer return to his office there. His store would have to close, and with it the loss of a substantial amount of income.[14]

In 1943, while in Switzerland, Weidner visited General A.G. Van Tricht, the Dutch Military Attaché in Bern, where he was pleasantly surprised to receive a commission as captain in the Dutch Army. The award was in recognition of his meritorious service in providing loyal service to his fellow Dutch countrymen and others who were led to freedom as a result of his efforts. Several other members of the Dutch-Paris Line received similar commissions.[15]

On a number of occasions, Weidner and members of his Underground group saved the lives of a number of Jews who were very likely to be sent to their deaths. In Switzerland, relatives of Jews being held in Holland in special detention camps were able to obtain falsified citizenship papers from consul offices of neutral countries for a financial consideration of between $100 and $500. These countries, such as Paraguay or San Salvador, would prepare what appeared

The Dutch-Paris Underground Line

to be a valid citizenship document unbeknownst to the home government in those countries. This made no difference to those who obtained the documents, because if presented to Nazi authorities in those detention camps, they just might be able to keep their loved ones from being deported to concentration camps in Germany. By carrying these forged documents from Switzerland through France and Belgium into Holland, Weidner and his operatives were able to save the lives of countless Jews.[16]

One of the most noteworthy experiences of the Weidner network was the unexpected meeting with escapees Pieter Dourlein and Johan Ubbink, the S.O.E. wireless operators captured in the *Englandspiel* who freed themselves from the Haaren Prison in Holland. The two agents were picked up and escorted across southern France into Berne Switzerland by efficient Weidner guides. By the end of November, they were in Spain and then on to London where they related to the British authorities the story of the incredible debacle that cost the lives of so many dedicated Dutch agents.[17]

One of the many agents who worked in the Weidner network was a young Dutch girl by the name of Suzy Kraay who had successfully carried out several escort assignments. However, in Paris as she was beginning a new assignment, which involved escorting a group of American airmen in Toulouse to Spain, she was arrested by the French police who mistakenly believed her to be Jewish. When she was accosted, she carelessly had in her possession a small book that listed the names and addresses of about 150 agents in the Dutch-Paris network. On the way to police headquarters in an attempt to conceal the list she accidentally dropped the book on the sidewalk, which was promptly picked up by one of the policemen. It was not long before the young resister's true identity was discovered.

Initially, Suzy believed the French policeman who interrogated her to be sympathetic to the Resistance. However, she soon realized he was a Nazi sympathizer, and refrained from disclosing what the names and addresses in the notebook meant. Consequently, she was turned over to the heartless Gestapo for further interrogation. The fear of breaking under torture was a constant concern to her as it was to all of those in the Resistance. When Suzy was ordered to provide more detailed information about the Dutch-Paris Line, and especially about its leader, John Weidner, and after repeated refusals to cooperate with her captors, she was taken downstairs to a room where she was forced to observe several male prisoners being brutally tortured and told that she would be subjected to the same treatment. Still, she refused to cooperate. Only after she herself was repeatedly tortured for hours without any letup, and after being forced to witness an even more grotesque form of torture that she was told would be inflicted upon her, did she finally break down and reveal the names of the members of the Weidner organization. Broken by the Nazi torture, Suzy was finally sent to the women's concentration camp at Ravensbruck in Germany.[18]

Meanwhile, the Weidner Underground was continuing to move refugees and airmen out of Paris into the south of France. Yet within the next two days, about half of the members of the entire Weidner network were arrested.[19] When it was clear that the arrests of the members of the network were taking place, Weidner realized that Suzy was the only person who had the names of the 150 members.

Numerous arrests took place in Holland and in Brussels, including a group of American airmen who were being led to Paris; so also were members taken into custody in Lyons, Annecy and Vichy. Some forty members perished, including Weidner's older sister, who died in Ravensbruck.[20]

The mass arrests were a disaster for the Dutch-Paris Line. Nevertheless, there were still 150 members who had not been taken, and new agents could be added to the group. Throughout France, the Gestapo posted a five million franc reward for information leading to Weidner's arrest. Complaints were even lodged with the Swiss Government because they had allowed the Resistance leader to take refuge there.[21]

Toward the end of 1943, while in Paris, Weidner met Christian Lindemans, an affable, flamboyant Dutchman who ran a small Resistance group that had been ushering refugees from Holland and Belgium into Spain for quite some time. "King Kong," as he was known because of his large size, needed money to obtain the help of guides in the Pyrenees. Weidner provided him with 50,000 French francs, but had no intention of merging his organization with Lindemans's. He found him extremely volatile, bombastic and subject to sudden changes of judgment. As an Underground agent, Weidner was shocked at Lindemans's careless manners and lack of security, which even went so far as dropping a revolver in a station waiting room while waiting for a train for Brussels. "King Kong" was also known for his numerous mistresses, one of whom bore him two children.[22]

In the spring of 1944, after Lindemans's brother and a mistress were captured by the Gestapo, he decided to work for the Germans as a double agent in exchange for gaining their freedom. The Germans agreed and from his change of sides 267 arrests of the traitor's own Resistance group were made. In October 1944, after numerous suspicions by British intelligence, Lindemans was brought in for interrogation at which time he readily confessed to being a German agent, and while awaiting trial he committed suicide.[23]

The Dutch-Paris Underground Line

In April 1944, while in Geneva, Weidner was instructed to deliver Gerrit van Heuven Goedhart, an important member of the Dutch Underground, to London.

As a leader of *Het Parool*, a leading Resistance newspaper, Goedhart had valuable information for the Allied High Command; Weidner's job was to get him safely out of Holland and into England. After being met and brought out by a Dutch agent, Goedhart was met by Weidner in Belgium, then on to Toulouse and finally the hazardous trek through the Pyrenees into Spain, whence he proceeded to Portugal and then to London. After his arrival he was appointed Minister of Justice of the Queen's Exile-Government abroad.[24]

Meanwhile, Weidner was busy contacting the various operations centers of the newly reorganized Dutch-Paris network. He was then summoned to England to discuss the escape line and also general conditions relating to the morale of the Dutch people with whom he had been in contact. Additionally, he was told to bring some highly classified information with him. He was first to go to Toulouse, where he would be given additional information for London, and then to Vichy where financial arrangements were to be made to help with furthering refugee work. Weidner made a final stop in Lyons where he provided funds to help out those families of the network members who had been arrested by the Gestapo after Suzy Kraay's confession.[25]

In May, Weidner and three other members of Dutch-Paris were having dinner in a restaurant in Toulouse when they were suddenly arrested by the dreaded *Milice*, often referred to as the French Gestapo, whose techniques and aim were the same as their German counterpart: to destroy the Resistance. The resisters all had false papers and when interrogated at the *Milice* headquarters, Weidner denied being the person whose papers he had in his possession.

He was then subjected to a bathtub torture in which he was stripped of his clothes and electrical wires were attached to more sensitive parts of his body. When a switch was thrown, a hot burning shock jolted his body with excruciating pain. Fortunately the torture was stopped after the French officer in charge remembered that the person they believed Weidner to be had fresh wounds on his shoulders. Upon inspecting the prisoner, it was obvious that they had the wrong man. Alas, it was not long before they discovered that they had accosted John Weidner, the most wanted man on the Gestapo list.[26] Again, he was taken to the torture room where he faced the combined water torture and electric shock after refusing to answer their questions. But just before he was subjected to the terrible anguish, Weidner insisted on speaking to the French Gestapo chief, whereupon his wish was granted.

DAWN OF COURAGE

Weidner appealed to what he hoped was the collaborator's better nature as a French citizen by expressing genuine concern for the French people and their safety, by refusing to disclose the names of people who were only interested in helping refugees find freedom in Spain and Switzerland, and by appealing to a trace of honor as one Dutch officer addressing a French officer. The *Milice* officer referred Weidner's case to a higher French authority in Vichy, since the request was beyond his authority; when submitted to Vichy, the appeal was rejected summarily. Even worse for Weidner and the other members of the network, the German Gestapo was informed of their capture in Toulouse and preparations were being made for their execution.

Meanwhile, one of the officers who arrested Weidner and his companions came to the Resistance leader's cell and asked him if he was a Christian. It so happened that the officer found a small Bible in the prisoner's pocket. The conversation between the two men then turned to a more personal and religious discussion. Their acquaintance began to develop, and when Weidner was informed that he was being turned over to the German Gestapo the next day, he managed to persuade the officer to help in an escape. The two prisoners were placed in a cell on the third floor of the prison where there was a window, and were given tools to force the cell door open. At just after 6:00 in the morning, just after curfew and not far from a guard who was asleep on the floor, the men escaped from a window, dropping three stories to the street. They then headed to the apartment of Abbe de Stegge, a Catholic priest who was also a member of Dutch-Paris, where three other escapees were hiding: a Dutch flyer in the R.A.F., a Dutch secret operative and a Catholic priest who was requested in England to care for the Dutch Catholics who were in the army there.[27] Weidner and the other member of the network went to Geneva after their escape in Toulouse; the others were successful in making it to England.

Back in Switzerland, Weidner re-established contact with the Dutch-Paris connections in Brussels, Paris, Toulouse and Lyons. He was later ordered to London where, in the closing months of the war, he met with Dutch officials, chief of whom was President Gerbrandy, the Dutch Minister-in-Exile, and had a private audience with Queen Wilhelmina. He also discussed arrangements for helping those men and women who were so devoted to the cause they embraced in the Dutch-Paris network throughout the occupied territories.

At war's end, Weidner was honored not only by the Dutch Government, but also by the Governments of France, England, the newly formed state of Israel and the United States for the selfless and courageous work he performed that helped save approximately 1,000 persons, including more than 800 Jews and more than 100 airmen who made their way safely back to England.[28]

Certainly there can be no more fitting eulogy to memorialize the life of John Weidner than these words, spoken by the man himself:

> *You can't help only when it doesn't cause you to suffer. When you want to help people in need, you can't be concerned if your hands get dirty, or if your life is in danger, for that matter. Helping those in need knows no bounds other than those of life itself.*[29]

14

The Carpet to the Rhine

"My country can never afford the luxury of another Montgomery success."
—Prince Bernhard of the Netherlands to Cornelius Ryan, author of A *Bridge Too Far*

In 1944, World War II was in its fifth year and German troops still controlled most of Europe. However, on June 6 of that year, all of that began to change when Allied troops landed on the beaches of Normandy in northern France.

Codenamed "Overlord," American, British and Canadian forces under the Command of General Dwight D. Eisenhower launched the greatest air, naval and ground assault ever to be mounted and executed. The objective of the invasion was to secure a firm base from which an Allied offensive would bring about the ultimate defeat of Nazi Germany and the liberation of the occupied countries of Europe.

In advance of the invasion, a successful major deception plan was put in place codenamed "Operation Fortitude," in which a phantom army was assembled on the English coast, including dummy installations, equipment and landing craft, fictitious camps and radio traffic. The deception was intended to reinforce the belief of the German Western Front Commander, Field Marshal Gerd von Rundstedt, that the main invasion would occur directly across the English Channel from the White Cliffs of Dover at its narrowest point at Pas de Calais.[1]

Several days prior to the invasion, tactical air attacks were ordered involving road and railway interdiction bombing, which eliminated rail sections and key bridges on the Seine and the Loire below Paris. This was augmented by members of the French Resistance who severed German supply and reinforcement arteries by numerous rail cuts, road blocks and acts of minor sabotage on the night of the landing, thereby harassing and delaying German troop movements.

The fact that the landings took place in France, not in the Low Countries, removed Holland as a consideration for the invasion planning of a Second Front. Quite apart from the internal dissention from within the Dutch and British intelligence communities, the lack of arms (most of what had been dropped in Holland went straight to the enemy), the still enigmatic shadow cast by *Englandspiel* and the continued pressure from an indigenous hostile police force, basic considerations of geography and logistics kept Dutch Resistance forces from playing a significant part in the "Overlord" operation at the start.[2] Nonetheless, as Resistance historian Michael Foot hastens to add, "it deserves to be remembered that the Low Countries' role was as difficult, as dangerous as anyone else's; and that the Low Countries' casualty rates—notably among S.O.E.'s agents—were often higher than the French."[3]

The Cross-Channel invasion was announced from London by the B.B.C. at 9:30 AM and later Prime Minister Pieter Gerbrandy addressed the people of Holland on *Radio Oranje*. That night, leaflets were dropped all over the Netherlands containing Eisenhower's assurance to the peoples of Western Europe of their deliverance from the Nazi yoke, along with copies of the Gerbrandy speech. Anton Mussert, the Dutch National Socialist leader, sent a telegram to Hitler reaffirming his "eternal allegiance" to the Nazi leader. For the people of Holland who had lived in virtual captivity for more than four years, liberation and the end of the war was a foreseeable certainty.

For almost two months, the conflict in the Normandy countryside persisted unabated. On August 15, additional American troops landed on the Riviera in southern France and began the advance northeastward. On August 25, Paris was liberated, preceded by an insurrection initiated by forces of the French Resistance.

By mid-summer, a consensus that the war would be over before Christmas was given credibility by a number of circumstances and events. German casualties had become enormous. Germany had lost 400,000 killed, wounded or captured. Half the totals were prisoners of war, and 135,000 of these were taken in the month subsequent to July 25. Additionally, the German Air Force suffered extensively by the loss of 3,500 aircraft, even though the *Luftwaffe* had been severely depleted before the invasion began.[4]

By the middle of July, while the American and British troops were rapidly driving across Western Europe, German forces on the Eastern Front were shrinking. The Red Army was sweeping the Germans out of Russia, had overrun half of northeastern Poland and Lithuania, and was approaching the East Prussian frontier, barely a hundred miles from Hitler's headquarters in Rastenburg.[5] Enemy morale was at an all time low. This was underscored by the attempted July 20 assassination coup against Hitler by high-level military conspirators who were already convinced that Germany had lost the war.

August continued to witness the eclipsing of Hitler's mechanized armies both in the West and in the East. The fall of Paris highlighted the disintegration of the German forces in the Battle of France. The *Wehrmacht* had neither the reserves nor, because of a chronic shortage of oil, the mobility to counter a concentrated offensive. Hitler was forced to deploy his forces strung out all the way from the Swiss border to the North Sea. Without reserves, and unable to shift forces rapidly from one sector to another, he refused to risk leaving a part of the German frontier unguarded.[6]

On the Eastern Front, the Russians marched into Rumania on August 27 and within three days occupied the great Ploesti oilfields; the following day they entered Bucharest. Within several days, the Red Army invaded Bulgaria, which offered no resistance and announced its own declaration of war against Germany. Farther north on the Eastern Front in the Baltic, Germany's defeats elsewhere prompted Finland to bow to Russian armistice terms.[7]

On September 3, the British captured Brussels; the following day, they entered Antwerp, and with the courageous help of the Belgian Underground, some 36 hours later, advanced another 54 miles along the Schelde Estuary and captured the critically important Antwerp harbor and port facilities. The British troops were now just twenty miles south of the Dutch border. On September 1, *Reichskommissar* Seyss-Inquart, swayed by the succession of Allied victories throughout France and Belgium, ordered the departure of thousands of German civilians to the east of Holland close to the German border.[8] The mass evacuation, characterized by heightened fear, uncertainty and disorganization, also included the withdrawal of large remnants of German military forces and Dutch Nazis. In the south of Holland, the Dutch who lived in the towns and villages near the Belgian border who witnessed this mass migration were exceedingly jubilant. The Germans were in full retreat and the happy prospect of liberation was just a few days away. The expectation of what seemed to be immanent deliverance from the Nazi yoke reached its peak on September 5, 1944, amidst the waving of Dutch flags, orange banners and crowds carrying flowers on what came to be known in Dutch history as *Dolle Dindsdag*, "Mad Tuesday."

While Dutch crowds were celebrating what they believed to be the beginning of the end of the Occupation in Holland, most of the Underground units within the organized Resistance remained calm and watched the situation with circumspection. Underground leaders knew that the Germans lacked the troops capable of halting a determined Allied drive. On September 3, the day after the German retreat began, freedom throughout the Netherlands appeared imminent. Amidst the confusion and elation, many members of the Resistance were anxious to fight as they waited for the arrival of Allied forces from the south. Messages that the German forces were retreating back toward Germany and the belief that the country could be liberated "in a matter of hours" were sent to Field Marshal Bernard L. Montgomery, Commander of the British 21st Army Group.

On September 4 at *Wolfsschanze* (Wolf's Lair), Hitler's headquarters in East Prussia, Field Marshal Gerd von Rundstedt was called out of a two-month retirement after being relieved from command of German forces in the West in the aftermath of the Normandy invasion and reappointed Commander of the Western Front.[9] Von Rundstedt was ordered to produce a strategic plan to hold the West Wall that extended from the North Sea to the Swiss border. The 400 mile front, better known as the Siegfried Line, was an obsolete concrete belt of fortifications that had remained unmanned, neglected and without guns since 1940. In fact, the concrete casements, designed for what were now antiquated anti-tank guns, could not contain the more modernized weaponry needed to deal with the updated Allied armor of 1944.[10]

Even more difficult and more urgent was the problem of acquiring sufficient men to garrison the Line and to rebuild and reinforce the disorganized units that were streaming back to the German frontier. In addition, German panzer units were virtually nonexistent. Along the entire Western Front, the estimated Allied strength consisted of more than 2,000 tanks as opposed to only 100 panzers.[11] The *Luftwaffe* was totally destroyed, giving the Allies complete aerial supremacy and von Rundstedt's demoralized troops were outnumbered more than two to one.

Given these circumstances, the Field Marshal could not create an armored reserve powerful nor mobile enough to deal with another Allied breakthrough. He reported that it would take six weeks to modernize the fortifications. Nevertheless, the Fuehrer ordered him to fight a delaying action until the Line could be made fit for defense. He believed that the Allied advance into Holland could be stopped and that a successful counterattack could thwart what were no more than Allied "armored spearheads." Hitler knew that with the exception of the port at Antwerp, all the other ports were still being held by rear-guard German units even though surrounded and cut off. Consequently, he expected the Allied drive to come to a halt as the result of overextended supply lines.[12]

Von Rundstedt came to the same conclusion when he realized why the British waited another 36 hours before mounting a drive from Antwerp to the great Antwerp harbor facilities some 54 miles away. He reasoned that the British slowdown was the result of an Allied headlong pursuit that had overextended itself. The British were successful in seizing the harbor docks intact, but made no effort to secure the bridge approaches over the Albert Canal, and these were blown up by the time a crossing was attempted two days later. As a result, the harbor, which could have served as a major port for providing Allied supplies along the front, was useless.[13]

On September 5, although not immediately noticeable by most of the casual Dutch spectators, roads from the Belgian border north to Arnhem were still crowded, but the German troops that had been heading back to Germany had halted and were slowly regrouping. Eleven miles to the south in Nijmegen, German military police were closing off all roads leading to the German border. The town was now serving as a troop-staging area. Farther south in Eindhoven, just ten miles from the Belgian border, the retreat had stopped. It was becoming increasingly obvious to the civilian population that Hitler had no intention of surrendering and wasted no time in redeploying troops where they were critically needed.

Even more depressing to Dutch observers was the large number of reinforcements coming from Germany. Disciplined formations of German paratroopers commanded by Colonel General Kurt Student were disembarking from trains farther south in Holland at Eindhoven, Tilburg, Weert and Helmond.[14] Many additional troops recalled were in various stages of training and refitting; *Luftwaffe* units such as flight crews and ground personnel whose air operations had been halted by the shortage of petrol were now being used for ground fighting. One division, formed in convalescent depots from men who were invalids, such as those with defective hearing or with ulcers, were hastily recalled from Germany to active duty. Student's Parachute Army was the only substantial reinforcement that Hitler was able to offer von Rundstedt.[15] Even though the situation looked especially bleak for Hitler and his armies, the inevitability of final German defeat was still a long way off, because the remaining German divisions were still capable of fierce resistance.

The Carpet to the Rhine

On September 6, German troops of the 15th Army, supported with artillery, vehicles and horses, were being brought into Holland through the mouth of the Schelde Estuary from the Pas de Calais by night via a hastily consolidated fleet of Dutch freighters, barges and sundry boats and rafts. Yet despite the presence of Allied coastal artillery on Walcheren Island, which served to guard entry into the estuary from the North Sea, nothing was done to stop the convoy. The Germans presumed that the Allies underestimated the size of the evacuation and made no effort to interfere. Equally perplexing was the failure of the British to make any serious effort to cut the base of the isthmus where the German force was following the single main road running east from Walcheren Island across the Beveland peninsula and making its way into Holland. Despite continuous Allied air attacks, the German 15th Army managed to make its way into the interior of Holland where in the days ahead it was to come face to face with the Allied forces.[16]

After their breakout from the Normandy beaches and an accelerated run of 250 miles through northern France and Belgium, the Allied pursuit was weeks ahead of schedule, but in the all-important area of supply they were badly behind. After six weeks of almost nonstop movement against little opposition, Eisenhower's armies were suddenly faced with a serious maintenance and supply problem. The logistics estimate, especially for fuel, which was calculated to support a long-term advance, had now been stretched dangerously thin. As the Supreme Commander of Allied forces later wrote: "Because almost the entire area (the Seine) had been captured in the swift movements subsequent to August 1, the roads, railway lines, depots, repair shops, and base installations, required for the maintenance of continuance forward movement, were still far to the rear of the front lines."[17]

Holding up the Allied advance were not supplies, but rather the Channel ports, from where supplies would be shipped, which were still being held by the Germans. Most of what was needed was stockpiled in Normandy and being brought through the only viable port controlled by the Allies at Cherbourg. Thus, providing supplies was an enormous task. The crisis was worsened by the lack of transportation. The disruption of the French railway system by the Resistance, an asset to the Allied success just prior to the invasion in Normandy was now, under changed circumstances, a liability to the Allied advance toward the Rhine. Railway engineers worked night and day to repair broken bridges and track and to restore the operational efficiency of rolling stock.

Supplies would have to be driven some 450 miles to the forward elements at the Belgian-Dutch border. The urgent need was met by seemingly endless convoys of trucks known as the "Red Ball Express," which made grueling, round-the-clock trips of between six and eight hundred miles. By using relief drivers, every vehicle ran at least twenty hours a day. Even then, the demand was not adequately met because of the critical shortage of gasoline. Infuriated by the fuel shortage, General George S. Patton, Commander of the American 3rd Army, appealed to Eisenhower: "My men can eat their belts, but my tanks have gotta have gas."[18] Gasoline and fuel oil had to be brought onto the Continent by means of flexible pipelines laid under the English Channel. From the beaches, the gas and oil were pumped forward through pipelines laid on the surface of the ground to main distribution points. The laborious tasks undertaken by those men who provided the means necessary to continue the Allied advance against what seemed to be insurmountable odds was the highest expression of morale and devotion to duty, and equal to the efforts of those troops fighting on the front lines. Clearly, the herculean efforts of those unsung heroes that resolved the transportation problem during those first hectic weeks in September will go down in history as an incredible *tour de force*. As well they should.

After having learned of the Allied capture of Antwerp, and of German V-2 rocket attacks against London being launched from sites located near The Hague, Field Marshal Montgomery sent a message to Eisenhower indicating that the time had come for a major all-out Allied offensive from Holland into Germany that he believed would end the war before the end of the year. The British commander's proposed objective was to send his army group through Holland on a "single-thrust" end-run securing a bridgehead before the winter began and then to quickly seize the highly industrialized Ruhr.

Conversely, Eisenhower favored a "broad front" policy. He considered the bulk of the German Army in the West already destroyed, and that the Allied success should be exploited by promptly breaching the Siegfried Line, crossing the Rhine on a wide front and attacking the Saar and the Ruhr. The Supreme Allied Commander believed that by seizing the two largest industrial areas in western Germany, Hitler would no longer have the capacity to wage war. Montgomery claimed that such a plan would involve a long winter campaign that would not succeed.

The British field commander indicated to Eisenhower that of the two strategic pursuits available to the Allied armies—the Saar and the Ruhr—only one such drive could successfully be made because there were not enough supplies to handle both drives. In Montgomery's opinion, the northern drive toward the

The Carpet to the Rhine

Ruhr was the most expeditious, and would bring the best results. The operation would involve crossing the Rhine north of the Ruhr. This would mean facing three major river barriers—the Maas, the Waal, and the Neder Rijn or Lower Rhine—and five other smaller canals.

To breach the water barriers, Montgomery formulated a plan in which a carpet of airborne forces would be laid along an 80-mile corridor in Holland to capture the road bridges that would secure the crossings over the three major river barriers, thus providing a narrow corridor for tanks of the British Second Army moving up from the south, which would race across the captured bridges seized by the paratroopers. After crossing the Lower Rhine Bridge at Arnhem, the major objective, the troops would dash into Germany.

Eisenhower approved the plan and treated the combined airborne-ground operation as simply an extension of the northern advance to the Rhine and the Ruhr.[19] The airborne proposal was especially favored by the War Department in Washington, chiefly from the Chief of Staff General George C. Marshall and Air Force Chief of Staff, Henry "Hap" Arnold, who had been insisting that the highly-trained First Allied Airborne Army be used at the earliest opportunity.

The two-fold plan was code-named Operation Market Garden—"Market" was the airborne drop and "Garden" the armored drive. The daylight aerial drop would consist of three and a half separate parachute divisions laid down along a northerly line extending from Eindhoven to Nijmegen to Arnhem. The monumental operation was to include a total of 35,000 paratroopers, one-third of which would be glider-borne infantry; an estimated 5,000 fighters, bombers, and C-47 Dakota troop-transports and over 2,500 gliders that also included hauling jeeps, artillery and other heavy equipment. To command the operational phase of "Market," Lieutenant General Frederick Browning, head of the British I Airborne Corps, was appointed.

The American 101st Airborne Division, commanded by Major-General Maxwell Taylor, was assigned to capture the canal and river crossings just north of Eindhoven; Brigadier-General James Gavin, who headed the 82nd Airborne Division, was assigned to seize the river crossings between the Maas and the Waal south of Nijmegen; the third objective, the capture of Arnhem and seizure of the vital 400-yard-wide river crossing over the Lower Rhine was given to the British 1st Airborne Division, under the command of Major-General "Roy" Urquhart and, under his command, the Polish 1st Parachute Brigade commanded by Major-General Stanislaw Sosabowski.[20] Arnhem and the Rhine bridge crossing were indispensable to the success of Market Garden, the ultimate aim of which was to seize the industrial Ruhr, which would seriously weaken

Germany's war producing capability.

While plans for the Market Garden offensive were unfolding, British military authorities in London informed the Dutch Minister of War and Dutch intelligence that a railroad strike throughout the Netherlands would be an asset in hastening an Allied victory. As part of Montgomery's strategy to cut off the Germans in western Holland and to halt the transport of the dreaded V-weapons to the Dutch coast, the strike would hinder enemy transport and troop concentrations.

Moreover, over the past two years, Dutch trains had carried more than half a million Dutchmen to Germany for forced labor, more than 120,000 Jews to extermination camps, and tens of thousands of political prisoners to concentration camps. This move would be one of the most important acts of defiance against the Nazis that the Dutch were asked to make. Since it was believed that the strike would be of short duration and liberation no more than several weeks away, Prime Minister Gerbrandy agreed with the Allies to proceed with the strike. The response by the Dutch workers in favor of the strike was overwhelming: only 1,500 to 2,000 out of a railway workforce of 30,000 refused to participate in the strike.[21]

On September 10, preparations for Market Garden began. The following evening the American 1st Army crossed the German frontier and within two days faced German defenses at the Siegfried Line. On September 13, Maastricht was the first Dutch city to be liberated with little enemy resistance. Approaching the German city of Aachen, they were pushed back against the Belgian border as German defenses showed signs of stiffening. Nevertheless, the consensus among the Allied leaders was that the enemy was still weak and demoralized after the earlier German retreat was halted. Eisenhower's headquarters reported that there were "few German infantry reserves" in Holland, and those that were in the area were not capable of any serious organized resistance. Despite undeniable reports from the Dutch Underground that rapidly increasing German strength was developing in the area of the planned airdrop, the intelligence was disregarded because it lacked any backup endorsement from Montgomery or his staff. One such authenticated report from the Resistance was that "battered panzer formations had been sent to Holland for refitting." This report was also discounted. Alas, those "battered" formations, which were in fact the veteran elite 9th and 10th SS Panzer divisions, were the desperately needed reinforcements that Army Group B Commander Field Marshal Walter Model had conveniently hidden in a densely wooded region of Arnhem. Nevertheless, at the British 21st Army Group headquarters, optimism for Montgomery's brilliant scheme continued to prevail.[22]

The Carpet to the Rhine

❁ ❁ ❁

On September 17, 1944, at 10:45 AM, the largest air armada ever assembled lifted into the air from 24 bases in England. More than 2,000 troop-carrying planes and gliders were escorted by 1,240 British and American fighters. In the earlier predawn hours, the way was prepared for by 1,400 Allied bombers that targeted German anti-aircraft batteries and troop positions en route to the drop zones. There was no serious enemy opposition during the Channel crossing, because practically the entire *Lutwaffe* fighter force was situated in central and southern Germany.

United States 82nd Airborne troops and elements of the British First Division flew along a northern track, while the U.S. 101st Airborne followed a southern route. As the latter approached the Dutch coast, they encountered black puffs of flak—German anti-aircraft fire coming from the outer Dutch isles. In the vanguard, special pathfinder teams were dropped to locate and mark areas for the artillery and equipment drop and landing zones. Altogether, 4,600 aircraft took part in the airborne operation on this first day, of which 73 were shot down, almost all due to flak.[23]

On the night before the invasion, Allied bombers conducted widespread pre-assault aerial attacks against Arnhem, Nijmegen and Eindhoven. The following morning, extensive bombing continued, augmented by fighters that began strafing enemy machine-gun and flak positions all over the area. The feeling of the townspeople was one of ambivalence. Moods alternated between exaltation and fright. People hurried into churches, homes and cellars or wherever they could find shelter. No one was certain of what would happen next, but most of the Dutch people believed that the bombing was a prelude to an Allied ground offensive. The Dutch people, like the Germans, had no idea that an air attack was imminent.

At half past one in the afternoon, the sky over Arnhem, Nijmegen and Eindhoven was an incredible sight to behold. When the vast formation swung north across the Dutch border, people in the towns and villages below looked up from rooftops and balconies at the persistent droning of aircraft, what for them was a rhapsodic anthem that signaled the dawning of liberation. Throughout the entire Market Garden area, 20,000 American and British soldiers had landed in Holland, heading toward the bridges to safeguard the corridor for the Garden ground forces whose lead tanks were expected to connect with the 101st Airborne paratroopers by nightfall.

At 2:15 PM, General Brian Horrocks, commander of the British XXX Armored Corps positioned just inside the Belgian border, gave the order to lay down a barrage of artillery fire five miles deep along the fifteen-mile Eindhoven corridor. Within ten minutes, hundreds of tanks, half-tracks, armored cars, personnel carriers and armored vehicles supported by air cover provided by British typhoon fighters began the slow move northward toward Eindhoven. Soon after crossing over the Meuse-Escaut Canal bridgehead and into Holland, the spearhead was halted by a barricade of German gunners who succeeded in knocking out nine tanks. The rocket-firing Typhoons were called in, and as they were targeting in on the enemy gunners, the burning tanks were being pushed off the road. Tank crews followed by British Grenadier infantry disposed of the remaining German anti-tank positions and concealed snipers behind the barricade and cleared the road for the armored advance. Further German opposition was encountered as they moved up the road, and the tanks came under heavy fire, especially from bazookas, but with the help of the Typhoons, the enemy was eventually overcome. Because of the unexpected German resistance, which was far tougher than the British anticipated, Horrocks's XXX Corps was only able to reach Valkenswaard by nightfall, some five miles south of Eindhoven.

Meanwhile, paratroopers of the 101st Airborne Division met very little German resistance at the dropping zones. Acting independently for longer than anticipated due to the armored delay, they quickly captured the railroad and highway bridges north of Eindhoven over the Willems Canal amidst heavy fighting; farther south between the towns of Veghel and Son, the town of St. Oedenrode was captured. Heavy German resistance was met at Son, where the bridge over the Wilhelmina Canal was blown up. A temporary crossing was established by engineers from the 101st until equipment could be brought up to rebuild the bridge. This would delay even further Horrocks' armor. By midday of September 18, the British armored battalion met the 101st and the way was clear for the armor to continue north through the corridor to Nijmegen.

Responsibility for the middle sector of the Market Garden corridor was left to General Gavin's 82nd Airborne Division. The objective was to secure a ten-mile corridor from the Maas River to the Waal River including the 1,500-foot bridge near the town of Grave and the half-mile-long highway bridge at Nijmegen, the most important of all the division's objectives and crucial to the entire Market Garden operation. Some 2,000 paratroopers of the 504th Regiment were dropped about 500 yards southwest of the Grave Bridge. They worked their way toward the bridge in deep drainage ditches; and despite harassing enemy fire from a flak tower across the river, they held the bridge and were able to prevent its demolition. Additional units secured a crossing over the Maas-Waal Canal. Within six hours, Gavin's troops cleared the way over which the British ground forces would travel.

The Carpet to the Rhine

The largest numbers of airborne troops, battalions from the 505th and 508th Regiments, were dropped approximately one and a half miles from the German border between the Dutch Groesbeek Heights area and Reichswald, which was just five miles inside the German border. The drop zones were purposely left unmarked by pathfinders so as to keep the Germans from knowing where the paratroopers and gliders were to land. Gavin's main concern was the possibility that enemy tanks would suddenly counterattack from the Reichswald.[24] To protect his glider-borne men, a complete battalion of field artillery and General Browning's Corps headquarters staff that were also aboard, the men were instructed to jump close to the anti-aircraft batteries, overtake the enemy and silence the guns that were in the drop zone area as quickly as possible. One member of the 505th Parachute Infantry Regiment, squad leader, Sgt. (now retired Colonel) Spencer Wurst, remarked that the sudden appearance of three or four American parachute infantry battalions landing in such a close area could not help but create a rather sudden morale problem for the enemy.[25] Nevertheless, the men of the 82nd encountered a considerable amount of anti-aircraft fire and small-arms fire from woods surrounding the drop zones, as did several P-47 and P-51 fighter planes providing air cover that were hit by German gun emplacements during low-level attacks. But in less than an hour, the paratroopers assembled into small groups and managed to suppress the remaining German resistance and took a number of prisoners.

On Monday, September 18, overwhelming numbers of Germans launched a counterattack from across the German frontier out of the Reichswald forest and the town of Wyler and overran the landing zones that were to receive the glider reinforcements of desperately needed artillery, ammunition and men from England.

Although outnumbered five to one, the late arrival of the glider-borne troops enabled General Gavin's force to hold out for more than four hours under heavy enemy fire before the situation was restored.

On the morning of September 19, spearheaded by Grenadier Guards, the British Armored XXX Corps continued the drive toward Nijmegen. In a combined attack with British tanks intent on capturing the highway and railroad bridges, General Gavin had only one battalion of troops with which to enter the city, because his Glider Infantry Regiment had been unable to take off from England due to heavy fog lying on the airfields. As the troops entered the outskirts of the city there was some fighting in the streets, but they did not encounter any serious resistance. They were met by Dutch civilians out on the sidewalks and streets cheering and applauding the American troops. Members of the Dutch Resistance, identified by orange armbands, were quite helpful to the Allied units; they guarded prisoners, acted as guides and performed other duties as well.[26]

By mid-afternoon, because both the road and rail bridges were intact, Gavin's force, supported by British armor, divided; one column headed for the railroad bridge and other approached the main highway crossing over the Waal River. At both locations some five hundred SS troops, well-positioned and supported by artillery and armor, were waiting. One column of troops whose mission it was to secure the railroad bridge encountered buildings on the river's edge that were set afire by the Germans; additionally, enemy fire from machine guns, anti-aircraft and 88 mm dual purpose guns made it impossible to overrun artillery positions and other enemy opposition at the approach to the bridge.

The second column that headed to the highway bridge ran through some ornamental gardens called Huner Park. Close to the park was an old medieval fort, the Valkhof, situated on a large wooded knoll; on the elevated bank leading to the medieval structure the Germans were heavily fortified. The American troops and British tanks that tried to get to the bridge were halted by a punishing artillery barrage as well as small arms and mortar fire. Amidst disastrous casualties—in nearly three days, upwards of 200 dead and almost 700 injured—tanks that tried to rush the bridge were knocked out.[27] By late evening, the Anglo-American assault was stopped some 400 yards from the Waal River bridge, the last water obstacle on the road to Arnhem. Throughout the night, the Allies expected the bridge to be destroyed. What they did not know was that the overall German Commander, Field Marshal Walther Model, had given explicit instructions prohibiting its demolition as he believed it could be used to counterattack the Allied forces.

General Gavin realized that because of the heavy German resistance at the bridge crossing, any further head-on attack would be an exercise in futility. Consequently, he proposed a plan designed to gain complete possession of the Nijmegen road bridge by simultaneous attacks from both the north and south ends of the bridge. This would require an assault crossing of the river a mile downstream by men of the American 504th Parachute Regiment. They would seize the northern end of the bridge while an attack of German defenses on the southern end by Grenadier Guards and British armor was also taking place. Gavin knew that heavy casualties could be expected even after having crossed the river, since the troopers would have to cross 200 yards of flat ground beyond which was an embankment where heavy enemy gunfire could hail down on the Allied invaders. That would also have to be overrun. If Market Garden were to succeed, the Waal River bridge would have to be secured.

The Carpet to the Rhine

The assault crossing took place the following afternoon, September 20, after some 28 small assault boats were rushed to Nijmegen during the night. The launching was a disaster from the start. The men had to use their rifle butts to paddle. Boats overturned as men tried to lift themselves aboard; some were put into too shallow and could not budge; others were overloaded and, caught by the current, began to circle out of control and sank under heavy loads. The mass confusion soon became a horrible disaster as the enemy mortars and heavy machine guns opened fire from the northern bank in front of them and from the railroad bridge. No more than half of the men in the first wave survived the severe enemy fire.

After those who survived the onslaught in the first wave reached the northern embankment, boats turned around and started back for the second wave. Undaunted by the ferocity of enemy resistance, some 200 men scrambled or swam ashore and with grenades, submachine guns and bayonets, continued their unrelenting assault against an enemy that was pulling back to secondary positions until ultimately the German defenders were forced to surrender. The unmatched gallantry of those men of the 82nd was nothing short of magnificent.[28] By 6:30 that evening, the Americans routed all enemy opposition and advanced toward the road bridge. On the way, they stormed the northern end of the railway bridge and after driving the Germans out, triumphantly hoisted the American flag.

Earlier that afternoon, fierce fighting occurred in Huner Park and in the Valkhof close to the southern approaches to the highway bridge. But after heavy murderous fire in close quarters house-to-house fighting, a battalion of the 505th Parachute Regiment and British Grenadiers broke through and opened the way to the bridge. By 7:15, after obliterating enemy artillery on the far bank and countering enemy small arms gunfire on the bridge itself, British tanks crossed the 600-yard bridge whereupon, inspired by the sight of the Stars and Stripes at the northern end of the bridge, connected up with the Americans. The Nijmegen Bridge was in Allied hands undamaged and Arnhem was only eleven miles away.

The British airborne units that landed at Arnhem that first day, like those at Eindhoven and Nijmegen, met little initial interference from the enemy. Major-General "Roy" Urquhart's First British Airborne Division of over 5,000 paratroopers landed on its drop zone approximately four miles northwest of the prized Arnhem Bridge, capturing the villages of Wolfheze and Heelsum.

DAWN OF COURAGE

The First Parachute Brigade under the command of Brigadier G. W. Lathbury assembled quickly and within an hour of landing headed for Arnhem. The brigade's primary task was to take and hold the road bridge over the Rhine River until relieved by the advancing tanks of General Horrocks XXX Corps after their arrival, hopefully within 48 hours.

Three battalions were to converge on Arnhem from three different directions. The prime objective was given to Lieutenant-Colonel John Frost's 2nd Battalion: a southerly route marching along a secondary road running beside the north bank of the Rhine and taking out the railway and pontoon bridges west of the main highway bridge. In advance of Frost's battalion, a reconnaissance squadron of armored jeeps brought in by gliders and commanded by Major Freddie Gough was to rush the road and railway bridges, and seize them by a surprise attack until Frost arrived to develop defenses at either end of the bridge. Lieutenant-Colonel J.A.C. Fitch's 3rd Battalion would move along the Utrecht-Arnhem highway and, approaching the main highway bridge from the north, would reinforce Frost. After these two battalions had moved out, Lieutenant-Colonel D. Dobie's 1st Battalion would advance along the Ede-Arnhem highway, the most northerly route and occupy the area north of the city.[29]

Unfortunately, in 38 of the 358 gliders that were transporting Major Gough's armored jeeps, most of them were lost. In almost every case the reason was the tow-rope broke, which was a common mishap in airborne operations. Frost would now have to take the main Arnhem Bridge on foot without the help of Gough's surprise attack.

What the British were totally unaware of was that the heaviest concentration of German troops was, quite accidentally, a few miles north of Arnhem where the 9th and 10th Waffen SS Panzer Corps were refitting after their retreat from France and Belgium. As was indicated earlier, before the air drops took place British intelligence had been warned by the Dutch Underground that there were tanks in the Arnhem area, but the reports were ignored as being vague and unconfirmed.

Although the landings caught the Germans by surprise, they were quick to react to the British presence. Field Marshal Model happened to be at his headquarters in the Arnhem suburb of Oosterbeek, just over a mile from where the landings were taking place. Model immediately ordered General Wilhelm Bittrich, commander of the II Panzer Corps, to deploy his two tank divisions against the airborne troops. In addition Model asked for infantry and panzer grenadiers, anti-aircraft units, mortars and self-propelled guns.

The Carpet to the Rhine

As the three battalions of the 1st Parachute Brigade were making their way toward Arnhem, the march was more of a victory parade. The men were met by cheering, exuberant crowds of Dutch civilians from the farms and neighboring villages. People on both sides of the road offered them beer, milk, fruit and other welcoming provisions. The troops found it difficult keeping attentive to the possibility of an attack from the enemy.

The first serious and unexpected German opposition was encountered after the first hour on the road. Both the 1st Battalion on the northern route and the 3rd in the center were suddenly engaged in fierce enemy attacks. Lt. Col. Dobie's 1st Parachute Battallion became heavily engaged with heavy enemy fire in a wooded area within two miles of its drop zone. The SS Panzer Grenadier Training and Reserve Battalion, numbering 435 men, led by Major Josef Krafft, located in the Oosterbeek-Wolfheze area, held up the advance of Lt. Col. Fitch's 3rd Battalion. This delay enabled Field Marshal Model to dispatch a battle group of half a dozen tanks and some armored vehicles of the 9th SS Panzer Corps to take up blocking positions north of Oosterbeek, and between that suburb and Arnhem.[30] With the exception of one company, which managed to get through by a separate way, the heavy German armor precluded any further advance to the bridge by either of the two parachute battalions.

With the few vehicles available, Major Gough's reconnaissance unit saw that the 3rd Battalion had run into enemy opposition. An effort was made to outflank the Germans and open the way for Dobie's 1st Battalion by taking the northernmost route—the Ede-Arnhem road—but it was not long before the lead jeeps of the unit were suddenly ambushed by German armored cars and heavy weapons.[31]

Lieutenant-Colonel Frost's 2nd Parachute Battalion set out along the southern route at the same time as the 3rd Battalion on the central route, and despite a few encounters with enemy fire, Frost's battalion, along with Captain Eric Mackay and his Royal Engineers, whose job it was to remove expected German charges on the bridge, pressed on steadily. One company was detached to seize the railway bridge, but just as the troops got there, the Germans blew it up. The battalion continued to press on through the streets of Arnhem to the pontoon bridge, which they discovered was useless, as the Germans had removed its center section. The two bridges were not the most important ones; nonetheless, their destruction kept Frost from sending a company across to the other side of the river to capture the southern side of the road bridge in Arnhem.

On the final approach to the city near the Oosterbeek railway bridge, they passed under an embankment, and when they were less than two miles from the road bridge they moved through a maze of side streets to avoid any organized resistance. Once on the bridge, the troopers were suddenly fired upon from an enemy pillbox at the northern end of the bridge and by a lone armored car at the southern end of the bridge. With the help of sappers carrying flamethrowers, the German pillbox was set afire, and shortly after 8:00 PM, Frost's 2nd battalion took control of the north end of the bridge However, on the south bank, a party of SS Panzer Grenadiers drove up from Nijmegen and secured the southern end. Frost now had a force of five hundred men and one anti-tank gun. He knew that he would have to wait for reinforcements another 48 hours for the arrival of General Horrocks's XXX Corps. Nevertheless, twice during the night, Frost's men tried to seize the southern side of the bridge, but were beaten back each time.

Earlier during the night, Airborne Commander General Urquhart and Brigade Commander Lathbury were stranded with the 3rd Parachute Battalion along the Utrecht-Arnhem highway. Unable to return to Division headquarters due to continuous enemy harassment, a temporary headquarters was set up in a private residence set back from the road. Conditions were worsened because of a communications breakdown at Division headquarters. Until the wireless failure could be corrected, there was no way of informing Corps Commander General Browning of the status of General Urquhart's three battalions. While Browning could direct the movements of the 82nd and 101st Divisions and the British XXX Armored Corps, the more critical fighting that was going on at Arnhem at this vital juncture was beyond his control. Consequently, they did not realize that the Germans had responded far more quickly and more strongly than could reasonably be expected, and they had no idea of what was happening in Arnhem.

By dawn on Monday, September 18, men from the 1st and 3rd Parachute Battalions, who had managed to fight their way through the German defenses northwest of Arnhem, and many of whom were severely wounded, hungry, cold and exhausted from the fierce German counter-attacks the previous day, somehow reached the bridge. Lt. Col. Frost estimated that he now had between 600 and 700 men on the northern end of the bridge. But as Frost's battalion was growing in number, so also were the mechanized German armored units entering the city and taking up positions.[32]

Meanwhile, Brigadier Philip "Pip" Hicks and his 1st Airlanding Brigade had the thankless job of holding those Arnhem dropping and landing zones for the expected air drop later that morning. All through the night, his men had held off a series of vicious enemy attacks. Hicks, who had now taken over command in the absence of General Urquhart, decided to reinforce the 1st Parachute Brigade immediately.

On the arrival of the second lift, which was scheduled to land at 10:00 that morning, he diverted part of Brigadier John Hackett's 4th Parachute Brigade to that task. However, due to heavy fog in England, their take-off was delayed, and the drop did not occur until 3:00 that afternoon. Despite continuous enemy opposition, the landings took place satisfactorily. By this time both the 1st and 3rd Parachute Battalions, which had run into such heavy German opposition the night before, continued toward Arnhem, but were cut to pieces in a series of bitter actions near the St. Elizabeth Hospital, less than two miles from the Arnhem Bridge. They had neither the troops nor the ammunition to break through to the bridge, where Frost with his 600 troops was maintaining a precarious foothold at the northern end. Particularly noteworthy was that throughout most of the battle in Arnhem the hospital was used by both the British and German doctors and medics to care for the wounded on both sides. Civilian patients were evacuated by the Germans.

On the following day, Tuesday, September 19, the besieged battalions along with the South Staffordshire Regiment of the 1st Airlanding Brigade and the 4th Parachute Brigade, hoping to gain a passage to the bridge, were halted by German tanks and heavy weapons. When the anti-tank ammunition was used up, the airborne troops were driven back street by street through Oosterbeek to the Hartenstein Hotel, where General Urquhart had by now rejoined his headquarters and was forming a tight perimeter while awaiting the arrival of XXX Corps.

The likelihood of Urquhart's 1st Airborne Division being reinforced or resupplied by air was remote. Bad weather and the sudden appearance of over 500 German fighter planes held up the reinforcement plan. Thick fog on the British airfields kept the Polish Parachute Brigade and the glider regiment of the 82nd Division from taking off. The failure of the Polish Brigade to arrive removed the last chance of any airborne troops coming to the aid of the paratroops at the Arnhem Bridge.[33]

Meanwhile, an even more serious setback had occurred. The prearranged supply dropping zone was on ground that the British no longer held. Urquhart requested changed dropping points for supplies, but the wireless link with the R.A.F. was not working. As a result, signals requesting changed dropping points for supplies were never received. The British forces on the ground were then forced to witness the cargo planes drop 87 tons of ammunition, food and supplies entirely into enemy hands. They tried by every means possible to attract the attention of the air crews, waving and by lighting beacons, but it was all to no avail.[34]

On Tuesday evening, the situation at the north end of the Arnhem Bridge was becoming desperate. Frost's 2nd Battalion was holding a dozen houses and a school building that were being shelled and mortared. The cellars were filled with the wounded and the surrounding houses were ablaze. They were almost out of anti-tank ammunition and the 400 men who were still able to fight were no longer able to drive off the tanks, which were demolishing their positions. They continued to hope that help would come from Oosterbeek, not knowing that they had been out of radio communication since Sunday evening.[35]

On the morning of Wednesday, September 20, contact was reestablished with Divisional Headquarters through the local telephone exchange in Arnhem, which had been seized by members of the Dutch Resistance. It was then that Frost learned that there was no hope of relief unless he could hold out until ground forces reached him from Nijmegen. By now the 2nd Battalion defenders of the road bridge had been reduced to between 150 and 200 men and Frost himself was wounded when shrapnel from a mortar shell tore into his ankle and shinbone. All day long the battle continued without letup. Perseveringly, the British repelled attack after attack fighting from houses in the bridge vicinity.

That afternoon, several tanks fired upon Frost's headquarters, forcing his men into the open streets fighting from house to house. British sniper fire was able to pick off the exposed drivers of the German vehicles as they tried to make their way across the bridge. The stench of battle in the town was appalling. Burning hulks of armored cars and half-tracks and overturned jeeps and trucks cluttered the bridge; collapsed buildings and smoking piles of debris made the streets indistinguishable from one another. Dutch citizens and members of the Dutch Resistance helped with the wounded and private homes were turned into aid stations providing a rapidly dwindling supply of medical supplies, especially morphine and field dressings. More than 300 British and German wounded filled the cellars. Food rations were practically gone and the Germans had cut off the water supply.

Among the many Dutch citizens who risked their lives to assist the British soldiers was a most extraordinary woman by the name of Kate ter Horst who, with her husband Jan, a leading member of the Dutch Resistance, and five children lived in a fourteen-room former vicarage in Oosterbeek. During the ferocious siege in that upscale suburb of Arnhem, their home became a refuge for the wounded. At one time Mrs. ter Horst harbored some 200 British troops as well as her own small children in the cellar. Despite her home being so heavily bombarded by German artillery that it was no longer recognizable, she recalled that "every foot of space in the main hall, dining room, study, garden room, bedrooms, corridors, kitchen, boiler room and attic was crowded with wounded. She hardly slept. Going from room to room, she prayed with the wounded and read to them from the 91st Psalm."[36]

Hour after hour, Frost waited for some relief from either the 1st or 3rd Battalions to break through the German barrier, and some further word from General Horrocks's XXX Corps whose tanks were still far down the corridor.[37] At about the time that Frost was wounded, the bridge force lost one of its most important positions. In the school building halfway along the eastern side of the ramp embankment running down to the town, Mackay's force of Royal Engineers and some members of the 3rd Battalion who had held this exposed position throughout the battle were barely positioned when the Germans launched a severe machine gun and mortar attack. One shell from a tank set the roof and the top story ablaze—where most of the defenders were positioned. There was no way of putting out the fire and it was obvious that the building had to be evacuated after more than sixty hours—the evening of the first day. The wounded were brought out from the basement and the seriously hurt carried out on doors or mattresses. Meanwhile, the shelling of the building continued. In an attempt to cross the road into the gardens of some homes, Mackay and about ten other men were captured by the Germans, but later escaped.[38]

At dusk on the morning of Thursday, September 21, Frost and his force of less than 100 men still fought fiercely trying to hold on, but it was clear that the end had come. All opposition at the bridge ceased. The task of the 1st Parachute Brigade had been to seize and hold this bridge. This they did for nearly four days under unrelenting attacks and against increasing and overwhelming odds.

Meanwhile, in England, the 1st Polish Parachute Brigade, which had been trying to lift off since Tuesday, was still delayed due to the heavy fog that covered the airfields. Major-General Stanislaw Sosabowski was opposed to the operation from the outset. Units of the Polish glider transport and artillery battery that were absorbed into General Browning's command experienced an earlier disaster on Tuesday when they landed in the middle of a fierce battle between the British and the Germans.[39] From the very beginning, and unlike the British High Command, the Polish General refused to underestimate the German strength in the Arnhem area; moreover, he was convinced that his drop zones were too far from the bridge to effect surprise. What angered him more was that since his brigade's original task—to land south of the Arnhem Bridge, cross it and occupy a position east of the town—could not be carried out because of the inability to leave England on the nineteenth, plans were changed. The brigade was now ordered to drop east and northeast near the village of Driel, where they were to gain a firm bridgehead on the south bank of the Rhine in that area.

Since no one in England seemed to know what was going on in Arnhem due to the communications breakdown at Division headquarters, all that was known was that the north end of the Arnhem Bridge was in British hands. The Polish Brigade had no idea that they were preparing to land on top of the 10th Waffen SS Panzer Division. Once over the drop zone, General Sosabowski and his brigade encountered a combined enemy anti-aircraft assault and merciless slaughter of swaying, defenseless men of the brigade who were being riddled by tracer bullets as they descended from the sky; many were dead before they hit the ground. Those that landed safely were shot at from all sides. Of 1,000 men in the brigade that fought that day, only about 750 men assembled, including scores of wounded.[40]

General Urquhart expected the Polish brigade to cross the Rhine the night of September 21/22 in boats or rafts, but when they failed to arrive, Sosabowski pulled his men back into a defensive perimeter. It was not until 9:00 PM on Friday, September 22, that the Polish soldiers were able to start across the 400-yard-wide Rhine. In a few rubber dinghies and several wooden rafts, the men proceeded to move across to the northern bank of the river, when suddenly the boats and rafts were attacked by enemy machine gun fire and mortars. The Poles suffered serious casualties throughout the night as they struggled to cross the river. As a result of the fierce enemy action and a shortage of boats, only fifty men and almost no supplies had been ferried across the river when the operation came to a halt. The following evening, Saturday, September 23, no major crossing of the Rhine could be attempted because General Urquhart's 1st Airborne Division was so desperately in need of ammunition that the relieving forces had to concentrate on ferrying supplies. Between dusk and dawn, after suffering many casualties, the Polish brigade was only able to ferry over an additional 200 men to the Oosterbeek perimeter.

On Sunday, September 24, at a meeting of Lt. General Miles Dempsey, Commander of the 2nd British Army and XXX Armored Corps Commander General Brian Horrocks, it was decided that on the night of September 25/26, a final attempt be made to gain a bridgehead north of the Rhine River. To succeed, the corridor would have to remain open so that ammunition, assault boats and bridging equipment would be able to move northward. Horrock ordered a relief force, the 4th Dorset Regiment of the 43rd Wessex Infantry Division, to join up with the remaining 250 men of General Sosabowski's Polish brigade and cross the Rhine to the aid of General Urquhart's men.

Sosabowski, a very able and experienced officer, believed there was still a chance to turn the tide in favor of the Allies. He proposed a better crossing point downstream, close to Wageningen, that would provide the opportunity to attack the Germans in the back and rescue the remainder of the 1st Airborne Division as well as establish a bridgehead farther upstream. He was ignored and sent away in disgrace. So on the night of September 24, the landings were scattered because of the heavy enemy fire and the battalion was never able to concentrate on landing. The failure to accept Sosabowski's view led to the sacrifice of the 4th Dorset Battalion.

On the morning of Monday, September 25, the ninth day of the battle, the shrunken defense perimeter at Oosterbeek was now manned by only 2,500 British and Polish troops.[41] Since the landings during the previous night failed, and heavy casualties, a lack of ammunition, food and water were taking their toll on the defenders at this last bastion of the 1st Airborne Division's defense line, it was increasingly obvious that their only option was withdrawal. In addition, British air reconnaissance reported that German infantry were digging in on the north bank of the Rhine and that panzer reinforcements were moving toward the only sector of the river where a crossing could be made. Reluctantly, Dempsey and Horrocks made the decision to withdraw the division on September 25 after receiving confirmation from Field Marshal Montgomery. The withdrawal of the fit and walking wounded that took place that night amidst driving wind and rain was aided by a gun barrage from Horrocks' XXX Corps that served as a screen for their departure. After arriving at the river's edge, two companies of Canadian engineers were there to ferry the men across the river in some amphibious and assault boats.

By dawn on the morning of September 26, the evacuation had to be stopped as German machine guns sweeping the river precluded a safe crossing. Out of an original force of 10,000 troops, 2,163 men of the 1st Airborne Regiment and a Glider Pilot Regiment acting as guides, 160 Poles and 75 members of the Dorset Regiment reached the safety of the south bank of the river.[42]

After an exhausting march in darkness and torrential rain through woods, streets, houses and gardens, the survivors, including the walking wounded, along with General Browning's Corps HQ, were reunited with elements of their units in Nijmegen and subsequently flown back to England. Other British prisoners, including those injured and unable to walk that were captured at Arnhem, were transported to Germany. In the nine days of Market Garden, the combined losses of Allied airborne and ground forces—killed, wounded and missing— amounted to more than 17,000. American losses including air crews totaled

3,974. German loss estimates were between 7,500 and 10,000 men, of which perhaps a quarter of those were killed.[43]

As to the number of Dutch civilian casualties, no known figures have been compiled. Those who died in Arnhem and Oosterbeek are estimated to number under 500, but no one knows for certain. Some have said that the total number of civilian casualty figures during the entire campaign, which included the forced evacuation of the Arnhem region and the terrible hunger winter that was soon to follow, was as high as 10,000.[44]

Why Did Market Garden Fail?

The remarkable speed by which the American and British forces advanced through France and Belgium after the Normandy breakout created an overly optimistic attitude on the part of Allied leaders, which generated a notion that the war in Europe could be over by Christmas. The hurried advance had almost reached the German border when it was suddenly halted by a temporary shortage of supplies. Nevertheless, a quick end to the war seemed possible; yet, given the circumstances of the time, even without the historian's benefit of hindsight, which often prompts oversimplification, the Market Garden proposal was itself a highly questionable undertaking.

Part of the fascination of Market Garden is over the speculation that had the operation been successful, an Allied victory at Arnhem would have resulted in potentially enormous post-war advantages. Even before Market Garden was launched, the Western Allies were closer to Berlin than the Russians. According to British historian Martin Middlebrook, a successful Rhine crossing and dash into Germany would have given the Americans and British more favorable bargaining conditions concerning the fate of half of Germany and all of Eastern Europe at the Yalta Conference in February 1945, and the West would not have had to face over forty years of the Cold War.[45] Not so. The Yalta Conference only formalized what Roosevelt had earlier promised Joseph Stalin at the Teheran Conference in November 1943: moral legitimacy to what the Soviet dictator had acquired by sheer force, Russian domination of practically all of Eastern Europe including East Germany.[46]

What is not debatable is that the failure of the ten-day struggle at Arnhem can in no-wise be attributed to the superb British 1st Airborne Division who fought so magnificently throughout the long, drawn-out campaign. The errors that contributed to the defeat of the British soldiers must lie at the feet of others, most of whom have been described in this brief narrative.

There was first the blatant ignoring of early intelligence received from both the Dutch Resistance and from reconnaissance flights that German armored units had moved into the Arnhem area. The failure to make use of sound Dutch information and advice was a prime source of weakness in the overall Market Garden operation.[47] Montgomery believed that the German opposition would be slight; that their troops were still disorganized after the earlier hasty retreat and that those that were still around were low-caliber troops; and that the few tanks that were identified in the area were heading back to Germany for refitting. Once the Panzer divisions were known by the British High Command to be in the Arnhem area, the 1st Airborne Division was not warned of their presence nor provided anti-tank weapons as part of their weaponry.

The failure of the air operation was the decision to spread the airborne drop over two days, which resulted in a prolonged dispersal of the division and a failure to achieve concentration of effort.[48] Additionally, the three British battalions that landed on the first day were dropped too far from the Arnhem Bridge. Had troops been dropped at both ends of the bridge, they would have had the advantage of surprise by a sudden attack in force. As Colonel John Frost wrote later, "The whole idea of parachutists was that they should land behind the enemy and not be forced to cross rivers in the face of intense fire."[49]

Success at the bridge could have been further strengthened by adequate air support provided by the 2nd Tactical Air Force. But it was not so ordered. Granted, an inherent weakness of the operation was the unpredictability and sudden worsening of the weather over England in September, which seriously hampered air operations. Nevertheless, according to the Official History, Major L.F. Ellis stated that the plan that was finalized was this:

> In the final plan the local Tactical Air Group 83 (a part of Fighter Command) was ordered to be grounded during the time of airlifts and resupply. When these were postponed for several hours because of bad weather in England, 83 Group's aircraft remained grounded till released from England. During those hours the whole Arnhem operation had no close air support from 2nd Tactical Air Force.[50]

An additional factor that must be considered was the lack of sufficient drive by British 2nd Army Commander, General Dempsey and by XXX Corps., whose commander, General Horrocks, readily admitted in his memoirs that there was little opposition ahead of him: "We still had 100 miles of petrol per vehicle and one further day's supply within reach. I believe that if we had taken the chance and carried straight on with our advance, instead of halting in Brussels, the whole course of the war in Europe might have been changed."[51] Montgomery's order to Dempsey that the ground attack should be "rapid and violent" was not complied with.[52] Thus the slow progress in moving up the highway to link up with Frost's 2nd Battalion at the Arnhem Bridge.

Moreover, granted the benefit of hindsight, the unexpected skill with which General Model used the sparse resources available to him and the rapid action by the two skeleton Panzer Divisions that set up a defense impossible for lightly armed British airborne troops to penetrate was a critical factor in the overall evaluation of the Arnhem operation.

A real drawback for the British Army was the river obstacles, for it was they, in the long run, that contributed to the delay of the main thrust of the XXX Armored Corps. But as Lieutenant General Lewis Brereton, the American Commander of the 1st Allied Airborne Army, wrote after the battle: "It was the breakdown of the 2nd Army's timetable on the first day—their failure to reach Eindhoven in 6 to 8 hours as planned—that caused the delay in the taking of the Nijmegen bridge and the failure at Arnhem."[53] The delay was due to a lack of awareness on the part of the British commanders of the urgency of the situation and to insist that their troops press on with maximum pressure regardless of losses. This was expected even in those operations that were likely to shorten the war and thus save casualties in the long run.[54]

Probably the greatest shortcoming of the British Army relieving force was the failure to make the drive from the Waal to the Lower Rhine on September 22. It was not until the following evening that the 43rd British Infantry Division succeeded in reaching the south bank of the Rhine west of Driel in force. By this time it was too late to rescue the remainder of the 1st Airborne Division.

The aforementioned analysis of the Market Garden operation is not new. It has, for the most part, long been discussed and much of it has been accepted by most military historians. That the operation should ever have been launched will always be open to question. The astonishing claim of Market Garden's chief architect, Field Marshal Bernard Montgomery, that "the battle of Arnhem was ninety-percent successful" is wholly unsupportable; unless, as British historian Chester Wilmot states, the success is judged solely by the capture of eight water crossings. But the inability to secure the ninth bridge at Arnhem meant the failure of the entire operational strategy.[55] Montgomery stated in his *Memoirs* that "in spite of my own mistakes, the bad weather, or the presence of the SS Panzer Corps in the Arnhem area," he laid a large portion of the blame on Eisenhower claiming that "if the operation had been properly backed from its inception, and given the aircraft, ground forces, and administrative resources necessary for the job—it would have succeeded."[56] Others who fail to share his assessment of Market Garden might call to mind Samuel Johnson's apt remark: *No man is defeated without some resentment, which will be continued with obstinacy while he believes himself in the right, and asserted with bitterness, if even to his own conscience he is detected in the wrong.*[57]

15

The Dutch Famine of 1944–1945

I queued for hours to get some salted endive or some beans. As always that hunger… And then there was less and less. There remained nothing, not even in the black market. Sugar beets from which we first made syrup and then some kind of cookies from the leftovers. Impossible to eat, but it kept many people alive. Fried tulip bulbs were the last resort.
—J. Vrouwenfelder, *Life in Western Holland,*
December 1944

The failure of the Market Garden offensive dampened the hopes of an early liberation for four and a half million people—half of the entire Dutch population—and for an earlier end of the war in Europe. After the Allied defeat at Arnhem, Holland became a divided country. The provinces north of the Rhine and Waal Rivers, which also included the densely populated western side of the country, were still in the hands of the Germans; south of those rivers fighting was still being waged.

The continued presence of the German Occupation Forces in Holland now presented the Allied military authorities in London and the Dutch Government-in-Exile with a serious dilemma: whether the railroad strike that was undertaken at the inception of Market Garden should now be continued. Because the offensive was originally expected to be of short duration and liberation at most a few weeks away, the general expectation was that the strike would then be ended. Sufficient numbers of railroad workers had gone on strike to bring practically all trains to a standstill with the exception of those border provinces in the northeast and the south. To some extent, the strike was an impediment to the Germans, but military operations were more seriously affected by Allied air attacks.

During the first week of the strike in the fighting around Arnhem, the Germans were hampered by the unavailability of Dutch trains. Moreover, the strike forced the Germans to use their own personnel in Holland to a far greater extent than if the Dutch had remained on the job. Many of the German railroad men became casualties from Allied bombing and sabotage; but now that the strike could no longer serve as a tactical deterrent because the offensive had failed, the decision to continue or end the strike had to be made. The defeat at Arnhem had changed the situation considerably.

If the strike was to be resumed, there were serious, practical problems that needed to be considered. There was the fear of German reprisals; there was the need of hiding places for the strikers and the matter of income and food for the duration of the strike.[1] On October 5, in a Radio Oranje speech, Prime Minister Gerbrandy explained to the people of Holland that ending the strike would do nothing to improve their situation. The Germans would use the Dutch railway network to rob Holland of what was left of its food, cattle, raw materials and machinery. Moreover, the coal supply, which came from the liberated province of Limburg, was no longer available since it was now in the hands of the Allies, and trains providing the remaining food stocks would be easy targets by Allied planes. Those trains that did survive air attacks would also be used by the Germans for transporting those menacing V-weapons to the Dutch coast for launching against England.[2]

Furthermore, the Dutch Government in London believed that the strike would uplift morale and raise Dutch prestige among the Allies. It would also be a successful act of defiance in the closing days of the war in which large segments of the population would participate by rendering assistance to the railroad workers.[3]

When the decision to continue the strike reached the office of Seyss-Inquart, the *Reichskommisar* reacted by immediately imposing a food embargo on all shipping in those areas still under German control. This meant all canals and barge transport including the Ijsselmeer waterway, which links the provinces of North Holland and Friesland in the northwest part of the country. The prohibition would have a particularly adverse effect on the densely populated cities of western Holland—Amsterdam, Rotterdam, The Hague, etc. Because of German exploitation, food had already become a scarce commodity in those areas, and when rations were cut even more, the situation became much worse. Not only would there be hunger, but for large numbers of the civilian population, the scarcity of food would create famine.

Shortly after the resumption of the strike, the Germans undertook a "scorched-earth" policy. The ports in Amsterdam, Rotterdam, Schiedam and Vlaardingen, which included the warehouses, offices, cranes, quays, docks and ships were destroyed; on the islands of Zeeland and South Holland, large portions of the land were flooded with fresh water by the Germans.[4] A fifth of that arable land had already been inundated by the Allies, hoping to flood the Germans out by bombing the dikes in the Walcheren close to the Scheldt estuary and letting the sea in.[5]

Better than one-fourth of Holland lies below sea-level, and for a people who rely upon a complex system of dikes, canals, floodgates and pumping stations to keep dry, flooding was a major concern. In the hope of stopping the Allied advance, large areas of western Holland were flooded by the Germans, and more inundations were being prepared by the mining of dikes and pumps. The destruction of those Dutch power and pumping stations would result not only in the flooding of certain areas, but also in a complete lack of fresh water, sanitation, lighting and heating. Now that liberation was no longer an early expectation, the people of western Holland were faced in the coming winter months with a problem of survival.

After the Germans had halted Allied resistance in and around Arnhem and the vast majority of the British soldiers had been captured, the Rhine was an unassailable barrier where the Germans felt reasonably secure. Families in Arnhem, who had been confined to living in cellars for ten days while the battle raged around them, had now hoped that since the fighting was over there would now be relative peace and quiet. Instead, the town's 100,000 inhabitants were ordered to evacuate their homes within 36 hours. The order to leave came as a tremendous shock to the inhabitants, who were still stunned and bewildered by recent events.

Thus an endless stream of refugees, instructed to carry only the barest necessities with them, began the march from Arnhem with no place to go. An effort by prominent Dutchmen in the town to prevail upon the Germans to rescind the order was answered with the rejoinder that a "blanket of bombs" would be laid over Arnhem if the order was disobeyed. Many of the evacuees headed toward Apeldoorn, 48 miles away. Those who tried to return to Arnhem were stopped by patrolling Germans and told that they would be shot if they made any further effort to re-enter.[6]

Amidst falling rain on an overcrowded road, streams of men, women and children continued to swell, walking on worn shoes and many with bleeding feet. The only sounds to be heard were baby buggies and carts bumping along the road with clothes, bedding, silver and china piled on top, and crying children lying on top of baggage, cold and hungry. Many of the refugees went to Ede and Barneveld and other small towns in the neighboring region where they were housed in schools and where the Red Cross provided blankets and food for those who slept on floors.[7]

What particularly affected the people was that every farm and every household in the surrounding region was suddenly contacted by the Germans, who would then evaluate the size of the homes and order the owners to accommodate so many people. The residents were simply commanded to open their homes to total strangers who could be criminals, Nazis or German collaborators. Dutch authorities were responsible for making the assignments of specific people to designated households.[8]

In October, the anguish and misery that was caused by the forced evacuations was intensified even further by a number of reprehensible reprisals. In the small village of Putten a number of small riots broke out between German soldiers and members of the Resistance. On one occasion during an ambush by a small Underground group, a German officer was taken hostage. The incident was avenged by the Germans, who rounded up 33 innocent farmers and passers-by who were lined up in the village square where it was announced that they would be shot if the ambushers were not found. When the German Military Commander, Friedrich Christiansen, was told of the incident, he ordered all the men between the ages of seventeen and fifty be turned over to the SS, the women and children evacuated and the village burned down.

A day and a half later the German officer was released by the Resistance in hopes of saving the village hostages, but nobody informed the Germans. The women were told to gather their belongings and leave the village with their children. The next day a few men stepped forward when asked by the SS who the attackers were, but they were not believed. Six hundred male villagers were arrested and after a temporary stay in a concentration camp in Amersfoort most were sent to Germany; only 49 returned to Holland.[9] This was an act of terror comparable in scope to the Lidice massacre in Czechoslovakia in June 1942, where the entire male population of the town was massacred and the women and children sent to concentration camps in Germany in retaliation for the assassination of the diabolical SS *Reichsprotector*, Reinhard Heidrich.

Additionally, in the town of Wormerveer, five citizens were chosen at random and executed after a policeman had been killed; in Rotterdam, three people were killed for trying to pick up anti-Nazi pamphlets in the street; later that same day four men were executed after 48 prisoners were freed from a police station by a Resistance group. One of the worst reprisals came after the murder of a valued German intelligence agent who had built up an intensive network of informers who had infiltrated a number of Underground groups, of which a number of members were discovered and killed. The intention was to kidnap the agent, because killing him could lead to severe reprisals. He was caught by members of the Resistance while having a drink in an Amsterdam bar, but in an attempt to desensitize him with chloroform, the bottle containing the liquid broke during a struggle, and the only expedient was to shoot him. The next day, 29 citizens of Amsterdam were executed in revenge, and several buildings were set on fire.[9]

The anxiety and despondency caused by the forced evacuations, reprisals and deliberate destruction of so much life and property—along with the increasing hunger—was compounded even further by the lack of transportation and power that resulted from the gas and electricity that had been cut off. This created an atmosphere of desperation, which in the words of one Dutchman, "covered the whole of western Holland like a thick grey blanket. Decay and poverty dominated. Hunger and cold leave their mark and the drabness increases by the day."[10] Central kitchen food distributions were expanded throughout all of western Holland. People waited in lines for hours for a plate of soup made from unpeeled potatoes. Soon, sugar beets and beetroot replaced potatoes. A food inspector reported that the central kitchen frequently served food, approved for human consumption, but which animals would refuse; the country was in desperate need of help.[11] One writer described culinary conditions in Holland this way:

> *The Dutchman, gastronomer by birth, had to live on three slices of dry bread and half a liter of soup a day, plus, if he was lucky, for breakfast a plateful of rye-in-water without sugar or salt. He came to swallow a product which, grown to maturity, used to provide the glory of Holland in red and yellow and violet: tulip bulbs. At the dining tables they took the place of the rare potato. But don't believe these bulbs were abundantly available. Oh no. Their nutritiveness once discovered by the mob, they became costly. You had to watch your garden closely. People learnt to celebrate the days on which bulbs were part of the meal.*[12]

In the large cities in western Holland, thousands were experiencing famine, and many sought help from outlying areas.

Hunger knocked more and more pressingly. Under-nourished men, women and children walked or cycled along the sad, wet country roads, trying to pick up some food in exchange for their wedding rings, their overcoats, for salt or yeast or a box of matches if they had it. Often their tyreless wheels broke down, often they themselves fainted with exhaustion. And often the things they had got were seized by ruthless Germans or quislings. Everywhere children begged for a slice of bread, for a single potato. Many died.[13]

In mid-October, Seyss-Inquart realized that the embargo on inland shipping did nothing to bring an end to the railroad strike. But he also realized that the military interests of the Reich were being adversely affected by the embargo. The Dutch barges were badly needed by the Germans for the transport of their own supplies as well as for the systematic confiscation of Dutch stores and material. He also knew that the strike and the embargo on the shipment of food into western Holland were responsible for the famine that was taking place in that same area.

The German army also took a hard look at the food situation and knew that the famine would result in widespread sickness and epidemics that would provoke even greater hatred, and could even lead to rebellion and a general demoralization among the German soldiers. The embargo was lifted in October, but the decision was met with resistance from Dutch barge owners, many of whom believed that the Germans would confiscate the boats needed for food transport in order to ship what they looted from Holland.[14] The Dutch Nazi party took this refusal by the barge carriers as an opportunity to blame them and the railway strikers for the serious food shortage. But further analysis clearly demonstrated that there were other causes of the shortage as well.

At the time of the invasion of Holland in 1940, because there was a concern over the future of food, the Dutch Government created a reserve of some 1.2 million tons of food. But when the Dutch farmers tried to rely upon production from their own soil, they were faced with serious problems. Not only were they forced to sell well in excess of fifty percent of their produce to the Germans, but there was also a great shortage of fertilizer, weed killers, insecticides and farm machinery. Many young agricultural workers were sent to work in Germany. And despite the fact that twenty percent of the livestock was killed off—mainly pigs and chickens because they consume many of the same foodstuffs as humans—food output went down year after year, until after the bad summer of 1944, reserves were almost nonexistent.[15]

Conditions worsened in November, when rain fell in unprecedented quantities, and flooding rose to unrestrained levels. No longer could people rely upon the central soup kitchens for food; those living in the cities reached out to the farms with one hope in mind: to acquire food. Neither was money nor the lack of it, goods to exchange, miserable weather, inadequate clothing nor the lack of shoe leather able to deter the hundreds of thousands from making what came to be called "hunger trips." Raids, road blocks, Nazi confiscations or even Allied air raids were unable to halt the human hemorrhage along the country roads searching and begging for food.

On the road a kind of matter-of-fact fellowship without introduction developed among strangers who showed concern for one another by passing on suggestions and rumors, and especially warnings of German roadblocks where men, bicycles, and even carts loaded down with contents might be taken by the guards. People would swap food for fuel, help each other push their carts up the steep slope of a bridge, exchange road directions and rumored weather forecasts. It was the elementary human values of mutual friendliness and helping and sharing with one another that made life bearable.[16]

In December, Holland experienced an exceptionally bitter winter accompanied by much snow and ice. There was no coal, gas or electricity. People had to go outside and search for wood from wherever they could find it. One observer noted that early in the morning or after sunset you could see respectable gentlemen creeping through parks and public gardens, past lanes and canals, judging everything on its combustible qualities. The result was that tree-lined streets became bare in one night, while bridge-railings disappeared, wooden street pavement was torn up and little parks were razed to the ground.[17] In Amsterdam, 22,000 of its 42,000 trees were cut down in just a few months. Wooden paving-blocks between tram-rails were lifted; and canals were dredged in the hope of finding something that would burn. In the Jewish district, which was now empty because the inhabitants had been sent away to death camps in Germany and Poland, 1,500 houses were robbed of joists, beams, staircases, door and window frames, much of which had collapsed in ruins, often killing the wreckers.[18]

Dutch morale was weakened even further after receiving word of the sudden, massive German offensive in the Ardennes in neighboring Belgium on December 16, which dispelled any hope for an early liberation. It was Hitler's last bid—just nine days before Christmas. As General Eisenhower later wrote, "the German attack quickly attained the popular name of 'Battle of the Bulge,' because of the rapid initial progress made by the heavy assault against our weakly held lines, with a resulting penetration into our front that reached a maximum depth of some fifty miles."[19] Maneuvers were made particularly difficult for the Americans because of the snow-packed roads and fields, and especially by the tremendous fog that was able to conceal the Germans and hide their movements in the woods; it also precluded Allied air attacks. A temporary change in the weather did come on December 23, which enabled the ground-air tactical team to plunge into battle, giving the initiative back to the American forces. By the middle of January, the Americans had sufficiently attained the offensive to drive the Germans beyond their initial lines. Moreover, the Russians had opened a long-awaited and powerful winter offensive, which contributed to a sigh of relief by the Dutch, knowing that the war was just that much closer to ending.

But for those in Occupied Holland, liberation was still a long way off. On December 24, an announcement by the Germans was made throughout the towns and villages that all Dutchmen between sixteen and forty years of age were needed for work in Germany. The increasing demand for cheap labor to replace those factory workers who had either been killed in Allied air raids or exempted from military service prompted Germany to seize young men from all the countries of Occupied Europe to work in German war plants, and to clear the rubble and debris left by Allied bombing raids. The Germans believed that with the promise of good food and the support for their families, Dutchmen would be enticed to respond favorably to the need for help in German factories and to dig defenses in eastern Holland.

The Dutch response was unequivocal. Members of the Resistance went about the towns covering Nazi posters with a proclamation encouraging women to support their husbands and sons in a "principled rejection" of the German action. The Underground paper *Trouw* encouraged its readers to sabotage the German recruitment efforts by all possible means.[20] Throughout Holland, posters and leaflets were widely distributed opposing any cooperation with the German authorities. To weaken the effectiveness of the German deception, the Resistance either destroyed or stole population registers, and stole or forged ration cards. In the first two months of 1945, 53 registers were attacked and robbed in North Holland alone. In Amsterdam, where members of the Dutch Nazi party were assigned to handle the registration of workers, eight N.S.B. members were shot by the Resistance. The Germans responded by killing five hostages the next day, but the spirit of Resistance remained unbroken.[21]

In addition to the dissuasion by the Underground, further warnings against registration were given by the churches. Archbishop of Haarlem Johannes de Jong wrote that "the best sabotage is that our whole nation, as one man, ignores the summons." He ordered his priests to hide all necessary documents "otherwise you will soon be rid of the books and your male parishioners."[22] And on January 9, to clarify the official position of the Dutch Government, Prime Minister Gerbrandy appeared on Radio Oranje and told the Dutch people that only by standing unified with the Allied effort could the enemy be defeated.[23] Thus, thousands of those expected to leave for Germany joined the tens of thousands of evaders who had already gone Underground. Of the 500,000 men wanted by the Germans, less than a tenth of that number registered, maintaining an inability to work because of hunger.

The inability to attract more than 50,000 Dutch workers for German labor prompted the Germans to forcibly round up those who refused to register voluntarily for obligatory labor. The Resistance tried to alert towns and villages before a raid took place, but in some places it was too late. In a raid in the town of Dordrecht 3,500 men were awakened from their beds in the early morning hours by banging on doors and the firing of guns in the air, and forcibly taken to work camps such as at Rees, just over the Dutch-German border, where conditions for both housing and food were despicable. In most places, the men were put into barracks, factory buildings or brickyards, where their beds were simply layers of straw, and their coats served as blankets. As most of the men were unprepared when taken, they seldom had sufficient clothing or decent shoes. Many of the men fell ill because of the cold and improper clothing, shelter and food. They all complained of maltreatment and beatings by the guards. Later reports revealed that of the 3,000 who worked at Rees, one-third perished or were mutilated for life. Conditions were essentially the same at other work camps in Holland; their fate was the result of forced labor, exhaustion, lack of clothes, hunger and disease.[24]

Outside of the work camps, conditions were not much better. The medical profession reached a point where it could no longer deal with the patients that multiplied on a daily basis. Surgeons had to work in unheated operating rooms and suffered as much as anyone else from the lack of food. Drugs, bandages and other medical supplies became unavailable. Many suffered from the effects of lack of food, such as apathy and pain in the limbs; skin diseases were caused by the lack of soap, hot water and vitamins. More serious were epidemics of diphtheria and typhoid fever, and most prevalent of all, starvation.

While most of the male population was either in the work camps or in hiding or on hunger trips, women, children and old people were struggling to survive at home. Wives and mothers would wake up in the morning and wonder what the family would eat that day. They would queue up in food lines where often nothing was available. Children would search trash bins for meager leftovers from the central kitchens. Cleanliness was another problem for housewives. There was a total lack of cleaning material. Soap was in very short supply and substitutes did not clean. Except for shoes, underwear and stockings, clothing was considered less important; outerwear was patched and darned repeatedly. As one older citizen remarked, "the clicking of knitting-needles in the long dark evenings was to me a very familiar sound."[25]

Many were concerned about their children and what they would be like after the war. Without fathers at home, and with mothers being busy all day, many of the children were left to fend for themselves. At first, schools operated on a half-day basis, but the bitter cold soon forced them to close completely. Demoralization among the youth was a commonplace occurrence. One official report to the Allies in February 1945 stated that "as long as hunger and cold rule, those who are in need will follow the rule of life, i.e., the urge to stay alive and try to defeat every obstacle in the way. This has to be done by means which are in conflict with normal standards of morality."[26]

Meanwhile, the Dutch living in the liberated southern provinces stood by helplessly listening to reports of conditions in the occupied provinces in the north and west where the daily ration of food had decreased to 460 calories, less than a fifth of normal needs. Just how seriously the death rate had risen was disclosed in a comparison report on February 27, where it was stated that in Amsterdam alone, 107 persons died in the first week of September 1944, as compared to as many as 517 in the first week of February 1945.[27]

By mid-January, the crisis in Occupied Holland had reached such major proportion that Queen Wilhelmina addressed notes to King George VI, Prime Minister Churchill and President Roosevelt in which she declared:

> Conditions have at present become so desperate, that if a major catastrophe, the like of which has not been seen in Western Europe since the Middle Ages, is to be avoided in Holland, something drastic has to be done now, that is to say, before and not after the liberation of the rest of the country.[28]

Prince Bernhard, the leader of the Free Dutch forces, also appealed passionately to the Allies to hasten the liberation.

Nevertheless, Eisenhower's position was unequivocal: "military factors and not political considerations" must determine Allied strategy.[29] Despite the fact that millions of people in Occupied Europe were anxiously awaiting to be freed of the Nazi yoke, the Allied leaders were convinced that the defeat of Germany was their overriding purpose and must take precedence over the needs of the Dutch people, just as it did over the plight of the Jews. Churchill also believed that a diversion into Holland would be a mistake when the whole German defense might collapse if the Allied armies pushed forward into the heart of Germany. To act otherwise by aiding special categories of Nazi victims would only deviate from that purpose and aid the cause of the enemy.

❁ ❁ ❁

When it seemed as if matters for the people of Holland could not be any worse, Radio Oranje announced on January 25, 1945, that the Gerbrandy Cabinet had fallen.[30] People were now asking how, in the midst of so much hunger and suffering, Dutch partisan conflict could destroy the unification of the Government-in-Exile. Even though the government was composed of men who were basically divided and mistrustful of one another, they were nonetheless bound by a single purpose: the defeat of Germany.

In November 1944, an advance group of government ministers decided to go to unoccupied Holland to make preparations for the return of the government to the liberated provinces. However, before leaving, the group met stiff opposition from the Netherlands Military Government (M.G.), which the ministers themselves had formed earlier in 1943 at the request of the Supreme Allied Command (S.H.A.E.F.) to serve as a link between the Allied Command and the Dutch Government-in-Exile. In May 1944, an agreement was concluded that gave S.H.A.E.F. full military authority in the liberated provinces while sovereignty was preserved through the M.G. Since it was earlier believed that the liberation of the country would occur before the end of 1944, the military government was only expected to exist for a short duration.[31]

Colonel H.J. Kruls was appointed head of the M.G., which consisted mainly of civil servants with little or no military experience who had suddenly been turned into officers and who had never been popular with the Dutch ministers in London, whose powers they now seemed to be usurping. The M.G. soon found itself alienated from the Dutch populace, who resented the impression that they needed strong military supervision. The relationship between the M.G. and the Forces of the Interior in the south (N.B.S.), the now-organized resistance forces under the command of Prince Bernhard, was even more unfavorable. Many of those in the N.B.S. were known as "Shock troops," a mixed group of resisters, many of whom disliked taking orders from the M.G., who they resented as having enjoyed the comforts of London during the war while they suffered its deprivation.[32]

Conversely, the military government viewed many of the resisters as just so many arrogant opportunists who obstructed law and order by the unjustified arrest of alleged German collaborators. These allegations were largely confirmed by Gerbrandy and his Ministers, who flew to liberated Holland in November to survey conditions in the provinces. Demands were then made for an end to the arrests and to the removal of the undesirable elements in the N.B.S. Prince Bernhard also stipulated that new Interior Forces units could not be formed without his personal approval. It was becoming increasingly obvious that Gerbrandy was losing his grip on authority by his failure to deal firmly with the military government or members of the resistance who regarded the ministers with indifference.[33]

On January 14, 1945, J.A.W. Burger, Minister of the Interior, made a speech that was heard throughout the Netherlands. In it he seemed to excuse those who had collaborated with the Germans as distinguishable from those who were declared Nazis, i.e., those who "made errors" as opposed to those who "completely erred." He said that "a nation does not consist of heroes alone, nor of diplomats, but of a majority of people with normal worries about their daily existence." To the people in Occupied Holland who were still suffering hunger and terror, the speech was inexcusable. In effect, it was the *coup de grace* of the existing Exile Government.

Burger was soon dismissed and accompanied by three other Socialist colleagues who resigned in protest. Gerbrandy offered his resignation to the Queen, who accepted it, but on further advice from her Minister of Foreign Affairs, the prime minister agreed to remain in office until the war was over.[34] But even more pressing and of greater concern for the 4.5 million suffering people in the occupied Dutch provinces was the question of when reassuring promises of help would translate into real help at last.

16

Holland Rejoices

Pilots who came to us while waging
The bloodiest war that ever yet befell
Mankind, and that for five years had been raging
Around and o'er us making life hell
Lo, how we wave at you, now all is well.
Look how we raise our children on our shoulders,
And they will tell their children's children
When they're old and wise
How man, like God, dropped Manna from the skies.
  —*Yge Foppema (1901-1993) Dutch poet of the Resistance*

The Way Back

While the Dutch in Occupied Holland were waiting for relief, and after the German counter-offensive into Belgium had been stopped in late January and pushed back to where it began on December 16, the Supreme Allied Command planned a massive American, British and Canadian offensive into the Rhineland between the Dutch border and the German industrial Ruhr as the first major step into the heartland of Germany. The failure at Arnhem in September and the subsequent flooding by the Germans of vast areas of southern Holland forced the Allies to bypass the Dutch cities as they advanced into northern Germany. Re-entry into Holland by British and Canadian armies would take place from German territory after an assault had been made across the Rhine River.

On February 8, the First Canadian Army, which was situated in the Nijmegen area, launched a five-hour barrage against the Reichswald, a large forested area that extends east of the Dutch border and just inside the German frontier. The Canadians advanced on an eight-mile front with the Rhine on their left flank and the Maas on their right, capturing the German town of Goch, but no actual breakthrough occurred. The Germans had flooded much of the countryside between the Roer and the Rhine Rivers and fortified the area with eleven divisions. According to one British officer, the Reichswald was one the most miserable and toughest battles fought since Normandy.[1]

Farther south, the 9th U.S. Army under General William Simpson was assigned the job of driving northeast across the Roer River to crush German resistance in the Dusseldorf, Krefeld, Munchen-Gladbach region. The object was to seize one of the Rhine bridges, which were not destroyed by the Germans, and which would enable Simpson's army to push on across Germany. However, the Germans had flooded the entire river valley, and the offensive had to be delayed two weeks until the waters subsided.[2]

While the Canadians were still bogged down facing a yet-unbroken German front, American combat engineers managed to span the Roer River with several pontoon bridges and larger treadway bridges, which would allow tanks, trucks and artillery to cross the river. By February 23, more than a thousand infantrymen crossed over to the east bank of the Roer, where the German troops were now retreating. Field Marshall von Rundstedt had urged an early withdrawal across the Rhine into the position between the natural defensive line of the Rhine River, but Hitler, true to form, refused to give in without a fight. As a result, the German troops, trapped between the Roer and the Rhine, were cut to pieces by the Allied advance. By February 25, the American troops were rolling toward the Rhine.

Between February 22 and March 10, a renewed British and Canadian offensive took place against heavy German mortar and artillery fire in the Hochwald, another heavily forested area, and where they continued the eastward march to the Rhine. On March 4, British and American forces met at Geldern on German soil. The following day units of the American 9th Army reached and cleared the west bank of the Rhine. Along the Maas River, Canadian and British forces engaged German pockets in villages where the latter were being forced to surrender. Though their resistance was virtually at an end, the Allied armies continued to encounter German opposition.

During the night of March 28/29, the Canadian Scottish Regiment experienced what they described as "probably the most vicious fighting of the battle for Emmerich," where on March 30, they faced a severe German counter-attack that was beaten back.³ The next day, Canadian engineers constructed a low-level pontoon bridge across the Rhine capable of carrying both infantry troops and tanks. Field Marshal Montgomery now ordered the Canadian Army to move steadily along the German coast on a northern front into Holland.⁴ By April 18, the Canadians had driven from Emmerich into Nijmegen, Arnhem and across northeastern Holland to the Zuider Zee. Two days later they reached the North Sea, bisecting the German 25th Army, trapping it against the sea near Amsterdam. At this point, Montgomery was fearful of a German threat to open the dikes and drown the Dutch populace if the Allied troops invaded the Grebbe Line, so he ordered the Canadians to hold up at Amersfoort.⁵ While the Canadians were making their way through the flooded land and swollen canals and streams of Holland, the full force of the Allied offensive was headed eastward into the heart of Germany.

By mid-April, General Omar Bradley's 12th Army Group was in the vanguard of three million Allied troops who reached the Elbe River and were only sixty miles from Berlin where they halted; in the southern sector the Germans were disintegrating in the face of General Jacob Devers' 6th Army Group.

Hitler had drastically reduced his remaining forces in the West, diverting the major part of them to the Eastern Front. Besides trying to hold the Elbe and the Oder River, they were also struggling to hold on to western Austria, the northwest corner of Yugoslavia, northern Italy, the western half of Czechoslovakia, all of Denmark and Norway and the Dodecanese Islands off the coast of Greece. Given the state of the German war economy and the food and material shortages in Germany and the occupied territories, these undertakings were an impossible task.

On April 16, the Russians broke out of their bridgeheads over the Oder and assumed the offensive against German armies that were collapsing. Within a week, they were in the suburbs of Berlin. By the 25th, the city was completely isolated by the Russian encircling armies. On April 27, Russian and American forces joined hands on the Elbe.⁶

Plans for Dutch Relief

The Combined Chiefs of Staff were acutely aware of the desperate situation in western Holland. On March 14, Eisenhower had been instructed to prepare a plan for the liberation as soon as practicable after the Rhine crossing was secured, introducing food supplies simultaneously with the arrival of the liberation forces.

Dutch Prime Minister Gerbrandy had pleaded with Eisenhower's Chief of Staff, Walter Bedell Smith, who made it clear that the Supreme Commander had no objections to providing assistance even if the Germans would profit from it, but that it was up to the governments involved to arrange how the supplies would be shipped to the Dutch.[7] Transport by both air and sea had been studied since late autumn; overland transport was not yet possible. By mid-December, of the many problems concerning Dutch relief, the chief concern was the uncertainty regarding German intentions: The enemy might continue to defend the western provinces, or carry out a complete evacuation, or leave immobile military units at certain locations. It would take at least three or four weeks to sweep mines out of the channel along the Dutch coast before relief supplies could be shipped to Holland from England.[8]

The Dutch Government had been in touch with neutral Sweden, who accepted the Dutch appeal for help as early as October 2, but the Germans refused to open the ports of Amsterdam or Rotterdam to ships providing relief. However, in mid-January an agreement was reached with the Germans in which the port of Delfzijl in the far northern province of Groningen could be used for shipment. On January 28, the first Swedish ships arrived with tons of flour, margarine and cod liver oil. However, because of delays by German authorities, it was not until February 15 that the shipments reached Amsterdam.[9] Early in March, another vessel operated by the International Red Cross delivered additional supplies.

By the end of March, a Red Cross delegate who had supervised the distribution of supplies reported:

> *The physical situation of the western provinces having reduced the inhabitants to a primitive state, they are obliged, in the struggle for existence, to engage in the black market, in usury and even in theft; men even eat flower bulbs. The bombed houses are pillaged and looted of all combustible material. The trees in the gardens are cut up by passers-by. The bread wagons in the cities can only circulate at 4:00 o'clock in the morning because if they go about in broad daylight crowds threaten to attack and plunder them.*[10]

On March 27, after further analysis, the Supreme Commander emphasized that operations west of Utrecht, where there were large concentrations of Dutch civilians, would involve heavy casualties from extensive bombing and shelling of towns and villages, as well as from starvation and flooding, and concluded that "the rapid completion of our main operation [defeat of Germany] may well be the quickest means of liberating the western Netherlands."[11]

On April 10, discussions in London prompted Prime Minister Churchill to write to President Roosevelt concerning Dutch relief. He told the president that the plight of the Dutch people was desperate; that between two and three million people were facing starvation. "I fear," he said, "we may soon be in the presence of a tragedy."[12] The prime minister believed that there was a need for immediate help and suggested proposing to the Germans through the Swiss government an arrangement whereby supplies from Sweden that were already being sent into Holland could be increased "by sea or direct from areas under military control of the Allies, subject to the necessary safe-conduct being arranged."[13]

While the Dutch relief proposal was being discussed among the Allied leaders, *Reichskommissar* Seyss-Inquart indicated a disposition to discuss measures for assistance, even though Berlin had told him to continue inundations and demolitions. On April 28, an unofficial meeting was held in the town of Achterveld where several British and German officers arranged a larger meeting. Full-scale discussions convened two days later in a schoolhouse on the outskirts of town. Chief among those present were Seyss-Inquart and his staff, Eisenhower's Chief of Staff, Bedell Smith, Montgomery's Chief of Staff, 21st Army Group, Major-General Francis de Guingand, Major-General Suslaparoff, representing the Russians, and Prince Bernhard, Commander-in-Chief of the Dutch Forces of the Interior.[14]

The *Reichskommissar* was prepared to agree to the importation of Allied supplies of food and coal into the western Netherlands if the Allies would halt their forces east of the Grebbe Line, i.e., the defensive waterline east of Utrecht. The Germans would continue to occupy the provinces of North and South Holland and Utrecht, but fighting would end and the people of those provinces would be fed.[15] The truce would be in effect a stalemate on the aforementioned front to which Seyss-Inquart would be willing to agree, provided this could be done without the knowledge of the German Government in Berlin. If the Allies would halt their advance, the Germans would cease executions, Gestapo interrogations, accord decent treatment to political prisoners and open the port of Rotterdam for the entry of supplies.

Although the American Chiefs of Staff doubted that the Germans would carry out further retaliatory measures against the Dutch civil populations, General Smith nevertheless stated to Seyss-Inquart in unequivocal terms that resisting the Allied effort to bring help to the people of Holland would mean the needless loss of Dutch civilian lives, which would make murderers out of him and those under his command, and which would subject them to trial for murder.

The *Reichskommissar* refused to agree to a formal surrender so long as the German authorities in Holland were in touch with their authorities in Berlin. Surrender would occur only when resistance was halted in Germany. The Allied governments authorized Eisenhower to negotiate a truce along these lines, provided this did not prejudice the principle of ultimate unconditional surrender of the German forces involved.[14]

Operation Manna

Henceforth, arrangements were made to provide food to the western Netherlands by air, sea, inland waterways and by road. Allied teams were to assist the Dutch medical services, and Seyss-Inquart agreed to stop further flooding, cease all repressive measures against the inhabitants and help to bring relief supplies.[15] Even before negotiations were completed, the British Air Ministry in consultation with S.H.A.E.F. ordered getting food to the starving population. The problem was met by the free dropping of food packages from Allied aircraft into the most densely populated part of the Netherlands, which included the three great cities of Amsterdam, Rotterdam and The Hague. The plan, designated "Operation Manna," was scheduled to begin on April 28, but because of bad weather the first flight was postponed until the following day, when 253 Lancaster bombers of the R.A.F. Bomber Command dropped over half a million rations close to Rotterdam, The Hague and Leiden. The U.S. Air Force joined the relief operations in "Operation Chowhound" on May 1.

To ensure greater accuracy of the drop and that the food parcels hit the ground undamaged, the planes flew at very low altitude over the Dutch countryside—500 feet or less—and at very slow speed. Seventeen-year-old Arie de Jong recalled in her diary:

> There are no words to describe the emotions experienced on that Sunday afternoon. More than 300 four-engine Lancasters, flying exceptionally low, suddenly filled the western horizon. One could see the gunners waving in their turrets. One Lancaster roared over the town at 70 feet. Everywhere we looked bombers could be seen. Everybody waved cloths and flags. What a feast! Everyone is excited with joy. The war must be over soon now.[16]

The Lancasters were accompanied by eight Mosquito bombers, which were responsible for marking the drop zones. Targets were marked by circles of green flares with red lights in the center to indicate the supplies were landing within the agreed drop zones, and red flares that they were straying into danger zones. The center of the drop zone was marked on the ground by a large white cross.

One Canadian pilot recalled, having flown by a windmill and people waving from their balcony, "You understand, we had to look up to wave back!" Sgt. Ken Wood, a rear gunner remembered, "People were everywhere—on the streets, on the roofs, leaning out of windows. They all had something to wave with; a handkerchief, a sheet—it was incredible." Another crew member wrote, "I will always remember seeing 'Thank you Tommy' written on one of the roofs, and recall those flights as a beautiful experience; it was as if we brought the liberation closer to reality." Relief continued in increasing amounts, and during a ten-day period that ended on May 8, over 3,100 sorties were flown by Bomber Command and an additional 2,200 by the American 8th Air Force. A total of more than eleven million British and American rations were dropped over Holland.[17] Due to the fact that most of the rations were originally intended for camps of Allied prisoners of war, they were packed in bulk, which caused some delay before they could be distributed as individual civilian rations.[18]

There were a few isolated incidents in which some of the Allied planes had been shot at by the Germans, but a telegram sent to Seyss-Inquart from the Allied High Command resulted in an immediate cease-fire. Otherwise, the agreement to stay away from the food supplies was kept. On the first day of the drop, the Germans encircled the dropping zones with both anti-aircraft guns and troops to determine whether any of the parcels contained arms. But on the following day both the guns and troops were nowhere to be seen.[19]

Amidst the excitement and jubilation caused by the air drops on that first day, rumors circulated that the Germans surrendered in Fortress Holland, i.e., Noord-Holland, Zuid-Holland and Utrecht, and that liberation by the Canadians was just a day away on April 30. The rumors, which were false, were anticipated by Radio Oranje, which announced that the help from the Allies was a separate operation and had nothing to do with surrender. Nevertheless, most all of the Dutch people were convinced that the end of the war was near and were ready to face the future with confidence.

The German Surrender and Liberation

That confidence was given reassurance on May 4, when negotiations were being conducted between Field Marshal Montgomery and representatives of Grand Admiral Karl Doentiz, who had assumed authority after Hitler shot himself on April 30. Negotiations involved the unconditional surrender of all remaining German forces in Northwestern Europe. All hostilities were to cease in Holland at 8:00 the following morning, Saturday, May 5, 1945, when General Johannes Blaskowitz surrendered all German forces in the Netherlands. Canadian

Holland Rejoices

Intelligence had estimated that there were still about 150,000 Germans in the western Netherlands; the actual strength on May 1 as supplied by the enemy was 117, 629 troops.[20] The terms of capitulation were accepted in quick succession by the German forces in southern Germany and Austria; at Rheims in the early hours of May 7, 1945, General Alfred Jodl surrendered all German forces to the Supreme Allied Commander, General Eisenhower, and all hostilities ceased on May 8. On the ninth, a second official surrender to the Russians was formally ratified in Berlin.[21]

Canadian forces liberated the remaining western Dutch territory still under German control on May 7–8. The route led through Amersfoort and Utrecht to Rotterdam. Throughout the cities, towns and villages, red, white and blue Dutch flags adorned the houses and orange streamers were flown everywhere. Radios blared the *Wilhelmus*, the national anthem, and the streets were lined with massive crowds ready to greet the liberating troops. The military convoy that entered the outskirts of Rotterdam soon became unrecognizable because of the shouting civilians who surrounded and climbed aboard the vehicles, shaking hands and hugging and kissing the soldiers as they made their way through the few miles of streets. The enthusiasm of the crowd seemed to have infected the German soldiers of the *Wehrmacht*; some of them, going in the opposite direction in wagons and on foot, waved and grinned.[22] This was the initial appearance one would receive upon entering the towns.

However, there was a different side of the liberation that showed the cheers, the bunting and festive celebrations as a façade, behind which an enormous amount of suffering was concealed. When Canadian Civil Affairs officers moved into the western provinces, they found numerous cases of starvation in houses; those who died from starvation were principally the very old, the very young and the very poor. A state of acute general starvation had only been avoided by a matter of two or three weeks. Conditions varied in the cities, but those living in Rotterdam were probably the worst. Later reports revealed that there were between 100,000 and 150,000 cases of starvation edema, with a death rate of ten percent in the more densely populated areas of western Holland. Food from the agricultural regions of the northeast was brought in to supplement the civilian rations.[23]

Although relief supplies had been coming into western Holland since May 2 by road, air and sea, there was scarcely any transport for their internal distribution, and it was not until May 10 that they began reaching the public in significant amounts. During the second half of May, arrangements for the relief of the inhabitants of Noord-Holland, Zuid-Holland and Utrecht began to work more smoothly. The planning and preparation that went into the relief was beginning to yield fruit.[24]

* * *

It has been estimated that between 120,000–150,000 persons were arrested in Holland on charges of collaboration with the enemy. In January 1945, the population of Holland was 9,220,000. Thus, roughly one out of every seventy Dutchmen was arrested. There were several reasons for these arrests. Many believed that they satisfied the sense of justice of the masses. Additionally, there was enough stored-up hatred by the population against suspected collaborators that mass arrests prevented mass lynchings. Others believed that the arrests were necessary to prevent sabotage and espionage against Allied military operations. This concern for security was no longer a factor after the German capitulation. When one considers the atmosphere in southern Holland in September 1944 and in the rest of the country after the liberation, when the details of what took place in the concentration camps and gas chambers were revealed to the people in Holland and other occupied countries, it is readily understandable that so many Dutch people associated collaborators with the brutalities of the Nazi occupiers.[25]

In May 1945, the Dutch public could distinguish only between black and white; between the "wrong" Dutchmen who had collaborated, and the majority, which had resisted. It was not possible to immediately comprehend certain extenuating circumstances, such as the spirit of defeatism in June 1940, and the partial acceptance by some people of the "New [Germanic] Europe;" internal divisions within the N.S.B.; various motives of the military volunteers; and differences between excusable and punishable collaboration by businessmen and civil servants.[26] During the liberation of Occupied Holland, all suspected pro-German elements in the liberated provinces were placed within one group and segregated in internment camps.

No one organization was more despised than the Dutch National Socialist Party (N.S.B.), which had come to symbolize collaboration and treason and whose members were hated even more than the Germans. In an adult population of approximately six million, membership in the party was comprised of some 50,000.[27] When the German soldiers were evacuated from Holland shortly after the capitulation, members of the N.S.B. were held to face their judges. All Dutch Nazis were potential informers whose disclosure to the German authorities could send ordinary citizens to a concentration camp or possible death for the most minor infractions. These included *anyone* who knew of a secret hiding

Holland Rejoices

place of a Jew or forced-labor evader; *anyone* caught reading an Underground newspaper; or *anyone* found having a radio or found listening to a B.B.C. broadcast.[28] Certainly the most contemptible member of the N.S.B. was its founder and leader, Anton Mussert. After the German capitulation, Mussert was arrested in The Hague on May 7, 1945. He was convicted of high treason after a two-day trial, and was sentenced to death. On May 7, 1946, he was executed by firing squad on the Waalsdorpervlakte, a site near The Hague where hundreds of Dutch citizens had been put to death by the Nazi regime.[29]

In September 1944, the Dutch Government issued a mandate that enumerated certain crimes of collaboration and treason. The following is a list of those offenses:

- Carrying arms for the enemy and spying, betraying persecuted persons to the enemy, and exploiting occupation circumstances to enrich oneself.
- Membership after February 1, 1941, in the Dutch National Socialist Party (N.S.B.), Dutch *Schutzstaffel* (SS), German Workers Party (N.S.D.A.P.), *Nationale Jeugdstorm* (N.S.B. Youth Organization).
- All volunteers for auxiliary police or paramilitary units.
- All Dutch officials in German organizations in the Netherlands.
- Those who held leading positions in pro-Nazi dailies or periodicals.
- Those seriously suspected of belonging to one of the previous categories.
- All those who because of their actions or sayings, might be expected to hamper the Allied war effort.

Milder restrictive measures were leveled against wives, fiancées or others who had close relationships with Germans or Dutchmen falling within the previous categories. Hatred against women who fraternized with the enemy was very intense; hence many of them were arrested for their own protection.[30]

In October 1945, a newer and more just policy concerning arrested collaborators was established. Pre-trial releases were granted to those who were simply innocent of any crime, those whose collaboration was so trivial that punishment was inapplicable, those who had served pre-trial internment lengthier than the prison term likely imposed by the court, and those who were in a physical or mental condition that justified release or had children whose interests justified it.[31]

It is somewhat paradoxical that the end of the war in Holland not only brought an end to the German Occupation and Dutch collaboration, it also brought an end to the unity that was engendered by the Occupation. For a time, the enormous task of rebuilding a devastated Holland held the disparate factions together, but beneath the surface the prewar political parties remained, along with their prewar political dissentions.

Queen Wilhelmina, who had been a rallying-point during the war, had hoped for a leadership position in the first post-war Parliament and a change in the Constitution in which the Cabinet members would be nominated, not elected. But her dreams of a new society were never realized. In May 1946, the first general election took place in which all prewar political parties except the National Socialist Party returned to Parliament. The country had been so accustomed to democracy with all its shortcomings that the return to a more autocratic system was no longer a consideration. The Queen reigned, but the country continued to be governed by the leaders of the pre-war political parties.

In September 1948, the beloved Queen Wilhelmina, after a successful reign of fifty years, abdicated in favor of her daughter, Queen Juliana, who succeeded to the throne. When the former Queen died in 1962, only one wreath was placed on her coffin; on its ribbon were the words "the united resistance movement of the Netherlands."

EPILOGUE

In these pages, I have tried to present to the reader some of the circumstances, events and characteristics of the Dutch Resistance. I should like to add a few final remarks by way of summary. To appreciate what took place in Holland between 1940 and 1945, the reader must be transported back to those difficult years and get below the surface of history to know what took place in the minds, hearts and emotions of the people involved.

To come to grips with the anxiety, fears, hopes and tribulations of those who endured those five long years, the experiences of individual resisters are required, for only they are able to elicit the empathy that will move the reader to that vicarious experience that leads to a better understanding of what were years of bitterness and sorrow, but also of courage and sacrifice. Those accounts that I have included in this book are but a few from the numerous participants who had some of the more active roles in the Resistance. I have also included the military phases of the Occupation, but as a student of the European Resistance, my main purpose was to undertake a closer survey of what the civilian population experienced who lived through that turbulent period.

The majority of Dutch men and women who lived through the Occupation were not active resisters, but simply ordinary citizens trying to cope with life as best they could in an extraordinary environment. Most of those who objected to the presence of the invading forces did so by making them feel unwelcome by low-profile behavior, such as walking out of a café when German soldiers entered, or by some small demoralizing gesture like giving wrong directions on the street; as a patriotic symbol of "keeping together," paper clips or safety pins were worn on outer garments. Some were brave and some were cowards, but most were neither. Yet many were forced to resist because of circumstances and events over which they had no control.

In a wartime population of more than nine million people, the number of both full-time and part-time resisters in the Netherlands was approximately 60,000. Approximately 5,000 belonged to Underground groups engaged in sabotage and some assassination activity; more than 25,000 men and women were involved in the illegal press as publishers, printers, distributors and couriers; additionally there were those who forged identity papers, ration cards and other Nazi documents, and those who had assisted escaped prisoners of war and Allied airmen who had either baled out or made forced landings in Holland; and another 30,000 people who provided aid and shelter to Jews, Dutch workers who escaped to evade the labor draft and others in hiding.

Additionally, the Underground was supported by a National Assistance Fund that was started during the first year of the Occupation, which sole purpose was to collect money needed to provide financial aid to the wives of Dutch sailors or merchantmen serving with the Allies, and which was later extended to include Resistance groups, and victims of German persecution, such as dependents of hostages and those who were arrested and those who were in hiding. A particularly noteworthy example of financial help were the weekly wages and even the Christmas bonuses that the 30,000 railroad workers received who had gone on strike in September 1944.

Of the 350,000 people known to have been in hiding during the last year of the Occupation, including the 35,000 Jews and remnants of the remaining British airborne troops after the defeat at Arnhem who were not captured, all were sheltered by thousands of Dutch families. Most of these families did not take an active part in the Resistance.

Of those men and women who did take part, the exact number of fatalities within the Resistance will never be known, but according to Dutch Professor Louis de Jong, the foremost authority on the Dutch Resistance, more than ten thousand were either shot by the Germans or died in concentration camps. And as in any war, countless other lives were adversely affected physically, mentally and emotionally by what they underwent on a day-to-day basis living under barbaric rule.

Many have questioned whether the incredible torture by the Gestapo or the fear of being caught and undergoing such treatment, which many surviving resisters endured and which resulted in severe post-war depression, or the ongoing ordeal of nightmares was really worth it; or whether the assassination of a high-ranking member of the German SS was worth the deaths of numerous innocent civilian hostages taken in reprisal. These are extremely difficult questions that were being asked during the Occupation.

To those who viewed the war in conventional military terms as a series of battleground engagements, and in which the Resistance played a very minor role, such questions were of little significance. But to those in Holland and elsewhere in Occupied Europe who dealt with those questions in moral terms—resisters, families and friends—they were issues of life and death. Chief among those issues was the fate of thousands of civilian lives who were saved by the fortitude, resilience and self-sacrifice exhibited by thousands of ordinary people. Perhaps the answer to the people of Holland and Occupied Europe was said best by the highly distinguished English historian, M.R.D. (Michael) Foot, who, in his distinguished work, *European Resistance to Nazism 1940–1945*, said:

> *If you who read this can say, I am not under fire; I am not under torture; I am not on the run; if I hear a noise at six in the morning, I know it is a neighbor or a milkman, not the secret police; no one in my country is arrested and held without prompt charge and trial; I can read newspapers, see and hear broadcasts of several different views; within the laws of libel, I can say what I like about anybody; then you owe it, in a larger degree than most historians have so far allowed, to the Resistance that Occupied Europe put up to Hitler. There is a Dutch saying worth recall: only dead fishes float down the stream, live ones swim against it.*

END NOTES

Chapter 1: The Innocent Years

1. Whitney R. Harris, *Tyranny on Trial: The Evidence at Nuremberg* (Dallas: Southern Methodist University Press, 1954), 139-40.
2. Fabian von Schlabrendorff, *The Secret War Against Hitler* (New York: Pitman Publishing Corporation, 1965), 24.
3. Herbert H. Rowen, *The Low Countries in Early Modern Times* (New York: Walker and Company, 1972), 85.
4. Werner Warmbrunn, *The Dutch Under German Occupation 1940-1945* (Stanford: Stanford University Press, 1963), 4.
5. Gerald Newton, *The Netherlands: An Historical and Cultural Survey 1795-1977* (London: Ernest Benn Limited, 1978), 54-57.
6. Robert den Boeft, "The Dutch Armed Forces in Exile," *Holland at War Against Hitler: Anglo-Dutch Relations 1940-1945*, ed. M.R.D. Foot (London: Frank Cass and Company Limited, 1990), 42.
7. Newton, *The Netherlands: An Historical and Cultural Survey 1795-1977*, 130.
8. Geert Mak, *Amsterdam* (Cambridge, Massachusetts: Harvard University Press, 1994), 247-48.
9. Henry L. Mason, *The Purge of Dutch Quislings* (The Hague: Martinus Nijhoff, 1952), 7.
10. In 1934, the N.S.B. was weakened significantly when the Netherlands government refused adherence to Mussert's party all civil servants, the military and the police forces. In the following year Mussert was dismissed from his position as engineer of the State's Waterways by the government who claimed that "his political views were incompatible with the dignity and patriotism required of any Civil Servant." L. de Jong, *The Lion Rampant* (New York: Querido, 1943), 130.
11. Mason, *The Purge of the Dutch Quislings*, 7.
12. Winston S. Churchill, *Their Finest Hour* (Boston: Houghton Mifflin Company, 1949), 34. The prewar Dutch Prime Minister must have had second thoughts about the seeming effectiveness of Dutch deterrence in the event of war, since in that same year the Colijn government

prepared a set of secret directives for the conduct of civil servants in the event of a military occupation. The directives assumed that the Occupying Power would respect the rules of the Hague Convention. Obviously, the author of the directive failed to anticipate the moral climate in the country dominated by a merciless Nazi enemy. Warmbrunn, *The Dutch Under German Occupation 1940-1945*, 121.
13. Newton, *The Netherlands: An Historical and Cultural Survey 1795-1977*, 123.
14. Boeft, "The Dutch Armed Forces in Exile," *Holland at War Against Hitler: Anglo-Dutch Relations 1940-1945*, 37.
15. Walter B. Maass, *The Netherlands at War: 1940-1945* (London: Abelard-Schuman, 1970), 16.
16. Boeft, "The Dutch Armed Forces in Exile," *Holland at War Against Hitler: Anglo-Dutch Relations 1940-1945*, 36-37.
17. *Ibid.*
18. Herman Friedhoff, *Requiem for the Resistance: The Civilian Struggle Against Nazism in Holland and Germany* (London: Bloomsbury Publishing Ltd., 1988), 1.
19. According to the distinguished British historian, Arnold J. Toynbee, history teaches that, once a nation wins wars or makes conquests by a particular ephemeral technique [Maginot Line], which may have been revolutionary in its formation, it ends by idolizing that technique and stubbornly adheres to it long after it has outworn its usefulness. F. Lee Bens, *Europe Since 1914 in its World Setting* (New York: Appleton-Century-Crofts, Inc., 1954), 318.

Chapter 2: The Winter of Deception

1. B.H. Liddell Hart, *History of the Second World War* (New York: G.P. Putnam's Sons, 1970), 33.
2. *Ibid.*, 21.
3. William L. Shirer, *The Rise and Fall of the Third Reich: A History of Nazi Germany* (New York: Simon and Schuster, 1960), 645.
4. Telford Taylor, *The March of Conquest: The German Victories in Western Europe, 1940* (New York: Simon and Schuster, 1958), 45.
5. Harris, *Tyranny on Trial: The Evidence at Nuremberg*, 141.
6. Hart, *History of the Second World War*, 35-36.
7. On May 23, 1939, in a military planning conference on the invasion of Poland, Hitler stated that "if England intends to intervene in the

Polish war, we must occupy Holland with lightening speed. We must aim at securing a new defense line on Dutch soil up to the Zuider Zee." Harris, *Tyranny on Trial: The Evidence at Nuremberg*, 140.

8. Newton, *The Netherlands: An Historical and Cultural Survey 1795-1977*, 134.
9. M.R.D. Foot, "Introduction," *Holland at War Against Hitler: Anglo-Dutch Relations 1940-1945*, xvi.
10. Shirer, *The Rise and Fall of the Third Reich: A History of Nazi Germany*, 653-54.
11. *Ibid.*
12. Harris, *Tyranny on Trial: The Evidence at Nuremberg*, 142.
13. M.R.D. Foot, "Introduction," *Holland at War Against Hitler: Anglo-Dutch Relations 1940-1945*, 38.
14. Warmbrunn, *The Dutch Under German Occupation 1940-1945*, 6.
15. Boeft, "The Dutch Armed Forces in Exile," *Holland at War Against Hitler: Anglo-Dutch Relations 1940-1945*, 39.
16. *The Historical Encyclopedia of World War Two*, ed. Marcel Baudot, Henri Bernard, Hendrik Brugmans, Michael R.D. Foot, and Hans-Adolf Jacobsen, trans. Jesse Dilson (New York: MJF Books, 1989), 163.
17. Paul Leverkuehn, "Battle in the West: To Dunkirk," *The Taste of Courage: The War, 1939-1945*, ed. Desmond Flower and James Reeves (New York: Harper & Brothers Publishers, 1960), 49.
18. Shirer, *The Rise and Fall of the Third Reich: A History of Nazi Germany*, 715.
19. von Schlabrendorff, *The Secret War Against Hitler*, 113.
20. *Ibid.*
21. Hart, *History of the Second World War*, 37.
22. Taylor, *The March of Conquest: The German Victories in Western Europe, 1940*, 155-180. See also Shirer, *The Rise and Fall of the Third Reich: A History of Nazi Germany*, 717-18.
23. *Ibid.*
24. *Ibid.*, 715-16.

Chapter 3: The Five Day War

1. Hart, *History of the Second World War*, 67. See also John Terraine, *The Right of the Line: The Royal Air Force in the European War 1939-1945* (Hertfordshire: Wordsworth Editions Limited, 1997), 124.
2. Taylor, *The March of Conquest: The German Victories in Western Europe, 1940*, 190.
3. Maass, *The Netherlands at War 1940-1945*, 31.
4. *Ibid.*
5. *Ibid.*, 32.
6. Terraine, *The Right of the Line: The Royal Air Force in the European War, 1939-1945*, 124.
7. Friedhoff, *Requiem for the Resistance: The Civilian Struggle Against Nazism in Holland and Germany*, 23.
8. Maass, *The Netherlands at War, 1940-1945*, 33.
9. *Ibid.*
10. Terraine, *The Right of the Line: The Royal Air Force in the European War, 1939-1945*, 126.
11. *Ibid.*
12. Taylor, *The March of Conquest: The German Victories in Western Europe, 1940*, 194. The Grebbe-Peel Line was a main Dutch defense position that extended from the south shore of the Zuider Zee, a huge bay that opens into the North Sea near Amersfoort, south and slightly east to the Belgian frontier. North of the Rhine the natural defenses of the line were augmented by extensive field fortifications with armored enclosures, bunkers and antitank obstacles.
13. *Ibid.*
14. *Ibid.*, 195.
15. Leverkuehn, "Battle in the West: to Dunkirk," *The Taste of Courage: The War, 1939-1945*, 49.
16. *Ibid.*, 50.
17. *Ibid.*
18. Maass, *The Netherlands at War: 1940-1945*, 35-36.
19. Taylor, *The March of Conquest: The German Victories in Western Europe, 1940*, 199.
20. *Ibid.*, 200.
21. Shirer, *The Rise and Fall of the Third Reich: A History of Nazi Germany*, 722.

22. Maass, *The Netherlands at War: 1940-1945*, 39.
23. *Ibid.*, 40.
24. Warmbrunn, *The Dutch Under German Occupation 1940-1945*, 9.
25. Shirer, *The Rise and Fall of the Third Reich: A History of Nazi Germany*, 722-723.
26. Warmbrunn, *The Dutch Under German Occupation 1940-1945*, 10.
27. Taylor, *The March of Conquest: The German Victories in Western Europe, 1940*, 202.
28. Warmbrunn, *The Dutch Under German Occupation 1940-1945*, 10.
29. Shirer, *The Rise and Fall of the Third Reich: A History of Nazi Germany*, 722.
30. Henry H. Adams, *Years of Deadly Peril: The Coming of the War 1939-1941* (New York: David McKay Company, Inc., 1969), 107.
31. Maass, *The Netherlands at War:1940-1945*, 42.
32. Allard Martens, *The Silent War: Glimpses of the Dutch Underground* (London: Hodder and Stoughton, 1961), 307.
33. F.J. Goedhart, *Nieuwsbrief van Pieter 't Hoen*. Translated by Joeri Hedwig Teeuwisse. Amsterdam: Historisch Adviesabureau 30-45, 2007.

Chapter 4: The Darkening of Occupation

1. Leesha Rose, *The Tulips Are Red* (New York: A.S. Barnes and Company, 1978), 16.
2. Louis de Jong, *The Lion Rampant: The Story of Holland's Resistance to the Nazis*, translated from the Dutch by Joseph W.F. Stoppelman (New York: Querido, 1943), 5, 25.
3. *Ibid.*, 5.
4. *Ibid.*, 6.
5. *Ibid.*, 8-9.
6. Warmbrunn, *The Dutch Under German Occupation 1940-1945*, 27.
7. "Within the German administration in the occupied territory two divergent tendencies became increasingly pronounced. The High Commissioner and his associates, while publicly asserting that the Netherlands would remain independent, hoped to postpone the entire issue until the end of the war. On the other hand, the German S.S. propagated the view of the race scholars that the Dutch were a Germanic people and therefore should become members of the Reich

at once.... Hitler consistently evaded the issue. ...Hitler, if victorious, probably would have annexed the Netherlands unless unforeseen political conditions had made annexation unprofitable." *Ibid.*, 25-27.
8. *Ibid.*, 24.
9. Friedhoff, *Requiem for the Resistance: The Civilian Struggle Against Nazism in Holland and Germany*, 66.
10. Warmbrunn, *The Dutch Under German Occupation 1940-1945*, 85.
11. Friedhoff, *Requiem for the Resistance: The Civilian Struggle Against Nazism in Holland and Germany*, 66.
12. Diet Eman with James Schaap, *Things We Couldn't Say* (Grand Rapids: William B. Eerdmans Publishing Co., 1994), 38-39.
13. de Jong, *The Lion Rampant: The Story of Holland's Resistance to the Nazis*, 28.
14. Louis de Jong, *The Netherlands and Nazi Germany* (Cambridge, Massachusetts: Harvard University Press, 1990), 34.
15. Werner Rings, *Life With the Enemy* (Garden City, New York: Doubleday and Company, Inc., 1982), 157.
16. Louis de Jong, "The Dutch Government in Exile," *Holland at War Against Hitler: Anglo-Dutch Relations 1940-1945*, ed. M.R.D. Foot (London: Frank Cass and Company Limited, 1990), 7.
17. Warmbrunn, *The Dutch Under German Occupation 1940-1945*, 134.
18. *Ibid.*
19. *Ibid.*, 44.
20. *Ibid.*
21. *Ibid.*, 135.

Chapter 5: The Plight of the Dutch Jews
1. Warmbrunn, *The Dutch Under German Occupation 1940-1945*, 165.
2. Maass, *The Netherlands at War: 1940-1945*, 111-112.
3. de Jong, *The Lion Rampant: The Story of Holland's Resistance to the Nazis*, 212.
4. *Ibid.*, 213.
5. Erik Hazelhoff, *Soldier of Orange* (Hastings on Hudson: The Holland Heritage Society, 1980), 60.
6. Rose, *The Tulips Are Red*, 29.
7. *Ibid.*, 33-34.

8. de Jong, *The Lion Rampant: The Story of Holland's Resistance to the Nazis*, 218.
9. *Ibid.*
10. Maass, *The Netherlands at War:1940-1945*, 65.
11. Warmbrunn, *The Dutch Under German Occupation 1940-1945*, 108.
12. Maass, *The Netherlands at War: 1940-1945*, 66.
13. Harry Paape, "How Dutch Resistance Was Organized," *Holland at War Against Hitler: Anglo-Dutch Relations 1940-1945*, ed. M.R.D. Foot (London: Frank Cass and Company Limited, 1990), 77.
14. Warmbrunn, *The Dutch Under German Occupation 1940-1945*, 110. See also Jorgen Haestrup, *Europe Ablaze: An Analysis of the History of the European Resistance Movements 1939-1945* (Odense: Odense University Press, 1978), 103.
15. *Ibid.*, 64-65.
16. de Jong, *The Lion Rampant: The Story of Holland's Resistance to the Nazis*, 217.
17. *Ibid.*, 218.
18. *Ibid.*, 221.
19. *Ibid.*
20. *Ibid.*
21. *Ibid.*, 223.
22. Shirer, *The Rise and Fall of the Third Reich: A History of Nazi Germany*, 965-66.
23. de Jong, *The Lion Rampant, The Story of Holland's Resistance to the Nazis*, 224.
24. Maass, *The Netherlands at War: 1940-1945*, 120.
25. de Jong, *The Lion Rampant*, 231.
26. Rose, *The Tulips Are Red*, 80.
27. de Jong, *The Lion Rampant*, 227.

Chapter 6: The Dutch Samaritans

1. Dr. Lawrence Baron, *The Dynamics of Decency: Dutch Rescuers of Jews During the Holocaust* (Canton: St. Lawrence University, 1985), 3.
2. *Ibid.*
3. *Ibid*
4. *Ibid.*, 4.

5. "Estimates remain problematic based as they are either on deducting the number of those deported from the 1941 census of the Jewish community, or on the number of the surviving Jews identified by Dutch authorities at the end of the war." Bob Moore, *Victims and Survivors: The Nazi Persecution of the Jews in the Netherlands 1940-1945* (London: Arnold, 1997), 146.
6. Bert Jan Flim, "Opportunities for Dutch Jews to Hide from the Nazis, 1942-1945," *Dutch Jews as Perceived by Themselves and by Others: Proceedings of Eighth International Symposium on the History of the Jews in the Netherlands*, ed. Chaya Brasz and Yosef Kaplan (Boston: Brill, 2001), 291.
7. Moore, *Victims and Survivors: The Nazi Persecution of the Jews in the Netherlands 1940-1945*, 151-52.
8. *Ibid.*, 156.
9. *Ibid.*, 158.
10. *Ibid.*, 150.
11. Ruud van der Rol and Rian Verhoeven, *Anne Frank* (Kampen, the Netherlands LRV-info, 1992), 37, 41.
12. Gay Block and Malka Drucker, *Rescuers: Portraits of Moral Courage in the Holocaust* (New York: Holmes & Meier Publishers, Inc., 1992), 5.
13. Andre Stein, *Quiet Heroes: True Stories of the Rescue of Jews by Christians in Nazi-Occupied Holland* (New York: New York University Press, 1988), 19-20.
14. Block and Drucker, *Rescuers: Portraits of Moral Courage in the Holocaust*, 34, 36.
15. *Ibid.*, 27.
16. Baron, *The Dynamics of Decency: Dutch Rescuers of Jews in the Holocaust*, 11.
17. Block and Drucker, *Rescuers: Portraits of Moral Courage in the Holocaust*, 81.
18. *Ibid.*, 62-63.
19. *Ibid.*, 66.
20. *Ibid.*, 12, 14.

Chapter 7: The Christian Church Reaction

1. Richard S. Fuegner, *Beneath the Tyrant's Yoke: Norwegian Resistance to the German Occupation of Norway 1940-1945* (Edina: Beaver's Pond Press, 2002), 68.
2. Friedhoff, *Requiem for the Resistance: The Civilian Struggle Against Nazism in Holland and Germany*, 38, 40.
3. "During the twenties, Berlin had been a splendidly cosmopolitan city, but she has never been *the* city that meant to all Germans what Paris meant to all Frenchmen, or London to all Englishmen. Saxons would rather go to Prague, Rhinelanders to Paris, Bavarians to Rome." Gudrun Tempel, *The Germans: An Indictment of My People* trans. from the German by Sophie Wilkins (New York: Random House, 1963), 7-8.
4. "Once the people feel helpless to solve their own problems, anyone who comes along with a plausible panacea can pick up the reins with his left hand. It was not Hitler's personality that appealed to Germans, but the simplicity of his proffered solutions to our problems, after years of bewilderment and frustration." *Ibid.*
5. J.H. Boas, *Religious Resistance in Holland* (Great Britain: The Netherlands Government Information Bureau, 1945), 7.
6. Warmbrunn, *The Dutch Under German Occupation 1940-1945*, 156-57.
7. Boas, *Religious Resistance in Holland*, 7.
8. Shirer, *The Rise and Fall of the Third Reich: A History of Nazi Germany*, 235.
9. Boas, *Religious Resistance in Holland*, 17.
10. *Ibid.*, 8.
11. *Ibid.*, 17.
12. *Ibid.*
13. *Ibid.*
14. *Ibid.*, 21-22.
15. J.H. Boas, *Resistance of the Churches in the Netherlands* (Great Britain: The Netherlands Information Bureau, 1944), 72-74.
16. de Jong, *The Lion Rampant: The Story of Holland's Resistance to the Nazis*, 194.
17. *Ibid.*
18. Warmbrunn, *The Dutch Under German Occupation 1940-1945*, 163.

19. de Jong, *The Lion Rampant: The Story of Holland's Resistance to the Nazis*, 205.
20. *Ibid.*, 265.
21. *Ibid.*, 205.
22. Boas, *Religious Resistance in Holland*, 26-27.
23. *Ibid.*, 27.
24. de Jong, *The Lion Rampant: The Story of Holland's Resistance to the Nazis*, 206.
25. *Ibid.*, 169. Though the Nazi party, according to N.S.B. leader Mussert's own statement, counted approximately 100,000 members with 30,000 men between the ages of 18 and 40, the total number serving the German war effort in any military capacity did not exceed 10,000 men. 185.
26. Paape, "How Dutch Resistance Was Organized," *Holland at War Against Hitler: Anglo-Dutch Relations 1940-1945*, 86-87. See also *Catholics Remember the Holocaust* (Washington: D.C. National Council of Catholic Bishops, 1998), 22.
27. Boas, *Religious Resistance in Holland*, 47.
28. Maass, *The Netherlands at War: 1940-1945*, 83-84.
29. de Jong, *The Lion Rampant: The Story of Holland's Resistance to the Nazis*, 207.
30. Boas, *Religious Resistance in Holland*, 54-55.
31. *Ibid.*
32. William C. Brennan, Ph.D, *The Abortion Holocaust: Today's Final Solution* (St. Louis: Landmark Press, 1983), 192.
33. Leo Alexander, M.D., "Medical Science Under Dictatorship," *New England Journal of Medicine*, Vol. 241 (July 14, 1949), 39-47.
34. Boas, *Religious Resistance in Holland*, 55.
35. Warmbrunn, *The Dutch Under German Occupation 1940-1945*, 162.
36. Boas, *Religious Resistance in Holland*, 61.
37. Warmbrunn, *The Dutch Under German Occupation 1940-1945*, 163-64.

Chapter 8: The Conscience of the Nation

1. In Poland about 1400 newspaper titles were registered; in France about the same number as in Holland. Haestrup, *Europe Ablaze: An Analysis of the History of the European Resistance Movements 1939-1945*, 224.

2. Friedhoff, *Requiem for the Resistance: The Civilian Struggle Against Nazism in Holland and Germany*, 110-11.
3. *Ibid.*
4. Warmbrunn, *The Dutch Under German Occupation 1940-1945*, 223.
5. *Ibid.*, 222.
6. *Ibid.*, 221.
7. R.A.H. Voss, "The Dutch Press Under the German Occupation 1940-1945," *Too Mighty to be Free: Censorship and the Press in Britain and the Netherlands*, ed. A.C. Duke and C.A. Tamse (Zutphen: De Walburg Pers, 1988), 179-80.
8. *Ibid.*
9. *Ibid.*, 185.
10. *Ibid.*, 182.
11. *Ibid.*, 193.
12. Harry Stone, *Writing in the Shadow: Resistance Publications in Occupied Europe* (London: Frank Cass & Co. Ltd., 1996), 10.
13. Anna E.C. Simoni, "Dutch Clandestine Printing, 1940-1945" Transactions of The Bibliographic Society. *The Library* 5 Series, Vol. 27, Issue 1 (Oxford University Press, March 1972), 3.
14. Stone, *Writing in the Shadow: Resistance Publications in Occupied Europe*, 25.
15. *Ibid.*, 19.
16. Bernard Ijzerdraat, *Geuzenactie Bericht No. 2*, translated by Joeri Hedwig Teeuwisse. (Amsterdam: Historisch Adviesbureau 30-45, 2007).
17. Bernard Ijzerdraat, *Geuzenactie Bericht No. 5*, translated by Joeri Hedwig Teeuwisse. (Amsterdam: Historisch Adviesbureau 30-45, 2007).
18. Warmbrunn, *The Dutch Under German Occupation 1940-1945*, 225.
19. Madelon de Keizer, *Het Parool 1940-1945: Verzetsblad in Oorlogstijd*, http://www.hetillegaleparool.nl/summary.html, 1-2.
20. *Nieuwsbrief van Pieter 't Hoen*, translated by Joeri Hedwig Teeuwisse. (Amsterdam: Historisch Adviesbureau 30-45, 2007).
21. Friedhoff, *Requiem for the Resistance: The Civilian Struggle Against Nazism in Holland and Germany*, 116.
22. Warmbrunn, *The Dutch Under German Occupation 1940-1945*, 230. See also Friedhoff, *Requiem for the Resistance: The Civilian Struggle Against Nazism in Holland and Germany*, 110-12.
23. de Keizer, *Het Parool 1940-1945: Verzetsblad in Oorlogstijd*, 3.

24. Stone, *Writing in the Shadow: Resistance Publications in Occupied Europe*, 173.
25. *Ibid.*, 84.
26. *Ibid.*, 88.
27. Warmbrunn, *The Dutch Under German Occupation 1940-1945*, 233.
28. J. Heyn, *Holland Hails You* (Wormerveer: Meijer's Boek-en Handelsdrukkerij, 1945), 13.
29. Stone, *Writing in the Shadow: Resistance Publications in Occupied Europe*, 106-07.
30. *Ibid.*, 90.
31. *Ibid.*, 124-25.
32. *Ibid.*, 126.
33. *Ibid.*
34. Warmbrunn, *The Dutch Under German Occupation 1940-1945*, 231.
35. *Ibid.*, 233-34.
36. Perry, "The Secret Voice: Clandestine Fine Printing in the Netherlands, 1940-1945," *The Holocaust and the Book: Destruction and Preservation*, 115.

Chapter 9: Resistance Initiatives

1. Haestrup, *Europe Ablaze*, 164. See also de Jong, *The Netherlands and Nazi Germany*, 31.
2. Paape, "How Dutch Resistance Was Organized," *Holland at War Against Hitler: Anglo-Dutch Relations 1940-1945*, 71.
3. *Ibid.*, 72.
4. *Biografie Bernard IJzerdraat*. http://oranjehotel.nationaalarchief.nlgevangenen/onderzoeksvoorbeelden/ijzerdraat.asp?
5. *Ibid.*
6. Simoni, "Dutch Clandestine Printing, 1940-1945," *Transactions of the Biblio-Graphical Society. The Library*, 10.
7. Eman with Schaap, *Things We Couldn't Say*, 391-92.
8. Sigrid Pohl Perry, "The Second Voice: Clandestine Fine Printing in the Netherlands, 1940-1945," *The Holocaust and the Book. Destruction and Preservation* (Amherst: University of Massachusetts Press, 2001), 109-11.
9. Hazelhoff, *Soldier of Orange*, 30-31.

10. Louis de Jong, director of the Netherlands State Institute of War Documentation editor, *Britain and Dutch Resistance* (Unpublished report) as cited in E.H. Cookridge, *Set Europe Ablaze* (New York: Thomas Y. Crowell Company, 1967), 248.
11. Hazelhoff, *Soldier of Orange*, 62-64.
12. Haestrup, *Europe Ablaze*, 165.
13. Cookridge, *Set Europe Ablaze*, 255.
14. *Ibid.*, 256.
15. Hazelhoff, *Soldier of Orange*, 92.
16. Haestrup, *Europe Ablaze*, 166.
17. M.R.D. Foot, *SOE in the Low Countries* (London: St. Ermin's Press, 2001), 79. The refusal of British intelligence to provide information to the Dutch intelligence community concerning their activities, despite their common goal, the liberation of Holland, was not unique to the Netherlands. A similar situation existed in Norway where friction and misunderstanding occurred between the British S.O.E. and the Norwegian Military Resistance, Milorg, principally over the latter's careless neglect of certain security measures which led to Nazi infiltration followed by a number of arrests. For a more in-depth study see this author's work, Fuegner, *Beneath the Tyrant's Yoke: Norwegian Resistance to the German Occupation of Norway* (Edina: Beaver's Pond Press, 2003) 141-45.
18. Hazelhoff, *Soldier of Orange*, 120.
19. Cookridge, *Set Europe Ablaze*, 257.
20. *Ibid.*, 259.
21. *Ibid.*, 256.
22. Hazelhoff, *Soldier of Orange*, 120.
23. *Ibid.*, 146.
24. Cookridge, *Set Europe Ablaze*, 260-61.
25. *Ibid.*
26. Hazelhoff, *Soldier of Orange*, 156-57.
27. Cookridge, *Set Europe Ablaze*, 257.
28. Allan Mayer, *Gaston's War: The True Story of a Hero of the Resistance in World War II* (Novato: Presidio Press, 1988), 123ff.
29. *Ibid.*, 130.
30. *Ibid.*, 125.
31. *Ibid.*, 184ff.

32. *Ibid.*
33. Haestrup, *Europe Ablaze*, 166-67. "In the summer of 1945 Gaston received an anonymous telephone call warning him to drop his inquiries. It was about this time that all of S.O.E.'s files having to do with WIM just happened to be destroyed in a mysterious fire that swept through the organization's London headquarters." The author goes on to state that "it is possible that the answer to what really happened lies in a dust-covered folder hidden among the British government's secret war archives. Unfortunately, those archives are sealed and will remain so until the year 2040." Mayer, *Gaston's War*, 195-96.

Chapter 10: A Dutch Calamity

1. Foot, *SOE in the Low Countries*, 131.
2. *Ibid.*, 133.
3. H.J. Giskes, *London Calling North Pole* (New York: The British Book Centre, Inc., 1953), 49.
4. *Ibid.* "The term *Englandspiel* – the game against England – is still in common use in Holland, where the idea that the German and the English secret services were playing a game, in which they used live Dutchmen as counters without much caring what happened to them." Foot, *SOE in the Low Countries*, 112.
5. *Ibid.*, 112-13.
6. H.J. Giskes, *London Calling North Pole*, 76.
7. Philippe Ganier-Raymond, *The Tangled Web* (New York: Pantheon Books, 1968), 34-37.
8. *Ibid.*, 43-44.
9. Taconis refused to become involved in Operation *NorthPole*. After having attacked an SS guard while in prison he was given the usual Gestapo treatment and kept in chains for many months. In November 1944, he was executed at the Mauthausen concentration camp. Cookridge, *Set Europe Ablaze*, 269.
10. Leo Marks, *Between Silk and Cyanide: A Codemaker's War 1941-1945* (New York: The Free Press, 1998), 98-99.
11. Ganier-Raymond, *The Tangled Web*, 51.
12. *Ibid.*, 59-60.
13. Giskes, *London Calling North Pole*, 83-87.
14. Foot, *SOE in the Low Countries*, 121.

End Notes

15. Cookridge, *Set Europe Ablaze*, 270. See also Marks, *Between Silk and Cyanide: A Codemaker's War 1941-1945*, 117-18.
16. Foot, *SOE in the Low Countries*, 123-24.
17. *Ibid.*
18. *Ibid.*, 125.
19. Marks, *Between Silk and Cyanide: A Codemaker's War 1941-1945*, 119.
20. Ibid., 120.
21. *Ibid.*
22. *Ibid.*
23. *Ibid.*
24. Giskes, *London Calling North Pole*, 105-06.
25. Foot, *SOE in the Low Countries*, 135.
26. Ganier-Raymond, *The Tangled Web*, 101.
27. Marks, *Between Silk and Cyanide: A Codemaker's War 1941-1945*, 121.
28. *Ibid.*
29. Giskes, *London Calling North Pole*, 117.
30. *Ibid.*, 121.
31. *Ibid.*, 118.
32. Professor M.R.D. Foot, "The Englandspiel" *Holland at War Against Hitler: Anglo-Dutch Relations 1940-1945*, ed. M.R.D. Foot (London: Frank Cass Company Limited, 1990), 127.
33. As cited in Cookridge, *Set Europe Ablaze*, 282-83.
34. Giskes, *London Calling North Pole*, 108.
35. Marks, *Between Silk and Cyanide: A Codemaker's War 1941-1945*, 122.
36. Giskes, *London Calling North Pole*, 106.
37. The Lysander was a single-engine high wing monoplane modified to serve as an air taxi service that landed and picked up agents in France on small fields that served as landing grounds. In Holland all agents as well as containers and packages were dropped by parachute. Heavy concentrations of German anti-aircraft artillery and large numbers of German night fighters stationed on Dutch airfields ruled out the use of British aircraft making landings on secret airfields in the Netherlands.
38. Cookridge, *Set Europe Ablaze*, 287.
39. *Ibid.*, 289-90.
40. Foot, *SOE in the Low Countries*, 130.

41. David Stafford, *Secret Agent: The True Story of the Covert War Against Hitler* (Woodstock: The Overlook Press, 2001), 150-51.
42. Russell Miller, *Behind Enemy Lines: The Oral History of Special Operations in World War II* (New York: St. Martin's Press, 2002), 138.
43. *Ibid.*, 136.
44. *Ibid.*, 139.
45. Marks, *Between Silk and Cyanide: A Codemaker's War 1941-1945*, 98.
46. *Ibid.*, 99.
47. *Ibid.*, 99-101.
48. *Ibid.*, 124.
49. *Ibid.*, 204-05.
50. *Ibid.*, 228.
51. *Ibid.*, 352-53.
52. *Ibid.*, 348.
53. Giskes, *London Calling North Pole*, 124.
54. *Ibid.*, 126.
55. Foot, *SOE in the Low Countries*, 186-87.
56. *Ibid.*, 194-95.
57. Giskes, *London Calling North Pole*, 135.
58. Cookridge, *Set Europe Ablaze*, 308.
59. Giskes, *London Calling North Pole*, 136.
60. Marks, "Englandspiel" *Holland at War Against Hitler: Anglo-Dutch Relations 1940-1945*, ed. M.R.D. Foot (London: Frank Cass Company Limited, 1990), 134.
61. Marks, *Between Silk and Cyanide: A Codemaker's War 1941-1945*, 101.
62. *Ibid.*
63. Leen Pot, "The Englandspiel" *Holland at War Against Hitler: Anglo-Dutch Relations 1940-1945*, ed. M.R.D. Foot (London: Frank Cass Company Limited, 1990), 142.
64. Patrick Howarth, *Undercover: The Men and Women of the S.O.E.* (London: Phoenix Press, 1980), 226.
65. Cookridge, *Set Europe Ablaze*, 309.
66. *Ibid.*
67. *Ibid.*
68. Ganier-Raymond, *The Tangled Web*, 191.

69. *Ibid.*, 192.
70. *Ibid.*, 190-91.
71. *Ibid.*, 192.
72. Marks, "Englandspiel" *Holland at War Against Hitler: Anglo-Dutch Relations 1940-1945*, 133.
73. Giskes, *London Calling North Pole*, 185.
74. Foot, "Englandspiel" *Holland at War Against Hitler: Anglo-Dutch Relations 1940-1945*, 127.
75. Giskes, *London Calling North Pole*, 200.

Chapter II: A Spirit of Defiance

1. "The eclipse of the German Navy and the inability of its U-boats to hinder the build-up of the Allied invasion forces in Britain made it more important that Hitler should quickly complete his preparations for the bombardment of the invasion base, and especially London with the flying-bomb (V.1) and the rocket (V.2). In July 1943, he ordered his Minister of Armaments and War Production, Albert Speer, to begin production of flying-bombs." Wilmot, *The Struggle for Europe*, 152-53.
2. Maass, *The Netherlands at War: 1940-1945*, 152-53. See also Wilmot, *The Struggle for Europe*, 170.
3. Elizabeth-AnneWheal, Stephen Pope & James Taylor, *Encyclopedia of the Second World War* (Secaucus: Castle Books, 1989), 450.
4. Warmbrunn, *The Dutch Under German Occupation: 1940-1945*, 113.
5. *Ibid.*, 114.
6. Paape, "How Dutch Resistance Was Organized," *Holland at War Against Hitler: Anglo-Dutch Relations 1940-1945*, 81.
7. Warmbrunn, *The Dutch Under German Occupation: 1940-1945*, 117-18.
8. Haestrup, *Europe Ablaze*, 105.
9. Warmbrunn, *The Dutch Under German Occupation: 1940-1945*, 187-88.
10. John Winthrop Hackett, *I Was a Stranger* (Boston: Houghton Mifflin Company, 1978), 76.
11. Interview with Gerda Leland, the daughter of James de Wit, February 20, 2007.
12. De Jong, "Anti-Nazi Resistance in the Netherlands," *European Resistance Movements 1939-1945: Proceedings of the Second International Conference on the History of the Resistance Movements*, 146.
13. Warmbrunn, *The Dutch Under German Occupation: 1940-1945*, 199-200.

14. H. Van Remmerden, *In the Shadow of the Swastika* (Boise: Lithocraft, Inc., 1996), 43-44.
15. Resistance Work: Hannie Schaft. http://en.wikipedia.org/wikiHannie_Schaft.
16. Warmbrunn, *The Dutch Under German Occupation: 1940-1945*, 196-97.
17. Van Remmerden, *In the Shadow of the Swastika*, 21-23.
18. Warmbrunn, *The Dutch Under German Occupation: 1940-1945*, 58-59.
19. *Ibid.*, 207-08.
20. *Ibid.*, 58.
21. *Ibid.*, 32, 60.
22. Stewart Bentley, "Of Market Garden and Melanie: The Dutch Resistance and the OSS," *Studies in Intelligence* (Washington, D.C.: Center for the Study of Intelligence, Spring 1998), 105-118.
23. Dutch Photographers: Emmy Andriesse. http://en.wikipeida.org/wike/Emmy_Andriesse.
24. *Ibid.*
25. *Ibid.*
26. De Jong, *Anti-Nazi Resistance in the Netherlands*, 138.
27. Dc Jong, *The Netherlands and Nazi Germany*, 47-48.
28. Block and Drucker, *Rescuers: Portraits of Moral Courage in the Holocaust*, 19.

Chapter 12: Brotherhood of Strangers

1. Liddell Hart, *History of the Second World War*, 599.
2. Army Air Forces *Official Training Film, TF 1-3384*, War Department 1944. According to British political journalist John Grigg, with so many targets to choose from it may not have been possible to be sure of which ones were, in fact, vital. However, "the Americans did come close to succeeding at Schweinfurt, and might have totally destroyed the target if their bombers had been able to fly the whole distance there and back with fighter protection, instead of losing it about half-way out." John Grigg, *1943: The Victory That Never Was* (New York: Hill and Wang, 1980), 134.
3. It was not until the late fall of 1943 that the Americans decided to mass-produce the P-51 Mustang that was as maneuverable as any fighter the *Luftwaffe* put in the air. It could escort bombers up to 600 miles from its bases as compared to the P-47 Thunderbolt whose limited range capac-

ity was only 375 miles. In view of the heavy losses sustained earlier by the bombers, it seems odd that the decision to produce the Mustang was not made earlier. *Ibid.*, 135.
4. *Signal* was a German pictorial propaganda publication published in all of the occupied countries of Europe.
5. Airey Neave, *Saturday at MI 9* (London: Grafton Books, 1989), 18.
6. *Ibid.*, 21.
7. *Ibid.*, 24.
8. By virtue of the armistice terms, France was three-fifths occupied by the Germans; the remainder known as Vichy was the unoccupied or "free zone," whose government maintained a policy of collaboration with Germany. After the Allied invasion of North Africa in November 1942, the Germans extended its occupation to Vichy.
9. Airey Neave, *Saturday at MI 9*, 97-100.
10. *Ibid.*, 60.
11. M.R.D. Foot and J.M. Langley, *MI 9 Escape and Evasion: 1939-1945* (Boston: Little Brown and Company, 1979), 67.
12. *Ibid.*, 132.
13. *Ibid.*
14. *Ibid.*, 134-35.
15. Vincent Brome, *The Way Back* (New York: W.W. Norton and Company Inc., 1957), 50-51.
16. Airey Neave, *Saturday at MI 9*, 117.
17. *Ibid.*, 156.
18. *Ibid.*, 161-62.
19. Edmund Cosgrove, *The Evaders* (Toronto/Vancouver: Clarke, Irwin & Company Limited, 1970), 18.
20. *Ibid.*, 19-21
21. *Ibid.*, 23.
22. Alan W. Cooper, *Free to Fight Again: RAF Escapes and Evasions, 1940-1945* (Shrewsbury: Airlife Publishing Ltd., 1988), 117.
23. M.R.D. Foot and J.M. Langley, *MI 9 Escape and Evasion: 1939-1945*, 136.
24. Airey Neave, *Saturday at MI 9*, 263.
25. *Ibid.*, 41.
26. *Ibid.*, 270

27. *Ibid.*, 271-72.
28. *Ibid.*, 356-57.

Chapter 13: The Dutch-Paris Underground Line

1. Herbert Ford, *Flee the Captor* (Nashville: Southern Publishing Association, 1966), 54.
2. Arthur Koestler, Hungarian author described life in a French detention camp both before and during the German occupation of Vichy in *Scum of the Earth* (London: Victor Gollancz Limited, 1941), 90ff.
3. Ford, *Flee the Captor*, 59-60.
4. John Weidner, *The Courage to Care*, ed. Carol Rittner and Sondra Myers (New York: New York University Press, 1986), 58-59.
5. Gay Block and Malka Drucker, *Rescuers: Portraits of Moral Courage in the Holocaust* (New York: Holmes and Meier Publishers, Inc., 1992), 54.
6. Ford, *Flee the Captor*, 74.
7. Block and Drucker, *Rescuers: Portraits of Moral Courage in the Holocaust*, 54.
8. Ford, *Flee the Captor*, 118-19.
9. *Ibid.*, 124.
10. *Ibid.*, 140-50.
11. *Ibid.*, 156.
12. *Ibid.*, 162-67.
13. *Ibid.*, 187-89.
14. *Ibid.*, 207-09.
15. Block and Drucker, *Rescuers: Portraits of Moral Courage in the Holocaust*, 54.
16. *Ibid.*, 234-35.
17. Foot, *SOE in the Low Countries*, 186-87.
18. Weidner, *Flee the Captor*, 245ff.
19. Block and Drucker, *Rescuers: Portraits of Moral Courage in the Holocaust*, 55.
20. *Ibid.*
21. Weidner, *Flee the Captor*, 277.
22. Foot, *S.O.E. in the Low Countries*, 212, 216.
23. *Ibid.*, 434.
24. Block and Drucker, *Rescuers: Portraits of Moral Courage in the*

Holocaust, 54.
25. Ford, *Flee the Captor*, 281, 283.
26. *Ibid.*, 224.
27. *Ibid.*, 301-02.
28. Block and Drucker, *Rescuers: Portraits of Moral Courage in the Holocaust*, 52.
29. Ford, *Flee the Captor*, 19.

Chapter 14: The Carpet to the Rhine

1. Dwight D. Eisenhower, *Crusade in Europe* (Garden City: Doubleday and Company, Inc., 1950), 231.
2. Foot, *SOE in the Low Countries*, 369.
3. *Ibid.*, 358.
4. Eisenhower, *Crusade in Europe*, 302.
5. Hart, *History of the Second World War*, 580. "For the German Army in the East, it was a catastrophe of unbelievable proportions, greater than that of Stalingrad, obliterating between twenty-five and twenty-eight divisions, 350,000 men in all." John Erickson, *The Road to Berlin* (Weidenfeld & Nicolson, 1983), 228. As cited in Terraine, *The Right of the Line*, 663.
6. Wilmot, *The Struggle for Europe*, 460.
7. Hart, *History of the Second World War*, 585-87.
8. Cornelius Ryan, *A Bridge Too Far* (New York: Simon and Schuster, 1974), 20.
9. *Ibid.*, 30.
10. Wilmot, *The Struggle for Europe*, 478.
11. *Ibid.*, 480.
12. Ryan, *A Bridge Too Far*, 37.
13. *Ibid.*, 60-61.
14. *Ibid.*, 48.
15. Wilmot, *The Struggle for Europe*, 479.
16. Ryan, *A Bridge Too Far*, 114-15.
17. Eisenhower, *Crusade in Europe*, 302.
18. Ryan, *A Bridge Too Far*, 70-71.
19. *Ibid.*, 89.
20. *Ibid.*, 123.

21. Henri A. van der Zee, *The Hunger Winter: Occupied Holland 1940-1945* (Lincoln: University of Nebraska Press, 1982), 30.
22. *Ibid.*, 113-14.
23. Wilmot, *The Struggle for Europe*, 501-02.
24. Spencer F. Wurst and Gayle Wurst, *Descending from the Clouds: A Memoir of Combat in the 505 Parachute Infantry Regiment, 82nd Airborne Division* (Havertown: Casemate, 2004), 168.
25. *Ibid.*, 171.
26. *Ibid.*, 176.
27. Ryan, *A Bridge Too Far*, 432.
28. Later, after the hard fought battle, British General Miles Dempsey remarked to General Gavin: "I am proud to meet the commander of the greatest division in the world today." Wilmot, *The Struggle for Europe*, 512 footnote.
29. Ryan, *A Bridge Too Far*, 257.
30. Martin Middlebrook, *Arnhem 1944: The Airborne Battle, 17-26 September* (Boulder: Westview Press, 1994), 116-42.
31. *Ibid.*, 137-42.
32. Ryan, *A Bridge Too Far*, 331.
33. Wilmot, *The Struggle for Europe*, 511.
34. Major-General R.E. Urquhart, "North-West Europe: Stalemate Before the Rhine," *The Taste of Courage: The War, 1939-1945*, 948.
35. Wilmot, *The Struggle for Europe*, 511.
36. Ryan, *A Bridge Too Far*, 548-49.
37. *Ibid.*, 397.
38. The next day, Mackay and three others escaped from the German town of Emmerich. They eventually made their way to the Rhine where they paddled downstream in a stolen boat to the Allied lines at Nijmegen. *Ibid.*, 482 footnote.
39. Tom Angus, *Men at Arnhem* (London: Leo Cooper, Ltd., 1976), 84-85.
40. Ryan, *A Bridge Too Far*, 502-07.
41. Wilmot, *The Struggle for Europe*, 520.
42. Ryan, *A Bridge Too Far*, 591.
43. *Ibid.*, 599.
44. *Ibid.*
45. Middlebrook, *Arnhem 1944*, 437.

46. Robert Nisbet, *Roosevelt and Stalin: The Failed Courtship* (Washington, D.C.: Regnery Gateway, 1988).
47. Sir John Hackett, "Operation Market Garden," *Holland at War Against Hitler: Anglo-Dutch Relations 1940-1945*, ed. M.R.D. Foot (London: Frank Cass and Company Limited, 1990), 162.
48. Middlebrook, *Arnhem 1944*, 443.
49. Peter A. Huchthausen, "A Drop Too Many," *Battlegrounds*, ed. Michael Stephenson (Washington, D.C.: National Geographic), 69.
50. Major L.F. Ellis, *Victory in the West: The Defeat of Germany* (London: Imperial War Museum), 53-54. As cited in Terraine, *The Right of the Line*, 670.
51. As cited in Ryan, *A Bridge Too Far*, 61.
52. Middlebrook, *Arnhem 1944*, 444.
53. Lt. General Lewis Brereton, *Diaries*, 360-61. As cited in Wilmot, *The Struggle for Europe*, 527.
54. *Ibid.*
55. Wilmot, *The Struggle for Europe*, 523.
56. As cited in Ryan, *A Bridge Too Far*, 597.
57. *The New Dictionary of Thoughts: A Cyclopedia of Quotations*. Originally compiled by Tryon Edwards, D.D. and revised and enlarged by C.N. Catrevas, A.B. and Jonathan Edwards, A.M. (New York: Standard Book Company, 1955), 122.

Chapter 15: The Dutch Famine of 1944-1945

1. Warmbrunn, *The Dutch Under German Occupation 1940-1945*, 142.
2. Van der Zee, *The Hunger Winter: Occupied Holland 1944-1945* (Lincoln: University of Nebraska Press, 1982), 36.
3. Warmbrunn, *The Dutch Under German Occupation 1940-1945*, 145.
4. Van der Zee, *The Hunger Winter: Occupied Holland 1940-1945*, 38.
5. *Ibid.*, 62.
6. *Ibid.*, 47.
7. Eman, *The Things We Couldn't Say*, 304-05.
8. *Ibid.*
9. Van der Zee, *The Hunger Winter: Occupied Holland 1940-1945*, 48-49.
10. *Ibid.*, 68.
11. *Ibid.*, 70.

12. J. Heyn, Jr., *Holland Hails You* (Wormerveer: Meijer's Boek-en Handelsdrukkerij, 1945), 3.
13. *Ibid.*, 2.
14. Warmbrunn, *The Dutch Under German Occupation 1940-1945*, 79.
15. Van der Zee, *The Hunger Winter: Occupied Holland 1940-1945*, 72.
16. Cornelia Fuykschot, *Hunger in Holland: Life During the Occupation* (Amherst: Prometheus Books, 1995), 100.
17. Van der Zee, *The Hunger Winter: Occupied Holland 1940-1945*, 77.
18. *Ibid.*, 78.
19. Eisenhower, *Crusade in Europe*, 353.
20. Van der Zee, *The Hunger Winter: Occupied Holland 1940-1945*, 81.
21. *Ibid.*, 120.
22. *Ibid.*, 121.
23. *Ibid.*
24. *Ibid.*, 124.
25. *Ibid.*, 153.
26. *Ibid.* 156.
27. *Ibid.*
28. Colonel C.P. Stacey, *The Victory Campaign: The Operations in Northwest Europe 1944-1945*, Vol. III (Ottawa: Queen's Printer and Controller of Stationery, 1966), 583.
29. Max Hastings, *Armageddon: The Battle for Germany 1944-1945* (New York: Alfred A. Knopf, Inc., 2004), 412.
30. *Ibid.*
31. *Ibid.*, 159-60.
32. *Ibid.*, 161-62.
33. *Ibid.*
34. *Ibid.*, 167-68.

Chapter 16: Holland Rejoices

1. Hastings, *Armageddon: The Battle for Germany 1944-1945*, 348-49.
2. *Ibid.*, 347.
3. Stacey, *The Victory Campaign: The Operations in Northwest Europe 1944-1945*, 542.
4. *Ibid.*, 539.

5. *Ibid.*, 587.
6. Hart, *History of the Second World War*, 680.
7. Van der Zee, *The Hunger Winter: Occupied Holland 1944-1945*, 41.
8. Stacey, *The Victory Campaign: The Operations in Northwest Europe 1944-1945*, 583.
9. Van der Zee, *The Hunger Winter: Occupied Holland 1944-1945*, 176.
10. Stacey, *The Victory Campaign: The Operations in Northwest Europe 1944-1945*, 583.
11. *Ibid.*, 584.
12. Winston Churchill, *Triumph and Tragedy* (Boston: Houghton Mifflin Company, 1953), 468.
13. *Ibid.*, 469.
14. F.S.V. Donnison, *Civil Affairs and Military Government North-West Europe 1944-1946* (London: Her Majesty's Stationery Office, 1961), 144-45.
15. Stacey, *The Victory Campaign: The Operations in North-West Europe 1944-1945*, 585.
16. Operation Manna, http://www.heureka.clara.net/lincolnshire/operationmanna.
17. *Ibid.*
18. Stacey, *The Victory Campaign: The Operations in North-West Europe 1944-1945*, 608.
19. Van der Zee, *The Hunger Winter: Occupied Holland 1944-1945*, 255-56.
20. Stacey, *The Victory Campaign: The Operations in North-West Europe 1944–1945*, 614.
21. *Ibid.*, 610-11.
22. *Ibid.*, 614.
23. *Ibid.*, 609.
24. Donnison, *Civil Affairs and Military Government North-West Europe, 1944-1946*, 148-49.
25. Mason, *The Purge of Dutch Quislings*, 40-43.
26. *Ibid.*, 39.
27. de Jong, "Anti-Nazi Resistance in the Netherlands," *European Resistance Movements 1939-1945: Proceedings of the Second International Conference on the History of the Resistance Movements*, 140.

28. Mason, *The Purge of the Dutch Quislings*, 19.
29. Martin Gilbert, *The Day the War Ended: May 8, 1945* (New York: Henry Holt and Company, 1995), 226.
30. Mason, *The Purge of the Dutch Quislings*, 45.
31. *Ibid.*, 54.

BIBLIOGRAPHY

Accattoli, Luigi, *When a Pope Asks Forgiveness*. Boston: Pauline Books and Media, 1998.

Adams, Henry H., *Years of Deadly Peril: The Coming of the War 1939-1941*. New York: David McKay Company, Inc., 1969.

Alexander, Leo, M.D., "Medical Science Under Dictatorship," *New England Journal of Medicine*, Vol. 241, July 14, 1949.

Andriesse, Emmy, *Dutch Photographers*. http://en.wikipeida.org/wike/Emmy_Andriesse.

Angus, Tom, *Men at Arnhem*. London: Leo Cooper Ltd., 1976.

Baron, Lawrence, *The Dynamics of Decency: Dutch Rescuers of Jews During the Holocaust*. Canton: St. Lawrence University, 1985.

Baudot, Marcel, Bernard, Henri, Brugmans, Hendrik, Foot, Michael R.D., and Jacobsen, Hans-Adolf, editors, *The Historical Encyclopedia of World War Two*. New York: MJF Books, 1989.

Bens, F. Lee, *Europe Since 1914 in its World Setting*. New York: Appleton-Century Crofts, Inc., 1954.

Bentley, Stewart, *Of Market Garden and Melanie: The Dutch Resistance and the OSS, Studies in Intelligence*. Washington, D.C.: Center for the Study of Intelligence, Spring 1998.

Block, Gay and Drucker, Malka, *Rescuers: Portraits of Moral Courage in the Holocaust*. New York: Holmes & Meier Publishers, Inc., 1992.

Boas, J. H., *Religious Resistance in Holland*. Great Britain: The Netherlands Government Information Bureau, 1945.

_____, *Resistance of the Churches in the Netherlands*. Great Britain: The Netherlands Government Information Bureau, 1944.

Brasz, Chaya and Kaplan, Yosef, ed., *Dutch Jews as Perceived by Themselves and Others: Proceedings of Eighth International Symposium on the History of the Jews in the Netherlands*. Boston: Brill, 2001.

Brennan, William C., Ph.D., *The Abortion Holocaust: Today's Final Solution*. St. Louis, 1983.

Brome, Vincent, *The Way Back*. New York: Norton and Company, Inc., 1957.

Churchill, Winston S., *Their Finest Hour*. Boston: Houghton Mifflin Company, 1949.

_____, *Triumph and Tragedy*. Boston: Houghton Mifflin Company, 1953.

Commission for Religious Relations with the Jews, *We Remember: A Reflection on the Shoah*. Boston: Pauline Books and Media, 1998.

Cookridge, E.H., *Set Europe Ablaze*. New York: Thomas Crowell Company, 1967.

Cooper, Alan W., *Free to Fight Again: RAF Escapes and Evasions, 1940-1945*. Shrewsbury: Airlife Publishing Ltd., 1988.

Cosgrove, Edmund, *The Evaders*. Vancouver: Clarke, Irwin & Company Limited, 1970.

Donnison, F.S.V., *Civil Affairs and Military Government North-West Europe 1944-1946*. London: Her Majesty's Stationery Office, 1961.

Duke, A.C., and Tamse, C.A., ed., *Too Mighty to be Free: Censorship and the Press in Great Britain and the Netherlands*. Zutphen: De Walburg Pers, 1988.

Edwards, Tryon, D.D., Catrevas, A.B., and Edwards, Jonathan, A.M., *The New Dictionary of Thoughts: A Cyclopedia of Quotations*. New York: Standard Book Company, 1955.

Eisenhower, Dwight D., *Crusade in Europe*. Garden City: Doubleday and Company, Inc., 1950.

Ellis, Major L.F., *Victory in the West: The Defeat of Germany*. London: Imperial War Museum, 1994.

Eman, Diet, *Things We Couldn't Say*. Grand Rapids: William B. Eerdmans Publishing Co., 1994.

Erickson, John, *The Road to Berlin*. Weidenfeld & Nicolson, 1983.

Flower, Desmond and Reeves, James, ed. *The Taste of Courage: The War, 1939-1945*. New York: Harper & Brothers Publishers, 1960.

Foot, M.R.D., *SOE in the Low Countries*. London: St. Ermin's Press, 2001.

_____, and Langley, J.M., *MI 9 Escape and Evasion*. Boston: Little Brown and Company, 1979.

_____, *Resistance: European Resistance to Nazism 1940-1945*. New York: McGraw-Hill Book Company, 1977.

Ford, Herbert, *Flee the Captor*. Nashville: Southern Publishing Association, 1966.

Friedhoff, Herman, *Requiem for the Resistance: The Civilian Struggle Against Nazism in Holland and Germany*. London: Bloomsbury Publishing Ltd., 1988.

Fuegner, Richard S., *Beneath the Tyrant's Yoke*. Edina: Beaver's Pond Press, Inc., 2003.

Fuykschot, *Hunger in Holland: Life During the Occupation*. Amherst: Prometheus Books, 1995.

Ganier-Raymond, Philippe, *The Tangled Web*. New York: Pantheon Books, 1968.

Gilbert, Martin, *The Day the War Ended: May 8, 1945*. New York: Henry Holt and Company, 1995.

Giskes, H.J., *London Calling North Pole*. New York: The British Book Centre, Inc., 1953.

Bibliography

Goedhart, F.J., *Nieuwsbrief van Pieter 't Hoen*. Amsterdam: Historisch Adviesabureau 30-45, 2008.

Grigg, John, *1943: The Victory That Never Was*. New York: Hill and Wang, 1980.

Hackett, John Winthrop, *I Was A Stranger*. Boston: Houghton Mifflin Company, 1978.

Haestrup, Jorgen, *Europe Ablaze: An Analysis of the History of the European Resistance Movements 1939-1945*. Odense: Odense University Press, 1978.

Harris, Whitney R., *Tyranny on Trial: The Evidence at Nuremberg*. Dallas: Southern Methodist University Press, 1954.

Hart, B.H. Liddell, *History of the Second World War*. New York: G.P. Putnam's Sons, 1970.

Hastings, Max, *Armageddon: The Battle for Germany 1944-1945*. New York: Alfred A. Knopf, Inc., 2004.

Hazelhoff, Erik, *Soldier of Orange*. Hastings-on-Hudson: The Holland Heritage Society, 1980.

Heyn, J., *Holland Hails You*. Wormerveer: Meijer's Boek-en Handelsdrukkerij, 1945.

Howarth, Patrick, *Undercover: The Men and Women of the S.O.E.* London: Phoenix Press, 1980.

Ijzerdraat, Bernard, *Geuzenactie*. Amsterdam: Historisch Adviesbureau 30-45, 2008.

Jong, Louis de, *The Lion Rampant*. New York: Querido, 1943.

_____, *The Netherlands and Nazi Germany*. Cambridge: Harvard University Press, 1990.

Keizer, Madelon de, *Het Parool 1940-1945: Verzetsblad in Oorlogstijd*. http://www.hetillegaleparool.nl/summary.html.

Koestler, Arthur, *Scum of the Earth*. London: Victor Gollancz Limited, 1941.

Maass, Walter B., *The Netherlands at War: 1940-1945*. London: Abelard-Schuman, 1970.

Mak, Geert, *Amsterdam*. Cambridge: Harvard University Press, 1994.

Marks, Leo, *Between Silk and Cyanide: A Codemaker's War 1941-1945*. New York: The Free Press, 1998.

Martens, Allard, *The Silent War: Glimpses of the Dutch Underground*. London: Hodder and Stoughton, 1961.

Mason, Henry L., *The Purge of Dutch Quislings*. The Hague: Martinus Nijhoff, 1952.

Mayer, Allan, *Gaston's War: The True Story of a Hero of the Resistance in World War II*. Novato: Presidio Press, 1988.

Middlebrook, Martin, *Arnhem 1944: The Airborne Battle, 17-26 September*. Boulder: Westview Press, 1994.

Miller, Russell, *Behind Enemy Lines: The Oral History of Special Operations in World War II*. New York: St. Martin's Press, 2002.

Moore, Bob, *Victims and Survivors: The Nazi Persecution of the Jews in the Netherlands 1940-1945*, London: Arnold, 1997.

Neave, Airey, *Saturday at MI 9*. London: Grafton Books, 1989.

Newton, Gerald, *The Netherlands: An Historical and Cultural Survey 1795-1977*. London: Ernest Benn Limited, 1978.

Nisbet, Robert, *Roosevelt and Stalin: The Failed Courtship*. Washington, D.C.: Regnery Gateway, 1988.

Remmerden, H. Van, *In the Shadow of the Swastika*. Boise: Lithocraft, Inc., 1996.

Rings, Werner, *Life With the Enemy*. Garden City: Doubleday and Company, Inc., 1982.

Rittner, Carol and Myers, Sondra, ed., *The Courage to Care*. New York: New York University Press, 1986.

Rol, Ruud van der and Verhoeven, Rian, *Anne Frank*. Kampen: LRV-info, 1992.

Rose, Jonathan, ed., *The Holocaust and the Book: Destruction and Preservation*. Amherst: University of Massachussets Press, 2001.

Rose, Leesha, *The Tulips are Red*. New York: A.S. Barnes and Company, 1978.

Rowen, Herbert H., *The Low Countries in Early Modern Times*. New York: Walker and Company, 1972.

Ryan, Cornelius, *A Bridge Too Far*. New York: Simon and Schuster, 1974.

Schaft, Hannie, *Resistance Work*. http://en.wikipedia.org/wikiHannieSchaft.

Schlabrendorff, Fabian von, *The Secret War Against Hitler*. New York: Pitman Publishing Corporation, 1965.

Secretariat for Ecumenical and Interreligious Affairs, *Catholics Remember the Holocaust*. Washington, D.C.: National Council of Catholic Bishops, 1998.

Shirer, William L., *The Rise and Fall of the Third Reich: A History of Nazi Germany*. New York: Simon and Schuster, 1958.

Stacey, Colonel C.P., *The Victory Campaign: The Operations in Northwest Europe 1944–1945*. Ottawa: Queen's Printer and Controller of Stationery, 1966.

Stafford, David, *Secret Agent: The True Story of the Covert War Against Hitler*. Woodstock: The Overlook Press, 2001.

Stein, Andre, *Quiet Heroes: The True Stories of the Rescue of Jews by Christians in Nazi-Occupied Holland*. New York: New York University Press, 1988.

Stephenson, Michael, ed., *Battlegrounds*. Washington, D.C.: National Geographic, 2003.

Stone, Harry, *Writing in the Shadow: Resistance Publications in Occupied Europe*. London: Frank Cass & Co. Ltd., 1996.

Taylor, Telford, *The March of Conquest: The German Victories in Western Europe, 1940*. New York: Simon and Schuster, 1958.

Tempel, Gudrun, *The Germans: An Indictment of My People*. New York: Random House, 1963.

Terraine, John, *The Right of the Line: The Royal Air Force in the European War, 1939-1945*. Hertsfordshire: Wordsworth Editions Limited, 1997.

Warmbrunn, Werner, *The Dutch Under German Occupation 1940-1945*. Stanford: Stanford University Press, 1963.

Wheal, Elizabeth-Anne, Pope, Stephen & Taylor, James, *Encyclopedia of the Second World War*. Secaucus: Castle Books, 1989.

Wilmot, Chester. *The Struggle for Europe*. Hertfordshire: Wordsworth Editions Limited, 1997.

Wurst, Spencer F. and Wurst, Gayle, *Descending from the Clouds: A Memoir of Combat in the 505 Parachute Infantry Regiment, 82nd Airborne Division*. Havertown: Casemate, 2004.

Zee, Henri A. van der, *The Hunger Winter: Occupied Holland 1940-1945*. Lincoln: University of Nebraska Press, 1982.

INDEX

A

Allies
  advance across Europe
    early days, 154–155
    in Germany, 190–192
    Operation Market Garden, 159–176
    refugees from, 180–181
    strategy, 158–159
    supply issues, 156, 157–158
  air forces
    bombing of German armaments factories, 128
    intelligence activities and, 103–104
    Operation Market Garden and, 161, 162, 163, 166, 169
    relief supplies, 195–196
    rescue of downed airmen
      described, 120–121
      general procedure, 129–131
      networks for, 132–137, 142–144, 146–151
    training to evade capture, 131–132
  invasion of Europe, 152–154
  liberation of Netherlands
    entrance from Germany, 192
    Plan Holland
      captured agents, 104–105, 111–113
      codebreaking and, 108–111
      German infiltration of, 94–104, 105–107, 113–116
      overview of, 93–94
    Royal Family appeals for, 187
  strategy priority, 187–188
  victory in Europe, 196–197

Amsterdam
  conditions in immediately after invasion, 29
  history, 54
  Jews transported to, 41
  onderduikers in, 47
  relief supplies to, 193
  riots in, 38
  strikes in, 38, 39–40
  Underground press in, 66
Amsterdam Scout (Underground newspaper), 66
Andringa, Leonard, 98–99, 100
anti-Semitism, 4, 36, 45
Arnhem Bridge, 159, 165–176
Arnold, Henry (Hap), 159
Aryan race, 53
Auschwitz, 42

B

Baasten, Arnold, 97, 98
"Banker of the Resistance," 122
Battle of the Bulge, 184–185
Becking, Baas, 84–85
Beckman, Wiardi, 89
Bedell Smith, Walter, 193, 194
Beggars' Action Resistance, 67–69, 79–80
Belgian Comet Line, 132, 133–137
Bergen-Belsen, 42
Bernhard (prince of Netherlands)
  flight to England, 18
  German background of, 2
  on liberation of Netherlands, 152
  Resistance and, 123, 188
Best, S. Payne, 9, 10
Beukema, Carl, 105
Bingham, Seymour, 110, 114, 115
Bittrich, Wilhelm, 166
black market, 122–123

Blaskowitz, Johannes, 196
Blizard, Charles, 110, 115
Block, Gay, 48
Boas, J.H., 53
Boden, Sergeant, 107
Bolshevism, 58–59
Bonaparte, Napoleon, 63
books, 76–77
Bouwma, Bill, 49
Bouwma, Margaret, 49
Bradley, Omar, 192
Brauchitsch, Walther von, 8–9
Brereton, Lewis, 176
Breznitz, Schlomo, 44
Brinkman, Albert, 115
Britain
    C.I.D. and, 86–87
    Dutch admiration for, 34–35
    escape to, 79
    evacuation of forces from Norway, 12
    German invasion of Netherlands and, 16
    intelligence operations, 9–10, 86, 88, 108–111, 132–133
    power of, 7–8
    Royal Family flight to, 18
    sea power, 3
    See also Plan Holland
Browning, Frederick, 159
Buizer, Johannes, 100
Bukkens, Joseph Jan, 101
Bulgaria, 45
Bureau Militaire Voorbereiding Terugkeer (M.V.T.), 87
Burger, J.A.W., 189

C

Calvinists. *See* Dutch Reformed Church (Calvinists)
Campert, Jan, 80–83
Canaris, Wilhelm, 18
Case Yellow *(Fall Gelb)*, 8–9
casualties, Dutch
    German invasion, 23, 24
    German reprisals, 124–125, 181–182, 185
    in Resistance, 202
    starvation, 197
    strike of 1943, 119
Catholic community
    deportation of Jewish converts and, 59
    in Germany, 56
    Jews and, 55–56, 57
    measures against N.S.B., 55, 56–57
    newspapers censored, 56
    number of believers, 54
    protests from pulpit, 55, 56, 59
    schools, 57, 58, 60
    youth league Underground group, 83
Catholic Guild of Israel, 56
Catholic University (at Nijmegen), 60
Central Intelligence Service *(C.I.D.)*, 84, 86–87
Choltitz, Dietrich von, 20, 23
Christiansen, Friedrich, 39, 65, 118, 181
Christmann, Richard, 107
Churchill, Winston, 13, 86, 187–188
Cleveringa, R.P., 37
Colijn, Hendrik, 5, 27
collaborators
    actions defining, 199
    informers, 30, 80, 94–95, 96
    number of, 198
    Resistance lists of, 79–80
    Resistance view of, 69–71
Comet Line, 132, 133–137
Communists
    strikes by, 38, 39–40
    Underground, 83
    Underground newspaper, 75–76
conscience, issues of, 28
conscripted labor for German factories
    Allied bombing and, 128
    Dutch army veterans as, 118–119
    Dutch students as, 126
    hiding of conscripts for, 121–122
    Jews as, 41–42
    number of Dutch sent as, 160
    Resistance response to, 122, 185–186
    round-ups for, 145

Index

Contact Holland, 88–90
courage and fear, 44
Crockatt, Norman, 131–132

D

D-Day, 152–153
De Achttien Dooden (*The Eighteen Dead*, Campert), 80–83
De Bezige Bij (The Busy Bee), 76, 82
de Brey, O.W., 115
de Bruyne, M.R., 87
de Geer, D.J.
    military preparedness and, 5, 27
    neutrality and, 10, 11
    policy of cooperation, 33
de Haas, Hendrik Jan, 99–100
de Jong, Arie, 195
de Jong, Johannes, 56, 59, 185–186
de Jong, Louis, 91, 126–127, 202
de Jongh, Andree (Dedee), 134, 135–136
de Jongh, Frederic, 134, 135, 136
de Quay, J. E., 33
De Unie (Netherlands Union publication), 34
De Waarheid (*The Truth*, Communist Underground newspaper), 75–76
de Wit, James, 121–122
Dempsey, Miles, 172, 173, 175–176
Denmark, 45
Department of Ungentlemanly Warfare. *See* Special Operations Executive (S.O.E.)
Devers, Jacob, 192
Dobie, D., 166, 167
Dolle Dindsdag (Mad Tuesday), 154–155
Dourlein, Pieter, 111–113, 147
Douwes, Arnold, 51
Drucker, Malka, 48
Dutch National Socialist Bond (N.S.B.), 4
    condemnation by religious leaders of, 55
    Gentile solidarity and, 45
    invasion and, 18, 29
    members assassinated by Underground, 125
    Catholic measures against, 55, 56–57
    number of, 198
    privileges of, 66
    Resistance lists of, 79–80
    Netherlands Union and, 34
    paramilitary branch, 35
    strikes against, 119
    Underground press and, 69–70
Dutch-Paris Line, 141–144, 146–151
Dutch Reformed Church (Calvinists)
    Jews and, 55, 57
    newspaper censored, 56
    number of believers, 54, 55
    protests from pulpit, 57–58, 59–60
    Underground press and, 72–73

E

Eastern Front, 154, 192
Ebenezer (code name), 97–99, 98, 100, 101–103, 105–106, 109, 110, 112, 116
    See also Lauwers, Hubertus
education
    denominational schools, 57, 58, 60
    institutions of higher, 37, 60
    of Jewish children, 37, 41
    lack of, 187
Einthoven, L., 33
Eisenhower, Dwight D., 152, 158–159, 187
Ellis, L.F., 175
England. *See* Britain
Englandspiel operation, 94–107, 137, 147
espionage. *See* intelligence activities
European Resistance to Nazism 1940-1945 (Foot), 203
extermination camps
    condemnation by Christian churches of, 59
    first transports to, 42
    number of Jews sent to, 160

F

Fall Gelb (Case Yellow), 8–9
fascism. *See* Nazi philosophy
fear and courage, 44
fifth columns, 10–11
final solution, 41, 44–45
First World War, 3
Fitch, J.A.C., 166, 167
Five Day War. *See* invasion by Germany
flags, 30, 32
flooding devices, 2, 3, 23, 26
food
    famine, 182–184, 186–187, 194, 197
    German embargo, 179, 183
    German scorched-earth policy, 180
    rationing, 122–123, 130
    relief supplies, 193–196, 197–198
Foot, Michael (M.R.D.), 104, 153, 203
Foppema, Yge, 190
"Fortress Holland," 17, 19
France, 8, 17
Francois, Duc de La Rochefoucauld, 7
Frank, Anne, 46–48
Friedhoff, Herman, 28, 63, 78
Frost, John, 166, 168, 169, 170, 171, 175
Fund for Special Emergencies, 57

G

Garrow, Ian, 132–133
gasoline rationing, 30
Gavin, James, 159, 162, 163, 164
Gentiles
    married to Jews, 37, 42
    solidarity with Dutch Jews
        examples of, 38, 41
        motivations of, 48–51
        religion and, 55–56, 57
        strengthened by N.S.B. actions, 45
        strikes to express, 38, 39–40
geography
    invasion and, 3–4, 5, 6
    Resistance and, 4, 79
    sea level, 2
    survival of Jews and, 45
Gerbrandy, Pieter S.
    fall of government, 188
    intelligence activities of, 88, 89
    made head of Government-in-Exile, 33
    Operation Market Garden strike and, 160, 179
    passive Resistance and, 120
    relief supplies and, 193
Germany
    air force
        bombing of Rotterdam by, 19–23
        destroyed, 155
        invasion, 1, 14–16, 17, 19, 20
        preparedness, 6
    Allies in, 190–192
    Catholic Church in, 56
    D-Day and, 153
    Dutch reaction to rise of Nazis in, 4
    history, 54
    intelligence activities
        counterintelligence, 88–89, 148
        Englandspiel, 94–107, 137, 147
        fifth column, 11, 85–86
        infiltration of Underground, 30, 80
    prewar relations with, 2, 3
    surrender of, 196–197
Gestapo (Staatspolizei,), 30
Geuzenactie (Beggars Action), 67–69, 79–80
Giocoechea, Florentino, 135
Giraud, Henri, 17
Giskes, Hermann, 90, 94, 95–99, 101–107, 110, 112, 113
Goebbels, Joseph, 65
Goedhart, Frans J., 69–71, 72, 89
    See also Hoen, Pieter 't
Goedhart, Gerrit van Heuven, 149
Goering, Hermann, 20
Golf operation, 106
Gough, Freddie, 166
Government-in-Exile
    call for passive Resistance, 120
    funds to aid refugees, 140
    intelligence activities, 84–88, 89,

108–111, 132–133 (*See also* Plan Holland)
    official Resistance of, 123
    proclaimed, 18
    Radio Oranje, 32, 58, 90
    See also Gerbrandy, Pieter S.
Gravemeyer, K.H.E., 57
Greater German Reich/Realm, 31, 53–54
Green Police, 30
Guerisse, Albert-Marie, 132–133
guilt and innocence, 1

H

Haarlem Daily (newspaper), 75
Hackett, Sir John W., 116, 120–121, 169
Halder, Franz, 9
Hart, B.H. Liddell, 7, 128
Heinrich, Lieutenant, 96, 97
Hepburn, Audrey, 74
Het Bulletin (Underground newspaper), 69
Het Parool (The Watchword, Underground newspaper), 71–72, 119, 149
Heydrich, Reinhard, 41
Hicks, Philip (Pip), 168–169
history, 2–3, 54
Hitler, Adolf
    conspiracies against, 11
    Dutch reaction to rise of, 4
    neutrality of Low Countries and, 1, 10
    role of Netherlands in Greater German Reich, 31
    suicide of, 196
    Western Front strategy of, 14, 117–118
Hoeben, Hein, 60
Hoehne, Commander, 22
Hoen, Pieter 't, 24–27, 69–71
Homan, J. Linthorst, 33
Horrocks, Brian, 161–162, 168, 172, 173, 175
House of Orange
    appeals for liberation, 187
    flag, 30

    German promises about, 15
    history, 2
    postwar, 200
    royal colors, 33
    See also Bernhard (prince of Netherlands); Wilhelmina (queen of Netherlands)
Howarth, Patrick, 115

I

I Was a Stranger (Hackett), 121
Ijzerdraat, Bernard, 67, 69, 79, 80
innocence and guilt, 1
intelligence activities
    Allied air losses and, 103–104
    Allied invasion and
        captured agents, 104–105, 111–113
    codebreaking and, 108–111
    German infiltration of, 94–104, 105–107, 113–116, 137, 147
    overview of, 93–94
    British, 9–10, 131–132
    of Dutch Nazis, 11
    German
        counterintelligence, 88–89, 148
        fifth column, 11, 85–86
        infiltration of Underground, 30, 80
    Government-in-Exile and, 84–88, 89
    Operation Market Garden and, 160, 166, 174–175
    Underground operations, 83–84, 88–90, 126
invasion by Germany
    air war, 1, 14–16, 17, 19, 20
    analysis of, 23–27
    Britain reaction to, 13
    casualties, 23, 24
    conditions immediately after, 28–32
    ground fighting, 16–18, 19–20
    purported reason for, 30
    topography and, 3–4, 5, 6
    warnings about, 11–12, 13

J

Jambroes, George Louis, 101, 103, 105–107
Jansen, Jules, 126
Je Maintiendrai (*I Maintain*, Underground newspaper), 66, 75
Jews
    anti-Semitism and, 45
    escape networks for, 141–144, 146–151
    funds to aid, 140
    Nazi view of, 36, 40
    treatment in Occupied Europe of, 44–45
    in Vichy France, 139–143
    See also Jews, Dutch
Jews, Dutch
    anti-Semitism toward, 4, 36
    assimilation of, 44, 45
    Catholic mission to, 55–56
    converts to Christianity, 59
    deportation of, 41–42, 59, 146–147, 160
    escape networks for, 141–144, 146–151
    funds to aid, 57, 140
    Gentiles married to, 37, 42
    in hiding, 45–48
    Jewish Council, 40, 41–42
    measures against, 32, 37–42
    rescue of, 45–51, 82–83, 126, 127
    resettlement to Amsterdam of, 41
    solidarity with
        examples of, 38, 41
        motivation for, 48–51, 55–56, 57
        strengthened by N.S.B. actions, 45
        strikes to express, 38, 39–40
    suicides, 42
    topography and survival of, 45
Jodl, Alfred, 196
Jones, Patricia, 108
Jongelie, Christian, 105
Jordaan, Hendrik, 99, 100

K

Kelder, Margarethe, 126
Kesselring, Albert, 20, 22
Killick, John, 115
"King Kong," 148
Kist, Jan, 106, 107
Kloos, Barend, 99
Klop, Dirk, 9, 10
Knokploegen (K.P. or L.K.P., action groups), 38, 122–123, 126
Knoppers, Hendrikus, 106–107
Kraay, Suzy, 147–148
Kraemer, Hendrik, 60
Krafft, Josef, 167
Kragt, Dignus (Dick), 137
Kruls, H.J., 188
Kuechler, Georg von, 17
Kuipers-Rietberg, Helena Theodora, 120

L

labor conscription. *See* conscripted labor for German factories
Lathbury, G.W., 166, 168
Lauwers, Hubertus, 94–98, 100, 101–103, 105–106, 116
    See also Ebenezer (code name)
liberation
    entrance from Germany, 192
    Plan Holland
        captured agents, 104–105, 111–113
        codebreaking and, 108–111
        German infiltration of, 94–104, 105–107, 113–116
        overview of, 93–94
        Royal Family appeals for, 187
Life in Western Holland (Vrouwenfelder), 178
Lindermans, Christian, 148
Low Countries
    Churchill on German invasion of, 13
    German invasion of, 8–9
    neutrality of, 1, 3, 10
    strategic location of, 25
Lubberhuizen, Geertjan, 76

Index

M

M19, 131–132, 136
Maasbode (Catholic newspaper), 56
"Maastricht Appendix," 17
Mackay, Eric, 167, 171
MacLean, Angus, 134–135
Mad Tuesday, 154–155
Manstein, Erich von, 12
Mansum, Arie van, 50
map of The Netherlands, viii
Marks, Leo, 108, 109–110, 114, 116
Marshall, George C., 159
May, Ernst, 88, 89, 96
medicine, 60–61, 186
Memoirs (Montgomery), 176
Menander, 139
Michel, Henri, 117
Middlebrook, Martin, 174
military, Dutch
    air force, 16, 19
    analysis of performance of, 24–27
    army, 15
    defense strategy, 2, 3, 5–6
    navy, 21–22, 24
    preparedness, 5–6, 11
    strategy of flooding, 2, 3, 23
    surrender of, 22, 23
    warnings about German invasion, 11–12, 13
Military Preparation for the Return (*M.V.T.*), 87
Mink, A.B., 115
Mit Brennender Sorge (With Burning Concern, Pope Pius XI), 55
Model, Walter, 160, 166, 167, 176
Molenaar, Jan, 98–99
Montgomery, Bernard, 152, 158–159, 175, 176, 192
Mussert, Anton, 4
    D-Day and, 153
    execution of, 199
    political ambitions of, 31
    safety of, immediately after German invasion, 29

N

National Assistance Fund, 202
National Organization for Assistance to Onderduikers (L.O.), 120–121
National Support Fund (N.S.F.), 122
Nationale Dagblad (Dutch Nazi newspaper), 37
Nazi philosophy, 53–54
    Bolshevism and, 58–59
    Catholic opposition to, 55, 56
    medical practice and, 60–61
Nazis, Dutch. *See* Dutch National Socialist Bond (N.S.B.)
Neave, Airey, 136
Netherlands Forces of the Interior, 123
Netherlands Union, 33–34
neutrality
    First World War, 3
    German strategy and, 25
    Hitler and, 1, 10
    military preparedness and, 6, 11
    Underground and tradition of, 78
    Wilhelmina and, 9
newspapers. *See* press; Underground press; *specific publications*
Nieuwsbrief van Pieter 't Hoen (Underground newspaper), 69–71
    See also Het Parool (The Watchword)
Norway, 12, 31, 53–54

O

Occupation
    Allied relief supplies, 193–196
    conditions immediately after invasion, 28–32
    daily life, 186–187
    departure of German civilians, 154–155
    documentation of, 125
    famine, 182–184, 186–187
    German reprisals, 39, 124–125, 181–182, 185
    as God's will, 32
    government, 30, 31

measures against Jews, 32, 37–42
newspapers, 56, 64–65, 66
police, 30
policy of cooperation, 33
political parties, 33–34
rationing, 30, 122–123, 130
solidarity of Dutch (*See also* strikes)
   examples of, 201
   increase in patriotism, 34–35
   with Jews, 38, 41, 45, 48–51, 55–56, 57
O'Connell, Barbara, 108
O'Leary, Patrick, 132–133
O'Leary Line, 132–133
onderduikers
   conscripted laborers, 121–122, 126
   described, 46
   feeding, 122–123, 130
   Jews, 45–48, 82–83
   number of Dutch aiding, 202
   organization formed to aid, 120
   rescued Allied airmen, 120–121
Oorschot, J.W. van, 9, 10
Operation Chowhound, 195–196
Operation Erica, 105
Operation Fortitude, 152
Operation Market Garden, 159–176, 178–179, 183
Operation North Pole, 94–107
Operation Overlord, 152–153
Oranje Hotel, 37, 80
Oranjebode (Message of Orange, Underground newspaper), 73
   See also Trouw (Loyalty)
Order Police, 30
Order Service *(Orde Dienst, O.D.),* 83, 84–85, 114–115
   See also Plan Holland
Oster, Hans, 11–12, 13
Otten, Seine, 51

P

pacifist movement, 3, 5, 32
Parlevliet, Herman, 100, 103
Partisan Action Netherlands (P.A.N.), 126

Pat Line, 132–133
Patton, George S., 158
Pax Germania, acceptance of, 28
Phony War, 7
physicians, 60–61, 186
Physicians Chamber, 60–61
Pius XI (pope), 55
Plan Holland
   captured agents, 104–105, 111–113
   codebreaking and, 108–111
   German infiltration of, 94–104, 105–107, 113–116
   overview of, 93–94
Poland, 6, 7, 45, 63
population of Netherlands, 3
press
   censorship of, 56, 65–66
   Nazified during Occupation, 64–65, 66, 70, 75
   in 1930s, 64
   See also Underground press
Pritchard, Marion van Binsbergen, 49–50, 51
Protestant community, 54–55
   See also specific sects
publishing houses, 76–77

R

Raad van Verzet (R.v.V., Council of Resistance), 123–124
radio
   intelligence activities and, 84–85, 87–89, 90, 94–95, 108–111
      Englandspiel operation, 94–107, 137, 147
   Jewish ownership forbidden, 38
   prohibited stations, 65
   Radio Oranje, 32, 58, 90
Ras, Gerard, 99, 100
rationing
   of food, 122–123, 130
   of gasoline, 30
Rauter, Hanns Albin, 30, 41, 119, 125
"Red Ball Express," 158
refugees
   from Arnhem area, 180–181

escape networks for, 141–144, 146–151
funds to aid, 140
Jewish, 36
suicides immediately after invasion, 29
religion
    aid to Jews and, 50, 55–56, 57
    censorship of Christian newspapers, 56
    Christian communities, 54–55
    funds to aid refugees, 140
    under Nazism, 54
    pacifism and, 32
    See also Resistance, religious
Resistance
    aid to *onderduikers*, 48
    Allied invasion and, 93–94
    anti-Nazi graffiti, 118–119
    black market farmers and, 122–123
    conscripted labor for German armaments factories and, 122, 185–186
    fatalities, 202
    forces under Prince Bernhard, 188
    funding, 122, 202
    Government-in-Exile call for passive, 120
    growth of, 117, 126
    main focus of, 126, 127
    neutrality tradition and, 78
    number of participants, 126–127, 201
    Operation Market Garden and, 160, 164, 166, 170–171, 174–175
    overview of activities of, 201–202
    rallying, 80–83
    symbolic, 32–33
    topography and, 4, 79
    Underground press and, 67–72
    unification of, 123–124
    view of collaborators, 69–71
    See also Resistance, religious; Underground; *see* specific groups
Resistance, religious
    aid to Jews by, 55–56, 57

    in educational institutions, 58, 60
    measures against, 58, 59, 60
    motivation for, 53, 128
    from pulpit, 55, 57–58, 59–60, 61–62, 120
    to sterilization, 61
Ridderhoff, Georges, 94–95, 96, 106
Rietschoten, Jan, 113
Roelfzema, Erik Hazelhoff, 88–90
Rotterdam
    German bombing of, 19–23, 56
    Resistance and, 69
    riots in, 38
Rouwerd, R.W., 111
Russia, 34, 58–59, 154

S

sabotage
    of German military installations, 124
    of registers for conscripted labor, 122
    as response to force labor calls, 185–186
    See also Plan Holland
Saint Josemaria Escriva, 128
Sas, G.J., 12, 13
"Schaemmel (Major)", 9–10
Schaft, Hannie, 123
Scharroo, Pieter, 20–21
Schellenberg, Walter, 9–10
Schmidt, Rudolf, 20, 21
Schoonhovense Courant (newspaper), 75
Schreieder, Joseph, 88, 89, 104–105, 106, 107, 112
SD *(Sicherheitsdienst)*, 30, 88, 89
Sebes, Hendrik, 99, 100
Secret Intelligence Service (SIS, British), 9–10
Seyffardt, Hendrik, 125
Seyss-Inquart, Arthur
    Allied relief supplies and, 194, 196
    assurances given by, 31
    German civilians ordered to leave by, 154–155
    German food embargo, 179, 183
    government established by, 30, 31, 53

on Jews, 36, 40
physicians and, 61
on reason for invasion, 30
Siegfried Line, 155–156
Simpson, William, 191
Slomp, Fritz, 120
Slovakia, 45
Sobibor, 42
Social Democrat youth league, 83
Sosabowski, Stanislaw, 159, 171–172, 173
Special Operations Executive (S.O.E.), 86, 88, 108–111, 132–133
  See also Plan Holland
Speelman, Wim, 72–73
Sponeck, Hans Graf von, 14
SS *(Schutzstaffel)*, 30, 37, 44–45, 80
Standaard (Calvinist newspaper), 56
Stein, Edith, 59
sterilization, 61
Stevens, R.H., 9, 10
Stijkel, Johan, 85–86
strikes
  against Nazi regime, 119–120
  against N.S.B., 119
  to protest treatment of Jews, 38, 39–40
  in support of Operation Market Garden, 160, 178–179, 183
  by university students, 37
Student, Kurt, 14, 23, 156
Sweden, 193, 194

T

Taconis, Thijs, 94, 95, 96, 97, 102
Taylor, Maxwell, 159
Tazelaar, Pieter, 89–90
ter Horst, Kate, 170–171
ter Laak, Johannes, 89
Terwindt, Beatrix (Trix), 136–137
Theresienstadt, 42
Tijd (Catholic newspaper), 56
topography
  invasion and, 3–4, 5, 6
  Resistance and, 4, 79
  sea level, 2
  survival of Jews and, 45

"Trojan Horse" operation, 18
Trouw (Loyalty, Underground newspaper), 73, 74, 185

U

Ubbink, Johan, 111–113, 147
Underground
  Beggars' Action Resistance, 67–69, 79–80
  early actions by, 83
  funding, 202
  German infiltration of, 30, 80, 94–95, 96, 142
  intelligence activities by, 83–84, 88–90, 126
  number of participants, 201
  political assassinations by, 125
  press (*See* Underground press)
  rescue of downed Allied airmen
    described, 120–121
    general procedure, 129–131
    networks for, 132–137, 142–144, 146–151
  sabotage by, 124 (*See also* Plan Holland)
  See also Resistance
Underground Camera, 125
Underground press
  dangers faced by, 73–74
  importance of, 63, 77
  news coverage by, 75–76
  number of participants, 201
  number of publications, 63
  publication and distribution of, 64, 66–67, 74–75
  Reformed Church and, 72–73
  Resistance and, 67–72
  See also specific publications
Union. *See* Netherlands Union
Urquhart, "Roy," 159, 168, 169, 172

V

V-men, described, 30
van der Giessen, Aat, 113
van der Reyden, Willem, 88, 89, 96

van der Wilden, Pieter, 106
van der Wilden, Willem, 106
van Hamel, Lodo, 84–85
van Hemert, G.J., 102, 103
Van Kleffens, Eelco, 15
van Os, Gerard, 106
van Papendrecht, Hoynck, 126
van Rietschoten, Jan, 100
van Steen, Antonius, 100, 103
Van Tricht, A.G., 146
Vander Burg, Theresa, 50
Vandermeersche, Gaston, 90–91
Van't Sant, Francois, 87
Venlo Incident, 9–10
Vichy France, 139–143
von Rundstedt, Gerd, 155–156, 191
Voor Waarheid, Vrijheid en Recht (*For Truth, Liberty and Right*, Underground newspaper), 66
Vos, Aart, 50–51
Vos, Johtje, 50–51
Vrij Nederland (*Free Netherlands*, Underground publication), 72
Vrouwenfelder, J., 178

W

Waal River bridge, 164
Waffen-SS, 30
Walther, Wilhelm, 18
Warmbrunn, Werner, 22
Weer Afdeling (W.A.), 35, 38
Wegner, Anton, 113
Weidner, John, 139, 140–141, 143–145, 146–151
Westerbork, 36, 42
Western Front
  Allies
    advance across Europe
      early days, 154–155
      in Germany, 190–192
      Operation Market Garden, 159–176
      refugees from, 180–181
      supply issues, 156, 157–158
    strategy, 152–154, 158–159

German strategy, 7–9, 14, 25, 117–118, 184–185
Whately, Richard, 93
Wilhelmina (queen of Netherlands)
  Dutch intelligence activities and, 87
  first broadcast of Radio Oranje, 32
  flight to England, 18
  German background of, 2
  German measures against, 34
  intelligence activities and, 90
  neutrality and, 9
  postwar, 200
  support for Russia and, 58
Willis, Nathaniel P., 1
Wilmot, Chester, 176
WIM intelligence group, 90–91
Winkelman, H.G., 17, 19, 21–22
Wood, Ken, 196
World Council of Churches, 140
Wurst, Spencer, 163

Z

Zech-Burkersroda, Julius von, 15
Zomer, Hans, 87–88

WORDS OF PRAISE FOR BENEATH THE TYRANT'S YOKE

"I must compliment you without reservation. The book you have written is according to my judgment the best book that has ever been written concerning the German occupation of Norway and the Norwegian Resistance. You have a total grasp of the situation in this country in the years 1940-1945. Very good indeed!"

—*Kristian Ottosen, Service in British-Norwegian Intelligence Service 1940-1942*

"Fuegner's work tells the story of a heroic people's confrontation with the Nazi regime and its collaborators. Along with information on the men and methods of sabotage against the German occupiers, there are valuable insights into the ideological struggle of the Norwegian Church and the establishment of an illegal press."

—*Jose M. Sanchez, Professor of Modern European History – St. Louis University*

"I have greatly enjoyed reading this book. A thorough account, well researched, compellingly told, and helpfully illustrated. I will certainly mention it to audiences when I do my presentation on the war."

—*Kathleen Stokker, Professor of Norwegian – Luther College*

"Breathtaking! Exciting!! Daring!!! Fuegner does with a typewriter what an artist does with a brush. Students of World War II should indeed be grateful for the extensive detail the book provides. Clearly, this is a meaningful contribution to the written history of World War II."

—*Dr. R. Frank Harwood, Brigadier General (Retired) and Professor Emeritus, Business Administration – University of Mississippi*